ALSO BY ELLEN MELOY

Raven's Exile: A Season on the Green River

The Last Cheater's Waltz:
Beauty and Violence in the Desert Southwest

The Anthropology of Turquoise:
Meditations on Landscape, Art, and Spirit

EATING STONE

ELLEN MELOY

EATING STONE

Imagination and the Loss of the Wild

PANTHEON BOOKS, NEW YORK

Pantheon Books and colophon are registered trademarks
of Random House, Inc.

Grateful acknowledgment is made to Kenneth W. Brewer
for permission to reprint the poem "Sheep."
Reprinted by permission of the author.

Library of Congress Cataloging-in-Publication Data

Meloy, Ellen.
Eating stone : imagination and the loss of the wild / Ellen Meloy.
p.   cm.
ISBN 0-375-42216-1
1. Bighorn sheep—Southwestern States.   2. Animals—Psychological
aspects.   I. Title.

QL737.U53M44 2005   599.649'7'0979—dc22   2004061210

www.pantheonbooks.com

Printed in the United States of America
First Edition
2   4   6   8   9   7   5   3   1

FOR MARK

Chidí naa'na'íísh
t'áá naach' idgi
nił bééhózin?

I have always longed to be a part of the outward life, to be out there at the edge of things, to let the human taint wash away in emptiness and silence as the fox sloughs his smell into the cold unworldliness of water; to return to the town as a stranger. Wandering flushes a glory that fades with arrival.

JOHN BAKER, *The Peregrine*

SHEEP

The Virgin River vanishes
in canyon rock
leaving tear stains
for the mountain sheep
who graze on stone,
who know the earth is steep
in every direction, who know
geometry is merely
the shape of stone,
empty space,
memory of hooves.

We want to ask
"How can you live here?"
But we drive fast
past their answer,
our attention always
ahead of us.

KENNETH BREWER

PROLOGUE

On one of my last winter days with the desert bighorns, they no longer kept me out of their world. With motions I had come to know as an exquisite union of liturgy and physics, they closed the distance between us and herded me toward a threshold, a place best described as a hairsbreadth.

Their slender legs rose like smoke from stone, curving into pale rumps. The rump carried all the muscle, the force that was capable of pushing their stocky bodies up a sheer cliff with nothing beneath their hooves but air and a foothold barely larger than my lower lip. This is what you will find at the center of the desert bighorn: dry, vertical space. On the flats, they seem as awkward as square wheels.

Their haunches held but small tensions now. The sheep stood about like mildly bored ballerinas. Black hooves found cusps of white snow. Breath condensed in milky wraiths. The wind did not matter to them. They moved serenely among themselves, brushing flanks warm with blood, weaving me toward that breach of transmutation.

Something in their amber eyes told me that I was about to change, to be given a language without tongues. I wanted to leap into that wild side—their side—then bring back their startling news from the other-than-human world. But I was weighted with a wobbly confusion about how to see, how to behave.

After so many days among the bighorns, in the end it seemed best to quiet the mind and act like a rock. I am simply here, I thought, here at the periphery of several hundred pounds of *Ovis* with lovely rumps and eyelashes as delicate as fish bones.

I then became the first rock in history to be overcome with feeling, a serene aching aimed at nothing in particular, only a cobalt sky with no edge but winter's cold and a river beside us that shook out its light in full dazzle, a river rimmed with ice and a band of rare mammals whose own biology and history could have lost them to the world.

EATING STONE

THE BLUE DOOR BAND

Homo sapiens have left themselves few places and scant ways to witness other species in their own world, an estrangement that leaves us hungry and lonely. In this famished state, it is no wonder that when we do finally encounter wild animals, we are quite surprised by the sheer *truth* of them.

Nothing speaks the truth quite like a 220-pound desert bighorn ram mounted atop a standing female, thrusting his heavy pelvis back and forth like there was no tomorrow.

It was the rut. Males, usually solo or in bachelor bands, had joined the females, which for the rest of the year lived separately with random groups of juveniles. The rams were glossy, fat, spirited. Their thick, curled horns and heavy testicles carried a few million years of evolutionary momentum. Here in the canyon, not much else mattered but the bone and muscle needed to transport these body parts. On four hooves rode massive sperm factories.

I had put the river between myself and the rutting grounds, not that I was much more than wallpaper as the sheep copulated. I shared guilt over trespass with other voyeurs: the few subdominant rams, unlucky in love; six nearby ewes; a pair of lecherous ravens perched on a boulder.

The mating unfolded quickly but with a ritualized certainty. Among a species with a complex repertoire of social behaviors, the penalty of ambiguity is reproductive failure.

As the ram dropped off the mount, the other males brawled in rushes, kicks, and threat displays. One lunged toward the ewe, only to have his butt smashed by her guardian, a ram of spent force but fixed vigilance. The ewe ran off and disappeared from view, pursued by the younger suitors. The snoopy ravens left their perch and followed. The remaining ewes, already inseminated or not yet in estrus and therefore not ready to breed, moved about restlessly, then settled down to feed.

The Colorado Plateau canyon country is one of several "wilderness" holdouts of this subspecies of a North American bovid family, genus *Ovis,* commonly known as mountain sheep. Strict regulations prohibit the hunting of desert bighorns except by special permit. Compared to their sport-celebrity hulky northern cousin, the Rocky Mountain bighorn (*Ovis canadensis canadensis*) of the intermountain West and Canadian Rockies, desert bighorns are smaller, paler, and longer in ear. They are more isolated and fewer in number. In some places, they face extinction on their native range.

Four races of desert bighorn sheep live in the arid wilds of the American Southwest and Mexico. Of these races, my momentarily sex-crazed sheep are Nelson's bighorns (*Ovis canadensis nelsoni*), occupants of the Colorado Plateau, Great Basin, and Mojave Desert.

The ewes that fed quietly on the talus of a river canyon had slender, upright horns that escaped notice, while the horns of males dominated one's gaze. Ram horns flare and curl. Aboriginal southwesterners took their form and gave them to their gods. For modern humans, this headgear is an icon of blood sport. To other sheep, ram horns are social organs.

Desert bighorns are blocky, long-necked ungulates, grayish brown in color, sometimes more gray than brown, or pale beige, or with a russet cast. Their noses are moist and their rumps are white. They eat dry, abrasive plants, digesting them with four-chambered stomachs and the help of protozoa and bacteria.

The five gaits of bighorn sheep reflect their mental state, from a pompous, show-offy walk to an exuberant trot down a near-vertical rock face or a twenty-five-mile-per-hour escape run. Their hearts pump at a rate of eighty beats per minute. The life of a bighorn sheep is a life spent on cliffs.

The rut marked the beginning of my year among desert bighorns, a calendar in which I matched my seasonal geography to theirs.

I made up a name of my own and gave it to the herd that lived in the river canyon: the Blue Door Band. Over the four seasons that I would spend with them, I would be their amiable, nosy neighbor. I peered at them through binoculars, spotting scope, and with naked eye. I watched them stare into space, fall asleep on their own feet, curl up in a tight sheep ball and nap with their chins on the ground. I watched them yawn, chew, stretch.

They scratched their backs on rocks. They hated brushy densities of trees. Their tongues hung out when they were thirsty. A few dropped dead. A few went swimming. The ewes raised a new generation. The rams roamed about alone or in ram bands, then came together and bashed heads, curled lips, and engaged in wildly testicular behavior.

True to their species, these animals loved bleak, hair-ball country. They were nervous, gregarious, hilarious. Agile, gorgeous, faithful to place to the point of disaster. They came with personalities: the bullies, the head bangers, the celibate pacifist ram, the barren ewes, the lambs perched atop sheer pinnacles of rock, leaping straight up in the air like toast popping out of a toaster. They were often elusive and spectral. To see them was a blessing.

As they entered the rut, the Blue Door Band numbered about eighty sheep. Out of this population, and depending on the season, I would sometimes see loners, trios, or groups that ranged from five to twenty individuals. I gave the sheep full, held-breath attention, sometimes lifting my binoculars to my eyes at midday, unaware of the passing hours until I dropped them, only then noticing that the sun had nearly set.

Or I would ignore the group completely and stick my head in a book, T. H. White's *The Goshawk,* trading ungulates for the arts of falconry. The wind whipped the pages. The sheep bleat-growled at my betrayal.

I gazed at distant mesas. Took naps. One minute, I swore eternal devotion to my little bovid band; the next minute, I entertained a feckless urge to hop in a boat and float down the river and disappear around the bend, ditching the sheep.

Sometimes I ditched the sheep. I left them for the seductive river or for other bighorns scattered in the far-flung deserts. I sent them postcards from New Mexico, California, Mexico.

For most of the year, though, I was loyal to the Blue Door Band, preternaturally attentive—how could anyone not be?—and shamelessly anthropomorphic. I wanted the bighorns to adopt me, a kind of reverse Bo Peep arrangement. Me, their lost human. Their pet. The primate among herbivores. The bovids' equivalent of a wolf boy.

Being with these wild animals was like prayer, a meditation that ranged from dopey to dreamy to absorption so profound, it stopped my blood. Their habits and motions formed a liturgy that mapped the prayer, liturgy as "the sanctification of time," a place where I was willing to wait in stillness, to count on nature's rhythms to calm my messy ones.

More often, it was the singular company of mammals I delighted in, just the sheep being sheep while I perched on a boulder or rock ledge, my feet falling asleep from sitting too long.

In the warm seasons, I could enter sheep company along the river. Winter conditions often kept me at a greater distance. I had to make long overland treks on foot to watching posts above a deep redrock canyon. The posts gave an unobstructed view of the Blue Door Band's range.

A remote fold of their canyon held a pile of stones that marked the remains of a hand-built shelter. Twenty years earlier, I had studied the shelter before it collapsed into an indeterminate pile of rubble. Then the shelter had a domed roof, a flat stone hearth, and a door frame that faced the sunrise. The door's milled boards were painted blue, the deep blue of the sky where it meets the canyon's redrock rims. This place gave me the idea for the sheep band's name.

On my watching days, I often found sheep all over the place, Velcro'd to the steep, rocky cliffs. Other times, I saw no sheep at all. I glassed the walls for hours. Both the day and the canyon felt empty. This was when sloppy meditation moved to true prayer, to words said against fear.

While you are among wild sheep, they can move out of sight the moment you bow your head to notice that the zipper on your jeans is open. Then you look up, look where they were or might be, and behold only rock and sky. When they disappeared for an entire day, or if I was at a post for several days and could not find them, I was alarmed.

Certain days, with sheep flesh present, were gifts set against a worrisome history, a past that might too easily repeat itself. Smack in the middle of the red-boned desert, these creatures lived an island life. They occupied a small enclave of wild country, surrounded by perils that could (and not for the first time) nearly decimate them.

The story of their precarious, marginal existence—the story of the continent's native fauna on their unstoppable trajectory from bounty to scarcity and even demise—was a familiar one, repeated over and over like a six-hundred-pound mantra lodged between the ears. How had this tribe of bighorns escaped the slide toward oblivion? No one could promise me that they would continue to survive.

As I sat contemplating this, the air had an edge of glass to it, the trees no burden of leaves. The light was thin and brittle. Scattered brush dressed the rust-colored canyon in brown, silver, and pale olive. For now, on this bright winter day on the Colorado Plateau, the river glistened in the sun and the sheep browsed nearby without fear. Several ewes interrupted their feeding and stared across the gorge. Their gaze gave notice of the direction they would soon take.

Then a pale turn of light, a shift of tectonic plate, some glimmer of a sheep idea, set them in motion. The animals glided down a precipice of jumbled boulders as if it were a wave of silk. I was not invited to go along. When the sheep disappeared from sight up a rocky arroyo, faith, more than sanctuary, affixed them to the canyon.

In the tensely vertical terrain of Utah's canyonlands, this band of desert bighorn sheep, creatures of considerable weight and evolutionary investment, had once vanished into thin air.

Their kind had likely been in the southwestern deserts since the late Pleistocene. Over the millennia, in a land of heat, drought, and food plants that resemble pot scrubbers, they had become a different race from that of their ancestors. Their pelage had paled in color and their bones had lightened. They had learned how to reduce body-water loss. They had struck ironclad allegiances to particular watering holes. They were, in short, *the locals.*

Barely a few decades into the twentieth century, we had the locals surrounded. Like every desert bighorn on the continent, the Blue Door Band lived on an isolated remnant of its former terrain. Intolerant of human activity, place-faithful to a fault, and with no other bighorns to naturally replenish them, they were, like many species on an island of habitat, vulnerable to catastrophe.

An aggressive predator, for instance, could wreak havoc if the bighorns were in weak condition or if their numbers were few. Contact with domestic sheep could expose them to debilitating disease. Competition for food could push them off their safe places to *no* place. There were few other places for them to go.

When the Blue Door Band declined in the early 1960s—too

few animals to keep the population viable—the word *extinct* was bandied about. Their passing garnered little notice from a public that barely knew the wild sheep existed in the first place.

Elsewhere in the Southwest, attentive shepherds—wildlife managers and advocates—nudged desert bighorns along through recovery and protection programs. But this band, as remote and as isolated as if stuck on an atoll in the middle of the Pacific, slipped through the cracks, their numbers likely fallen to a point of no return. They slid into a spectacular crash. Year after year, the river cliffs held their absence, air empty of blood and breath. The sheep were gone.

Then they came back.

TRIBE CAPRINI

These late-fall mornings have a weight to them, air pressed down by steel gray clouds. Storms cross the desert, but no rain falls, only this heaviness of air. Then a curtain of wind moves in from the high mesas and pushes the weight east, stripping the cottonwoods bare of their leaves in a single gust. Behind the wind, silver trees rise from islands of their own, shed gold, and the crickets lose their voices.

Migrating bluebirds, dozens of them, rest in the storms' wake, scattering electric blue shards in blond strands of salt grass. A single Russian olive tree holds some of the birds among its dried gold-green leaves, a Persian miniature I shall paint as soon as I study Persian miniatures for about ten years. The chile crop my husband, Mark, and I planted is harvested and dries to bloodred under a weakening sun, the summer's fire saved. From the Great Basin to Mexico, a high-pressure system settles over us. For several weeks, all edges will stay sharp. There will be no haze.

I try to spend most of my days with the sheep. November's thin light and ambient quiet make it easy to find them. They array themselves on a steep talus and stand at feed like perfect bighorns: heads down, all facing the same direction, shapely gray profiles against gray rock. Then they all turn to show white rumps atop graceful legs, more like glyphs than creatures.

At times, I post myself on a canyon rim and see no sheep.

Being with them spoils me for being without them. Then I hear a rock fall and clatter and, above the sound, I find a group clustered in a hanging arroyo, a vertical cleft in a cliff wall: *tsétah dibé,* in Navajo, sheep of the rock or mountain.

On one watch, I see fifteen ewes and juveniles bolt from their feed and run at top speed along a narrow horizontal ledge, single file, as if chased by a pack of starving panthers. The leader stops so suddenly—a panic-braking *ur-rrch*—her hooves leave skid marks in the limestone. Each one behind her crashes into the butt of the sheep in front of it: a pileup.

I spend an entire afternoon listening to horns clash, but I see no rams. The folds of the canyon hide them. I am so far from roads and humans, the only sounds are the river and the echoing impact of sheep skulls.

Another time, a thousand acres yields one bighorn. He is "skylining," standing atop an outcrop in ram supermodel profile. Head slightly raised, muscles tense, he does not move. Ten minutes pass without a twitch. The ram is frozen in place. I follow the direction of his stare. A half mile away, high above him on the canyon wall, one ewe feeds. He knows she is there.

Occasionally, I see a group of rams and ewes together in full rut. Most of the time, I see ewes and subadults in their eat-move-eat-rest mode. This can go on for hours. Yet they are there, the day's gift, and I watch them until I am stiff or the cold bites into my hands.

Whenever I drop the binoculars or spotting scope, take my eyes away from the world ringed by a lens, the sheer distance of the horizon startles me. Desert space is space that is felt, completely and with certainty. Out here, I feel like a small dot and a big voyeur. The bighorns are not harassed (I am too far away). In fact, sometimes I can barely see them. The sky and open desert are so enormous around us, who would know if we were out here anywhere?

A few hours before dawn, the waning moon rises as a disk of nickel cradled in a scimitar of silver. The slim crescent of light makes the moon strangely bright in its own darkness. The entire orb is visible: nickel moon against indigo sky. This is the last of it. The new moon is two days away.

I load for a long spell afield: camping gear and a day pack with binoculars, spotting scope, notebook, oranges, water bottle. After a hot summer of half-clad abandon, and October's gift of edible light, I try to wrap my mind around winter and the Concept of Socks, maybe gloves if the wind picks up.

The season of diminishing light never brings out the best in me. November feels like the portal of a tunnel. Sometimes when I walk through night-dark shadows in nearby canyons, the shadows come home with me, wrapped inside my heart as if I had drunk them. Hundreds of square miles of rough, remote desert surround me, yet at times the boundless space seems to lurch and creak and shrink, then implant its mass on my shoulder bones. When this weight descends, it is time to go to church.

As morning approaches behind the moon, a cluster of flashlight beams bounces around the ranch bottom below my house. From so far away, they come as pinpricks in the blackness, but I see them circle and fuss, then switch off. The hunters have returned.

My house sits on a bench above a broad alluvial valley framed by redrock cliffs. A river flows below the cliffs, breaking up the parched desert into possibility. Between house and river, on a neighbor's cattle ranch, more than a hundred Canada geese routinely stay the night in a dense flock of brown and gray against the pale fields.

During the winter months, the geese rest and feed on the ranch bottom until the morning sun burns off the night's chill and warms them. When the sun reaches a certain point above the red cliffs, they open wings as strong as sheet metal and as one thrumming mass rise and fly toward the river, carving a perfect arc in the cold blue air.

Several miles upriver, they settle down for the day on gravel bars and riffles of water over bedrock. Before dusk, they rise again and fly back to their resting grounds on the ranch bottom for the night.

You can set your clock by these daily risings and landings. The Canada geese will adjust for you the changing length of daylight as winter deepens. They begin and end days along the river, and that is all you need to know about time.

Although the hunters came from out of town, they know the habits of the river flock. From my window, I see their flashlights go dark and feel the tension of their waiting. I leave pack and preparations and slip out the door in a race with the light.

Would the geese forgive me, I wonder, for an act that I vowed never to commit: spooking them off their night roost, in the dense, confused dark, before they choose to go.

These are not golf course geese, the fat *Branta canadensis* that leave worm rolls of poop on fairways and lawns and wreak havoc on suburbia. These huge water-loving—shouldn't they be in Canada?—birds live in a desert.

They raise their goslings in a sandstone canyon and live by the miracle of the only wetlands for miles: the river and a few scattered farm ponds and livestock impoundments. They winter on the floodplain below our small town. Only the lack of open water—a rare, hard freeze—would spur them to migrate. They stay year-round. They live here.

The weekend before, the hunters had arrived before dawn and slipped behind a makeshift blind of dried brush piled high enough to hide them. I did not notice them until I heard the firing of shotguns. As soon as the morning gave enough light, the hunters shot a dozen geese off the ground like a skeet shoot, birds killed where they stood, bodies hitting the ground with heavy thuds.

"Jumping the roost," it's called, technically legal but "illegal by proclamation," say most sportsmen, and clearly unethical. Hunters of waterfowl usually fire at their prey on the fly. Airborne geese make ample targets. The birds plunge to the earth with a force of downward gravity that makes you gasp. But this is fair chase.

Jump-shooting wild geese off their night field is not fair chase.

Now, a week after the ground shoot, I thrash through rabbit-brush and tamarisk, which hit my face like whips. I am wearing a ragged sweatshirt, pajama bottoms, and socks. I am late for church.

I stumble through our cottonwood grove and by memory, more than light, make my way across the field at the low end of our property. Beyond the fence lie the ranch bottom and the geese; beyond them, the river. It is too dark to see the Mercedes in the field. In the middle of the open flats, far from any roads, sits the hulking wreck of an abandoned metallic blue 1965 Mercedes-Benz, its doors flung open as if gowned starlets would soon emerge.

The eastern horizon grows a band of light, whose strength the hunters await. I still move in the flat dimension of shadows and a fading moon, but I can hear the birds—low honks, feathers ruffling. What I need is a couple of the coyotes that live on the nearby river benches. *Help me out with this,* I say under my breath. But none appear.

As difficult as it is to sneak through brittle, crunching plant stubble in socks and pajamas, I sneak. I climb over the barbed wire and posts of a fence corner without suffering an embarrassing evisceration. At the edge of the flock, I lie flat on my stomach, my nose full of dust.

Among the dark bird shapes is a doomed glow of white: a

domestic goose, a lonely domestic goose, which joined the flock earlier in the fall. It mingles with a seething gaggle of gray-brown birds with jet black necks and ear-to-ear chin bands. I'm waiting for it to look around and suddenly shriek, My God, *I'm white!* On the ground, the snow-white goose stands out like a polar bear in the Kalahari, drawing every last photon of crescent moonlight into an explosive burst of shoot-me neon.

"*Up*," I rasp. "*Fly.*" Nothing happens.

Dawn washes out the moon and makes graceful necks and wings faintly visible. Knees knocking, teeth chattering, eyes bugged in fear, the rancher's Angus cows are worried, too. *We're black!* they cry. If mere minutes pass, a lot of us creatures will get our butts full of buckshot.

"*Up!*" I whisper again. The geese waddle about, all heads raised. Good, I think. Be nervous. Very nervous.

Muttering in a dust puddle in plaid flannel is getting me nowhere. I rise up on hands and knees and growl.

When a flock of wild geese takes flight all at once, you feel them press against your heart. I sit back on my heels as hundreds of wings push a mass of air toward me. The birds lift in raucous honking, giving sound, more than sight, to follow. Coyotes begin to yip and howl from the distant benches. I hear the geese bank a low turn over the Mercedes and fly in the direction of the river.

Can they see in the dark? Will they find the water before they bash their heads on the wall of sandstone on the far bank? The cliffs loom black and solid against a pale lemon sky. I put my trust in them. The geese tuck in their white chin straps and fly, carrying with them a bird the color of fresh snow.

Each time I look into the eye of an animal, one as "wild" as I can find in its own element—or maybe peering through zoo bars will have to do—and if I get over the mess of "Do I eat it, or vice versa?" and overcome any problems I might have with an animal's animality, or, for that matter, my own, I find myself staring into a mirror of my own imagination. What I see there is deeply, crazily, unmercifully confused.

There is in that animal eye something both alien and familiar. There is in me, as in all human beings, a glimpse of the interior, from which everything about our minds has come.

The crossing holds all the power and purity of first wonder, before habit and reason dilute it. The glimpse is fleeting. Quickly, I am left in darkness again, with no idea whatsoever how to go back.

The human body wants safety. The human mind longs for satisfaction—pleasure, love, affinity, experience, imagination. Whenever I tell people that the human mind, the imagination, depends on animals, they give me a stuffed teddy bear.

I suppose that being handed a vicarious imagination stimulant is better than being handed a live cheetah. Real animals, animals as beyond the reach of our dominion as they can be in today's world, no longer figure in our lives. Our distance from them, the thinkers say, has left us with the anguish of missing the wild that is no longer in ourselves. Peering into the lives of creatures not similarly deprived soothes some of this emptiness. Attention, for all its potent sensitivity, may be the spark that rekindles imagination. It may save a listless mind.

For British writer T. H. White, as I learn when I read while out watching bighorns, a mind activated by beasts was a rescued mind. White averted mental disasters by keeping a proximity to animals and sustaining a voracious appetite for knowledge.

Described by biographer Sylvia Townsend Warner as "chased by a mad black wind," this "hermetic and sometimes cranky man" wrote more than twenty-five books. He was an illustrator and calligrapher. He translated medieval bestiaries. He painted, fished, raced airplanes, built furniture, sailed boats, plowed fields, and flew hawks at prey. Late in life, he made deep-sea dives in a heavy old suit with a bulbous helmet, which made him look like a Zuni mudhead.

New skills "aerated his intelligence," Warner tells us. For his 1955 translation of a twelfth-century bestiary, he taught himself Latin. Through a character in one of his novels, he hinted at himself. "The best thing for being sad," the character says, "is to learn something."

Much of White's knowledge of the natural world resurfaced in his teaching—he was for many years a schoolmaster—although greater experts in his subjects accused him of smattering. "But smatterer or no," writes Warner, White "held his pupils' attention; their imagination, too, calling out an unusual degree of solicitude—as though in the tall gowned figure these adolescents recognized a hidden adolescent, someone unhappy, fitful, self-dramatizing and not knowing much about finches."

He wore scarlet. He was "nobly shabby." He drank, he said, "in order not to be sober." He kept owls and paid his students to trap mice to feed them. Fed, the owls perched on his shoulder as he sat under an apple tree, speaking to him in little squeals.

He wrote a story about geese and geese hunters, one of them a "mad general" who said one ought not to hunt geese and waved the birds away before anyone could. White's ardent love for natural beauty, his friends remarked, peaked in wild enthusiasm, then crashed into melancholy at beauty's transience.

The melancholy may have been clinical. In gloom, he sought air. In the late 1930s, he wrote:

I had two books on the training of the falconidae in one of which was a sentence which suddenly struck fire from my mind. The sentence was: "She reverted to a feral state." A longing came to my mind that I should be able to do this myself. The word "feral" has a kind of magical potency which allied itself to two other words, "ferocious" and "free." To revert to a feral state! I took a farm-labourer's cottage and wrote to Germany for a goshawk.

The Goshawk, published in 1951, chronicled White's seduction by a great and beautiful bird. He used his wits and books (one of them a treatise on hawking written in 1619) to train his goshawk, but mostly it was the bird itself who taught him. He had a way of looking, White noted. "It was an alert, concentrated, piercing look. My duty at present was not to return it."

Only several years after his time with the goshawk and other wild raptors—he called them his "assassins"—did White observe a professional falconer at work. With humility, he admitted his own errors and credited his instincts. "The thing about being associated with a hawk is that one cannot be slipshod about it. No hawk can be a pet. There is no sentimentality. . . . One desires no transference of affection, demands no ignoble homage or gratitude. It is a tonic for the less forthright savagery of the human heart."

Unlike White, I have few ambitions of the autodidact. I could never bobble under the sea in an iron mudhead suit. Yet something in the mind's structure, something physical, thrives on, depends on, the notice of other beings. Attention, fierce or dreamy, affixes my butt to sheep country, to long hours on bare limestone slabs in a chilly wind. Sometimes the sheep are completely boring. Sometimes their animation moves me beyond words. Our "companionship" closes the distance. I am here to learn something. I will need this knowledge. Time is running out.

When you truly understand one thing—a hawk, a juniper tree, a rock—you will begin to understand everything. To understand everything, to know the nature of a single living thing, the facts of a life other than my own, I chose desert bighorn sheep. Lucky me. As part of this quest, I watch very large animals having really wild sex.

Sheep sex is a fine place to go after crawling around a field with fat geese. For the goose "hunters," I had asked the gods for simple redress: Shrivel their testicles. I am not against hunting, only slob hunting. There is, out there somewhere, a rare breed of dignified, low-tech, traditional hunters who actually care about their own souls, who believe, as Montana poet Paul Zarzyski wrote, "We owe our prey some grace, / some contemplation of their lives / here with us."

Rescuing birds from slobbery has unnerved me. It has made me late for church—so late, the sheep may have disappeared.

At least once before, the bighorns had not simply walked over a ridge and out of sight; they had slipped away to a point of no return. They could do it again. I am accustomed to seeing them whenever I look, but is this experience trustworthy? These sheep, the Blue Door Band, are half flesh, half phantom. I witness them with astonishing calm and abject panic.

I drive miles and miles, loop around mesas, cross saddles and passes, backtrack in reverse gear, follow a map drawn on clear glass in colorless ink. After this expedition, foot travel is necessary. Pack slung on my back, I keep a brisk pace on the long hike into bighorn territory, a remote expanse of roadless desert. I move from a flock of one of North America's most ubiquitous species, Canada geese, to one of its rarest.

On this day, church has flying buttresses of upwarped sandstone and a ceiling of cornflower blue streaked with mare's tails. Vermilion mesas form transept walls. Nearly a hundred miles beyond, scattered mountain ranges raise their iris flanks into snowy peaks the shape of heaven.

Below my post, the river sings a robust hymn, flowing pale khaki with silt. Above the river, in a middle world partway up the canyon wall: eleven desert bighorns.

The sheep are animated by the motions of everyday behavior— eating, walking, resting—mixed with the conspicuous postures of a breeding group. The ewes and juveniles, here on their home terrain, try the hardest to attend to the normal. However, three rams have left their own range and now move among them.

A stocky ram lords it over the band with a sedate horniness. His headgear rolls from forehead to cheeks in a thick curl, heavy throughout the swoop and narrow at the broomed, or worn-off, tips. The round rump of his youth has taken a more angled slope and his withers are high.

While most desert bighorns are tan to gray, this ram is a dark chocolate brown. He appears to be about ten years old and, with maturity, has lost the paler hair on his belly and legs. With sleek coat, toned muscles, weight put on by summer's abundant food, this ram is in prime condition. His scrotum is the size of a ripe cantaloupe—a cantaloupe from Texas.

The sun rises to its midday height, slung low on its arc toward the winter solstice. Part of the canyon lies in shadow, but the bighorns keep to the light. In the sun, the ram's coat shines a burnished mahogany.

Over several seasons, throughout the Blue Door Band's range, I have seen a few young bighorns darken to brown as they matured, the pelage of this ram's line. In a population so small, it is possible to recognize progeny. The chocolate ram himself may be the offspring of a ram that lived in the canyon years before, a ram with a distinctive mahogany coat. For mysterious reasons, he fell off a cliff.

Today, his descendant pretends he is interested in bushes. Then he approaches a ewe in a low stretch and sniffs her hindquarters. The ewe squats and urinates. The ram nuzzles the urine and raises his head as if looking for passing aircraft. He peels back his upper lip and drops his lower lip, revealing a set of even leaf-grinding teeth. He moves his head from side to side.

The lip curl is both social gesture and chemistry test, likely related to a ewe's readiness for mating. As he nuzzled, the ram passed some of her urine through a duct to his vomeronasal, or Jacobson's, organ for analysis. Then he casually moved off, since lip curling is usually associated with ewes that are near estrus but not ready to mate.

Ewes in a desert bighorn population enter estrus at different times. This spreads the band's mating season over about eight to ten weeks, during which rams must keep up with ovarian activity and await, for each ewe, a receptive estrus period of only about forty-eight hours.

Like most older, full-curl rams, the chocolate male lip-curls randomly and wastes few calories until the time is ripe. He exercises a rather regal nonchalance, smitten by his own very large horns. How, I wonder, can he move with that pendulous cantaloupe between his legs?

The other adult rams in the group are smaller, younger, and more frenzied. The younger of the two noses around the ewes as they feed. He stands by one of them, then suddenly tries to jump on her. He butts another. All of the ewes evade him as if he were a large mosquito.

The third ram is between the mosquito ram and the chocolate ram in age. His substantial set of horns spreads out and away from his head as if a tight circular curl had somehow flared into a surprised sideways curl. The flared horns could level small trees each time he turns his head. But this is a desert, and the shrubs are sparse and low and hardscrabble. The only thing he is knocking over is air, and the females are not impressed. They want to eat. The younger rams want to butt and sniff. At one point, they encounter each other and rise up on their hind legs in a false charge. The chocolate ram remains oblivious of both of them. He is vastly interested in bushes again.

In lackadaisical strolls, the sheep cluster together and move apart. They pull at shrubs and grind mouthfuls of dry, abrasive plants with their hard teeth. Then, on a broad, flat shelf of rock, all eleven sheep lie down to rest.

At rest, they do not look into a companion's face, but appear to be concentrating on a thought or a bug not far from their foreheads. Several choose beds on the lip of the shelf and peer over the eighty-foot drop to a sandbar and the river.

A few of the nappers first paw their beds with a front hoof, scraping away rocks and duff. They like the dust. Day beds are not as complicated as night beds, so most of the sheep simply drop from standing position without pawing, lowering their front knees first, then settling their hindquarters. They tuck their legs under their bodies, a position that will let them rise up rapidly and flee. From my view, they look like eleven loaves of bread with horns. The flared-horn ram nods off sleepily until his chin rests on the ground, taking the weight of his rack off his neck.

Once in awhile, one animal stands up and butts another off its bed. Between naps, the two younger rams rise and look around, perhaps wondering if anyone has entered estrus since they last checked. Nearly every body gesture is a social one, drawing the attention of other sheep. The exchanges grow subtle. The group settles down.

Desert bighorns want a good view, and from their beds these sheep can gaze far upriver along a slender ribbon of khaki framed by canyon walls of red and gray, walls that seal them inside the universe.

Behind a gravel bar, a dense grove of tamarisk has turned the color of ripe peaches. An ellipse of pale rose sand lines the inside of a river bend of such beauty, you could set yourself on fire with the rapture of that curve. In it lies a kind of music in stone that might cure all emptiness.

At the mouth of a stair-stepped side canyon, the river tumbles over submerged rocks, a rapid I know how to run with raft and oars. Nothing moves but the water and two ebony ravens that glide along the chasm, their ebony shadows beside them.

I run my hand over my hair to understand the touch of sun on the bighorns' backs. Each day toward winter, the sun's heat weakens and slips away from the air. Because, on this afternoon, the desert has quieted so, the warmth seems to intensify. The sheep rest. They take the warmth into their woolly backs and watch the river.

When I was very young, wild animals came to me as they come to most children: in dreams. In zoos and "habitat" parks, even in their natural surroundings, real animals occupied a world that had become intolerably small for them and tragically disconnected from children. Yet somehow I acquired some knowledge about wildlife.

Some of it may have been digested from *Wild Kingdom,* a baby boomer–era television program and the forerunner of Disney specials, and an out-of-breath David Attenborough wheezing around some camel-infested wadi looking for pupfish. I cannot fully trust my memory of this source of wildlife information. I was quite young in *Wild Kingdom* days, and my parents restricted my brothers and me to one hour or less of television a week.

Perhaps I saw the show in reruns at a neighbor's when we were cheating. There in my memory is Marlin Perkins, a man with a zoo career, silver-haired and dressed in an impeccably ironed khaki safari suit, not in the Rockies with sheep, but in Africa, where he stands on safe ground beside a miserably fetid swamp while his burly, mute assistant, Jim, strangles turtles or thrashes angry hippos.

Or perhaps it's Marlin and Jim, hot and thirsty on some sun-baked plain. Before Marlin's hairdo can wilt, Jim has scrambled

around and dug up a *Chiroleptes,* or flat-headed frog, from the
sand, a frog that stores water in its body until it puffs up like a
water balloon. Jim hands the frog to Marlin, who squeezes it and
drinks, while we kids stare openmouthed at the screen, mesmer-
ized by the idea of drinking frogs, and one of my brothers, dead-
pan, says, "Jim is Marlin's boyfriend," although none of us knows
exactly what that means.

No, Marlin did not waste his time on sheep.

By the time I was in my early teens, animal information and
images from books and films, encyclopedic volumes of it, stuffed
my head and made me feel intelligent. It was a nature documen-
tary, one more sophisticated than *Wild Kingdom,* that first showed
me bighorns in rut.

Behind two rams the size of backhoes, there was snow on the
ground and a horizon of pines and craggy peaks. These were not
wimpy desert bighorns; they were cinematic Rocky Mountain
bighorns—larger, culturally emblematic, more Canadian-looking.
The footage hinted of frigid air and distance, of animals from a
difficult, untamed place, definitely not from a national park soon
to be engulfed by sprawling Denver suburbs.

The rams postured like cover boys in the latest hunter-training
DVD, *Kalashnikovs and Other Deer Rifles.* Rams are virtually syn-
onymous with wild sheep. Football teams do not name themselves Ewes, nor do ewes give their likeness to hood ornaments.
(Many people cannot easily identify a female bighorn. When they
see a picture of one, they mistake her for a mule deer that has
been left in the attic too long or for an ibex, a goat from Asia.) In
the film, there were no ewes, only the sense of them, off-camera
somewhere, batting their eyelashes, awaiting the victor in a fever-
ish heat.

The rams pulled their heads down in low, menacing stretches
and, muscles bulging, passed in opposite directions, as if pacing a
duel. Suddenly, they whirled around and rose up on their hind
legs, bodies rigid, forelegs extended.

They rushed forward on two legs, dropped their shoulders and heads, and pulled in their chins, adding downward force to the heavy horns. Across thirty feet of ground, they lunged at each other at twenty miles per hour.

Horns clashed violently, a blow described as a combination of karate chop and sledgehammer. For a long time, the sound of their clash reverberated in the mountains. The rams froze and looked off to the side in a present, or display.

Although this can happen, the wildlife films never showed it: The charging rams miss. Or they slip off one another and crash into the ground headfirst. Or one is knocked out cold by the other's blow.

Because neither of the movie-star rams missed, fell, nor passed out, no human male fantasy was cruelly demolished. The viewer had the impression that there was a victor, or more combat until there was a victor and some serious headaches. The loser would skulk away. The films implied that the triumphant ram would rest for about twelve seconds, then trot off and impregnate fifty ewes. In Rambo movies, the plot is remarkably similar.

Drawing us to the spectacular, such imagery selects—and often distorts—a fraction of bighorn behavior, a rare creature's life distilled into two males smashing heads. In real sheep life, described in detail by Valerius Geist in *Mountain Sheep*, the horn clash unfolds in a broader context; a horn battle is but a brief moment early in the rut. It can also happen outside the breeding season, year-round, when strange rams of similar age and size meet. It is not a direct fight for females, but a fight for rank. Ewes need not be present.

Earlier, on their bachelor grounds, the Blue Door Band's rams had changed passive tolerance of one another into ritualistic aggression. Those prerut encounters involved butting, kicks, neck stretches, body twists, grunts, huddles in tight groups, "homosexual" mountings, and other behavior that made their horn size—the quintessential focus of rank—conspicuous to one another.

Large-horned, older males seldom engage in full-force contests with small-horned, younger males, Geist has noted. Obvious differences in headgear translate into an obvious dominant-subordinate ranking. Instead, the most severe and lengthy confrontations occur between rams of similar physical size. Displays are not enough. These rams have but one means to establish dominance, to judge the other's clash force: fighting. Such contests culminate in hundreds of pounds of muscle and bone lunging at one another, skulls meeting in a violent crash amplified by the echo chamber of canyon walls.

Compared to wild sheep, elk are flatlanders. Elk organize their mating society by territory. A bull elk forms a harem by evicting other bulls and claiming all of the females in a certain area. His status is his plot of turf.

The harem strategy won't work on a bighorn's vertical terrain. The ewes favor cliffs and outcrops. They are not a very herdable mass; they are like a herd of popcorn. The dominant ram must guard them one at a time. He carries his status on his head, and shows it off. The mating behavior of elk and sheep tells us how closely land and biology are bound.

A prevailing bighorn ram gains temporary possession of receptive mates, moving from one female to another during a period of several weeks, with about thirty to sixty seconds per ewe in flagrante delicto. He is seldom alone with the ewes. Through blocking, horn display, and other interactions, he must remind the other rams of his dominance.

The desert bighorns above the river, though resting at the moment, have reached this courtship phase. Some of the head bashing will continue, but the rams' prerut activity has already established a somewhat organic hierarchy.

For this group, the chocolate ram has earned the role of tending ram—part inseminator, part guardian. Among bovids, his species has some of the heaviest testes relative to body weight.

His testicles have doubled, or perhaps even tripled, in size for the mating season. Although multiple rams may inseminate a ewe, the greater the sperm volume, the more likely the paternity. A flood of sperm drowns out the wimps.

In this corridor of stone, bighorn sheep propagation takes time. It is flesh, blood, and desert transformed into ritual. If the rituals succeed, the bighorns will have saved themselves.

The Blue Door Band's seasons are the desert's seasons. If you are living by a desert bighorn calendar, you will note that it is governed by the simple factor of birth. By timing the birth of the year's young when temperatures are moderate and food is abundant for lactating ewes, the lambs have the greatest chance to survive.

For the Blue Door Band, whose existence is governed by four distinct seasons on the high desert of the Colorado Plateau, these optimal conditions come in the spring; the ewes lamb from late April to early June. Subtract the 180 days it takes to gestate a lamb and you arrive back here in November and December, at the rut and period of conception, with eleven sheep napping in the dust like plump loaves of bread.

During the fall, temperatures have cooled and the days have shortened. Now the sun rises, barely pauses, then sets on its low arc. For mountain sheep, day length influences a ewe's readiness to conceive. Her estrus is induced by light.

The bighorns gather. They mate. Sperm pierce ovum, in time. Add 180 days and the northern hemisphere's longer ride through sunlight. The green returns, heavy and sweet. The air is warm, the light is long, and there is good food. The lambs arrive.

The symmetry of survival is nothing short of miraculous.

At my post across from the sheep, I feel squirmy. I do not have the stomach of a ruminant, a fermentation vat that needs repose for its digestive chemistry. I have not been eating dried grass and sticks.

I stretch my legs, then stand on the lip of a twenty-foot drop and look at the footholds that I would take if I were a bighorn sheep. The rock face plunges down an unbroken slab of limestone. Entirely unsuitable for bipeds. I would die.

At the edge of a higher cliff, I lower the binoculars straight down. The magnified abyss makes me queasy. I turn the binoculars around and aim them at my feet. How very far away they are, claustrophobic in their socks. I peer down at a blackbrush, all woody matter and nearly leafless: winter sheep food, the edible desert. In the faraway end of the binoculars, the bush looks like a tiny silver cage for a hummingbird.

The afternoon's long shadow swallows the canyon with an almost detectable speed. The sheep no longer lie in sunlight. One ewe rises quickly from her bed and looks at the river gorge as if suddenly remembering something she left on the bus. The others leave their beds and amble about. The flared-horn ram stands behind a bush, near the ewes, staring at their asses.

"Let's see you get that cantaloupe off the ground," I say to the chocolate ram as he rises. In one slow-motion push of his haunches, he leaps straight up a wall to a ledge above the bed area.

Map the day trails of a mixed group of desert bighorns and you will quickly see that ewes instigate "aimed" motion, the movement from one place to another. When a ram leaves a group, none of the other sheep follows. If you are anthropomorphizing about gender, this may set to rest once and for all who exactly is in charge around here.

Ears forward, body and stare fixed along a distinct line of sight, the first ewe off her bed now holds an attention posture.

With her gaze, she tells the others that she intends to move soon and which direction she will take. When she moves, the others follow . . . well, like *sheep.*

In their liquid leaps, eleven animals flow up a rock face to a narrow shelf below a steep arroyo. They pretend to act like a bunch of chewing herbivores. In fact, a bit of hell is breaking loose.

The flared-horn ram rushes at a female and singles her out from the herd. She bolts off at full speed. She careens and zigzags across the ledge, veering sharply around shrubs and boulders like a barrel-racing quarter horse at a rodeo. The ram is on her tail at every turn. When she pauses, he tries to mount her, but she wheels around to face him off and won't stand still.

Pursued closely by her suitor, the ewe weaves back and forth around the shelf of rock. Sometimes they pass within inches of its lip and an abrupt drop to the river, saved by their agility and the pure luck of galloping lust. The ram's strategy is called a "rape chase," or "coursing." In some cases, coursing works. Often the ewe rejects his attempts to mount, or the dominant, guardian ram broadsides the younger male and sends him sprawling.

The chase lasts for over eight minutes. Then the ewe leaps up a boulder, where the chocolate ram happens to be standing. There she stops, her sides heaving.

When the chasing ram spots the big chocolate male, I swear I hear a meek little *Oops!* bleat. In a split-second about-face, he whirls around and bolts straight toward the other ewes. His arrival splits the group apart and sends everyone fleeing in different directions. He dashes about, madly charging butts.

The chocolate ram, the tending, courting dominant, stands on the boulder with the tired ewe. He stretches his back and pees. He noses her flanks and pushes his chest against her rump. She half-jumps and lifts her tail. He noses and pushes her again. Then he mounts and humps her atop a rock the size of a Yugo.

Back at home, my services as goose whisperer are no longer required. The "hunters" have not returned, and the big birds peacefully track the arc of the day with their flights from field to river and back.

The canyon country sprawls under a tepid sun and ten years of drought, which has left hardly a stick of vegetation. I sit on the deck and draw optimistic pictures of desert bighorns eating the bounty of less desertified times. Below the house, across the valley, a coyote throws her song to the other side of the river. The high red bluffs throw the song back. The echo is so clear, at first I think I am hearing two coyotes.

The repeated song is purposeful; the coyote knows there is no other animal but herself. She is being a Zen coyote. She asks a question and receives the same question back as an answer.

She sings to the red wall for a long time, with lengthy pauses between howl and echo. When she finishes and moves on, I walk to the river and find the singing place. The coyote has taught me which piece of the escarpment has the best echoing wall.

"Rain," I cry.

Rain.

"Snow?"

Snow?

A few days later, clouds move in and a fierce windstorm whips through the valley, mocking us with its rainless fury. Among Indians of Arizona's Sonoran Desert, violent winds came when you did not handle your bighorn kill properly, when you hunted but failed to put the horns in the place set apart for them. Each hunter had such a horn place. If he brought the horns home, he would insult the wind.

One day, I walk along a stretch of river in the usual existentialist coma: Do rocks have souls? What is the meaning of life? A slow-moving glassy mirror of winter light, the river holds all of my attention. It carries everything I need to know. This kind of strolling reverie usually ends up with me walking face-first into a bush.

Instead, I come across a bighorn ram, ewe, and ewe lamb on a rocky slope above the riverbank. They lie on their day beds. Were a swarm of fundamentalist Christians to stroll by, they would see a trio presenting portrait-perfect *Ovis* family values. Meanwhile, the rest of the canyon hides the depraved orgies of mixed rutting groups.

I slowly move away from the riverbank and watch the three-some from a distance that will not disturb them. They are aware of me but not alarmed. The river flows between us as an agreed-upon boundary.

The ram has a hefty set of flared horns, horns that have been described as a "cast-iron jester's cap." From her distinctive gray-beige coloring and a radio collar and ear tag, I recognize the ewe from the summer. The lamb is likely her young of the year.

The adults lie on bare ground in oven-fresh-bread position. The lamb rests atop a horizontal slab of sandstone like a hood ornament. She still has a sweet young face and a dark brown neck cape with what looks like electrocuted fuzz.

When I first came to this canyon over twenty years ago, I saw thousands of desert bighorns. They ran single file across smooth faces of sandstone varnished by weather and minerals to a dark patina.

Some were simple rectangles with stick legs and arching horns. Others lifted their tails, spread cloven hooves, flattened their ears, and opened their mouths as if to tell you something, an anima-tion that barely seemed possible in the medium of stone pecked by stone tools. The style said a great deal about bighorn sheep anatomy and even more about stories, stories that were enigmatic or instructive of the things you must do if you are a hunter.

Up a canyon crack so steep and difficult that you have to spider up the rocks to reach it and earn the honor with bloodied hands, two bighorn petroglyphs attached themselves to the universe. A spiral emerged from a raised tail. The other figure exhaled (or inhaled) a wavy line from its mouth. The animals were contiguous with these lines, as if they trailed air or sounds.

The makers of the petroglyphs, pueblo dwellers who hunted and farmed the southwestern deserts a thousand years before, had left enough bighorn sheep to fill my dreams each night I slept in a canyon or on a mesa top. I never saw a real bighorn sheep. I never *looked*. The river blinded me with rapture. The river blinded me with rapture for twenty years.

Back then, I knew nothing of sheep scat, beds, and other signs. I saw no tracks, I found no bones. I met only their absence from a place where bighorns had once been, a past marked by their portraits on the canyon walls. Like most people, I presumed that overhunting, habitat loss, and the presence of domestic live-stock in the vicinity of this canyon had doomed its free-living native bighorns. I presumed "local extinction."

Beyond my notice, in those early years of river time, the Blue

Door Band would emerge, out of folds of sheer stone, from decades of absence. There would be wild sheep, like the three on the riverbank, in the flesh again, living on the cliffs that bore the images of their ancestors.

Now, the day is lazy and mild. The river sings a quiet song over submerged rocks. The bighorns stare into space, or at me. I am quite entertaining, but not entertaining enough for them to lift their butts off the ground.

NOVEMBER

The desert bighorn is an animal shaped by ice.

A creature that can break open and eat a spiky-bodied barrel cactus, that can go without water for days, then drink like a camel, that wears a fur coat in summer heat soaring beyond a hundred degrees—these are not images of an ice animal. Yet the design of wild sheep is very much an expression of arctic cold.

The route from ice to desert began in the early Pleistocene, in Asia, the ancestral grounds of ruminant mammals. About two million years ago, on the border between Pliocene and Pleistocene, a cooling climate and buckling mountain ranges saw an extraordinary expansion of mammal fauna from south of the Himalayas into Asia and central Europe. Among them were hoofed cud chewers, whose story you will know if you read the story of grass.

Ice ages, major episodes of advancing and retreating glaciers, marked the Pleistocene epoch, and mammals were the Pleistocene's art. At one time scrawny little beasts that scuttled under the palmettos, mammals had responded to changes in environment and climate with traits like flexible spines, young that nurse, jaws that chew sideways rather than chop, necks that move without turning the whole body. Four-chambered hearts pumped warm blood. Internally regulated body temperatures allowed survival from mountaintop to swamp, from the equator to the Arctic.

In the mammalian array came claws, hooves, toes, toed hooves. Aquatic rhinos, pigs of disturbing sizes, runt horses, rabbit-size camels, toothy grazers that ate whole nations of grasslands like huge lawn mowers. Efficient motion favored dispersal into new terrain; mobile creatures could spread until they reached a barrier of land or climate, ice or food supply. The migrating vegetarians took the meat-eaters with them.

The subfamily Caprinae, classified into tribes that include the Caprini (sheep, goats, sheep-goats), grew massive head ornaments and the skulls to carry them. By the late Pleistocene, caprid stock had arrived in North America by crossing the Bering land bridge between Siberia and Alaska. From there, they dispersed during interglacial, or warming, periods. Some of their descendants now occupy a range from Alaska to the tip of the Baja California peninsula.

Life in the Pleistocene's flux favored the biological complexity of herd life, translated not only as behavior but also in their very bodies—as color, coat patterns, manes, rump patches, and scent glands in the skin. The visuals, postures, and olfactory signs carried meaning within a close society of companions and competitors.

And in no other epoch but this one, in ice, cold, and oscillating climate, was there anything quite like the evolution of horns as elaborate social organs. While the tribe Caprini may show a variety of physical characteristics among members, its members all possess a solid common trait: social behavior that is overtly frontal—that is, concentrated on their heads.

Out on the rims, a hardening cold seeps into every surface. Already stripped by its very nature, the desert now seems skeletal. Brittle stems on the blackbrush snap against my pant legs as I walk. The rough dirt skates underfoot like stones inside a dry gourd. On the limestone slabs where I sit, the cold rises up from the rock into my spine. When I stand with my back to the sun, I cast a Giacometti shadow—thin, reedy, fourteen feet long— across dirt the color of sandblasted bricks. Around me, the sheep

are hairing up as they rut, and the ravens take perches on sandstone, warming their skinny toes.

This is not *cold,* I remind myself. Once, near Montana's Glacier
National Park, a snowstorm moved out of the night mountains.
Beneath the cloud cover, the temperature had hovered in the low
twenties. Mark and I put on our skis and slid cross-country under
a clearing sky and a full polar moon. Behind the storm, the air
suddenly dropped to fifteen degrees below zero. All moisture
converted to ice crystals. The cryogenic plunge was tangible, a
sharp sucking of air from the lungs. My hand and foot bones felt
like X rays look.

"That cold was an ice age," I declare perhaps a bit defensively
to the ravens, who know a doormat when they see one. This winter desert is an interglacial banana belt, made obvious by the fact
that I am hatless and wearing gloves with fingerless tips. I put my
notebook away and call it a day.

I stop for lunch at a small café by the river. The place is nearly
empty, the television tuned to the Weather Channel, which no
one is watching, perhaps because the meteorologist is obsessively
describing Chicago. The cook brings me a bowl of mutton stew
and a piece of fry bread the size of an inflated sombrero. Pow-
wow music plays in the kitchen. The stew is blow-on-the-spoon
hot. Finally, I warm up.

The next time you buff up the Hummer with an auto-detailing
cloth that came from the skin of a petite rupicaprid, bond with
the ungulates that share with us a molecular past.

The ice millennia gave the world hooved animals that range in
size from the thirty-one-pound female chamois, donor of the car
polisher, to the burly 660-pound male musk ox. They come in
brown, copper, black, gray, buff, and blond, sometimes two- or
three-toned.

The Himalayan blue sheep, or bharal, is neither blue nor a sheep, but slate gray and a perplexing combination of sheep and goat, at best an aberrant goat with sheeplike traits. The bharal is the favored prey of the snow leopard, a predator designed precisely to kill it.

Horns of Caprinae are short, long, very long, very short; smooth, bumpy, corrugated; spiraled, curved, curled, corkscrewed. The horns on the now-rare Marco Polo sheep curl, flip, then zap outward toward the horizon in a sort of soft slash, Zorro's Z. Horns on the giants of the group tend to look like melting Viking helmets. The smallest species favor straight-out-of-the-skull sabers that stab wild dogs. Some sheep are experts at an operatic flare and curl.

Bibs, beards, dorsal stripes, ruffs, manes; mantles of hair that drape over rumps and flanks; flicking tongues, stretched necks, and tense, stocky bodies that look like sneaky hay bales—such features convey rank and aggression in a realm where status gives access to mates. Appearance is language.

Some species are solitary. Others protect themselves from predators by a group, rather than a loner, life. Multiple senses—many eyes, ears, noses—detect danger. Snorts, grunts, alarm postures, and other signals transmit the alert instantly. As a communal defense against wolves, burly musk oxen stand shoulder-to-shoulder, looking like a cinder-block wall that overdosed on hairgrowth stimulants.

In North America, the thinhorn sheep took the northernmost kingdom—Alaska, the Yukon, northwest Canada—and, by the insularity of climate and distance, experienced the least human impact. Dall's sheep are golden-horned and snow-white, as one might expect for a subarctic world. The other thinhorn species, Stone's sheep, are nearly black.

In the Canadian and American West and in Mexico, the bighorns fell within reach of greater human activity. By the end of the nineteenth century, their numbers had plummeted and their range had diminished to scattered fragments.

Bound to the vulnerable geography of the plains, to the broken badlands and river breaks on the Upper Missouri and Yellowstone rivers, the Audubon's bighorn quickly walked into the crosshairs of American settlement. By the late 1800s, the subspecies was extinct. The California bighorn, Rocky Mountain bighorn, and the four desert bighorn races are still among us, but they have been extirpated on much of their former range. They have gone from ice to islands.

November slides toward December, tilting the balance of light further toward night. When I find a group of bighorns, I more often watch them in shadow than in sunlight. The canyon air turns frigid inside its chamber of stone. Cleared of much of its silt, the river flows verdigris against banks of salmon-colored sand, edged with the white lace of ice.

Bighorn sheep do not unfurl their breeding dramas in serene meadows or on the easy terrain of open flats. Imagine, instead, a six-hundred-foot-high wall of loose boulders, crumbling rock, and narrow, tiered wedding-cake ledges, you racing about in full-lust sprints, courting an evasive female while fending off rivals with your head.

Valerius Geist's studies of the rut suggest that older rams have a more refined courting technique than younger ones, with the effect of conserved energy, less stress for both ram and ewe, and, ultimately, more reproductive success. I do not see the archetypical full-curl, "Stay calm, then nail her," chocolate ram again. In most of the groups, the rams appear close in age and muster, the dominant-subordinate hierarchy more fluid, the fighting increasingly vigorous. There is more coursing than courtship. In short, the band is exhausting itself with aggression.

From a post high across the river one day, I watch five rams cut a young ewe away from a group and chase her up and down the cliff. In her attempt to shake them, she runs nearly half a mile upriver. On a terrace, she zigzags and barrel-races, all five rams at her rump. From the terrace, she jumps up a wall and perches on a foothold so narrow, it holds only her, a panting ewe with all four hooves on a footing the size of a teacup. The rams huddle below, breathing hard.

She jumps off her teacup and dashes away again. Whenever a ram closes in and tries to mount her, she wheels around and faces him. The other four circle her. The ewe lies down and tries to tuck in her rump. Divest yourself of all romantic notions. Sheep love is rough.

At one point, the ewe backs into a sumac bush so that none of the rams can reach her backside. Brief fights break out among the rams—kicks, shoulder heaves, horns slammed into flanks. Two rams face each other, tilt heads, and rise. They roar toward each other in a head-cracking clash that is so loud, I feel it in my teeth.

The rut is not without concussions, broken horns, broken legs, puncture wounds, bruised gonies, and other injuries. More often, aggression is literally absorbed by ritual, by behavior that appeases, by responses that quickly sort out status, and by the unequivocal language of head armor used like blocks of concrete. Today's rape chase is brutal. But no blood is shed; no necks are broken.

The rams pursue the ewe as she races toward a freestanding boulder with a narrow crack at its base. She drops to the ground on all fours and *crawls* into the crack to hide. All I can see is her face. Amber eyes peer out from this small cave: a ewe in a rock cubby. Five rams form a semicircle around the opening. They wait.

In a clumsy daydream, I am crashing my way through evolution at warp speed, as if all of time could fit inside a peanut. I go from slime to squid in a breath. The dinosaurs fall into a well. Dead ends and extinctions fly off like pits spit from olives. I zip over arboreal simians, crash through chimps, ignore the fruit-muncher hominid who peers through the leaves, blinks, and aims a hairy foot toward a pig carcass to grab a bite to eat.

In my crash through time, rock persuades itself into mountains, rivers carve through their heart, and closed basins hold immense lakes of silvery blue. A continent swarms with creatures, many of them overtly large, many of them horned and hooved, some of them headed toward oblivion: giant bears, dire wolves, saber-toothed cats; an American cheetah, a shrub ox, a species called yesterday's camel; mountain goats that eat the bark of Douglas firs, giant sloths foraging near the Grand Canyon.

Behind retreating ice, a wave of Siberian *Homos* spreads southward, jabbing Pleistocene megafauna with their little spears, dragging bloody mammoth haunches off to shelters of rock and laying them at the feet of their *enamorada*.

For 99 percent of our existence as humans, we lived as nomadic hunters and foragers. That leaves barely a blip for sedentary agriculture, written language, armies, and serious biological amnesia. Yet a river of creatures lives inside our cranium—reptiles in our brain stem, ocean life in our olfactory nerves, the whole of primate evolution in our sexuality, boldness, and self-awareness.

Paul Shepard calls the Pleistocene "the era of our becoming," a formative period for slow-breeding, bipedal, hunting omnivores. He uses this Cenozoic moment to underscore a central tenet of his work: The structure of the human brain, the very evolution of intelligence, depends on animals.

Although some of his arguments have been shown to be flawed, Shepard's words illuminate the context, if not the biology. "Animals are among the first inhabitants of the mind's eye," he wrote in *Thinking Animals*. "They are basic to the development of speech and thought. Because of their part in the growth of consciousness, they are inseparable from a series of events in each human life, indispensable to our becoming human in the fullest sense."

In the daydream, I am looking through the wrong end of the binoculars. I see the pale retreating rumps of the Blue Door Band. They are the size of dissolving pollen grains. What if you scan the land for these wild sheep, and for the other descendants of the ice mammals, but find none? What happens when, as the experts tell us, at the end of the current millennium most of the plant, animal, and bird species we know today are gone? Will this leave us brain-damaged?

In between sheep visits, I was under the impression that my life was every bit as ordinary as other people's lives, typical lives, with a Mercedes in one's field, Zen-trained coyotes in the river bottom, and ice-age mammals in the canyons, eating cactus.

Part of my life was the typical middle-aged gut-churning panic of riding a globe through space, a globe that spins through time with utter indifference to one's being. All over America, millions of fellow baby boomers were standing in front of the mirror in their jammies, utterly astonished to discover that dissipation and disintegration—of mind, of body, of matter—are essential elements of existence, and that the slide toward them is ever quickening and inevitable.

Watching wild animals intensely, like prayer, somewhat tempered the panic. At home, however, I paid far too much attention to my own cerebral senescence. I noticed peculiar episodes in brain activity.

It began one day in the post office. I stood at the counter, wearing an old teal-colored Eddie Bean barn coat over my jammies, a letter in hand. Suddenly, a meteor struck my head and erased 40 percent of my vocabulary. The *D* words slid down the Formica counter and headed toward the stamp drawer. The *B*'s formed snowdrifts against the postmaster's government-issue steel gray desk. My numb tongue flung participles at the MOST WANTED posters. Nouns fled in great chunks.

For three panicked minutes, eyes wide in horror, I was unable to pluck the word *certified* from the cosmos. The postmaster politely rumbled a barrage of questions at me: "Stamps? Parcel post? Delivery confirmation?" Speechwise, the tip of a peninsula broke off from my mainland brain and the sea flooded into the breach behind it.

In the days that followed, a kind of sonic language began to spill all over my paragraphs and conversations. I was a walking factory of messy homonyms, wacky neologisms, and absurd errors. "Ceiling wax" for sealing wax. "Plankton" for parking lot. The living room became "the basilica," Mark's circular saw "the cyclical saw." I said the human body had "Olympic nodes," then "lint nodes"; the navel harbored "an admiral's fleet." This was not the cleverness of puns or wordplay. The words that flew from mouth and pen were simply a train wreck.

Lamanites. I could not wrap my tongue around the Lamanites. According to my local duo of puppy-faced Mormon missionaries, the Lamanites were the sons of Laman, a lost tribe of Israelites who, in biblical times, had been cursed with dark skin for their sinful wickedness.

Mormon theology says that the Lamanites somehow found themselves nowhere near the Holy Land any longer. They ended up in North America as Indians, morally and geographically astray, running around wild and barbaric and godless in the New World until their unfallen (Latter-day Saint) brethren arrived to rejoin them to their lost faith. The puppies talked a lot about separation and rejoining.

"The Laminates?" I yelped to the missionaries, expressing the lunatic disbelief of one so obviously hell-bound that her undies were incinerating. "Do you mean to say that the Apaches are Laminates?" As in: Don't laminate me to your church. I was one speech-impaired Episcopalian.

This outburst quickly deteriorated into an assortment of imperfectly remembered Bible stories and the compulsion to tell them that I had married a man who was once expelled from Presbyterian Sunday school for coloring the face of Jesus with a purple crayon. I let them in on a tiny secret. "My purple-Jesus husband," I whispered, "thinks we live in this remote, isolated place because we're under a Jehovah's Witness protection program."

This pathetic monologue drew pitying looks from the puppies. They looked at their Rolexes and wondered how long it would take to ride their bikes to the next batch of Laminates on the nearby Navajo reservation.

Then the ear worms arrived. Silently, I began to count everything. An involuntary static of numbers rolled across my cranium as I walked up the steps. Down the trail to the gardens on the lower end of our property, I counted each rabbitbrush along the way, left and right, returning to the top of the trail when I lost track. I counted the times I stuck the shovel into the frost-covered potato bed. I measured fence posts, the distance between lightbulbs in the living room.

In junior high school, I loathed math, and the feeling was mutual. Mathematics attacked me at every opportunity. My algebra teacher made it his mission to make a girl cry whenever he started the class hour. For him, it was a warm-up exercise and, by persistent humiliation, it worked. He disdainfully called his female students "amphibians," neither girl nor woman, but in between. He told us we were innumerate by gender and always would be.

When he was lazy or anxious to get on with it, the math teacher would simply look at me, and I'd conveniently burst into tears. Then on we went to negative exponents. The math itself—

the numbers on the blackboard, the numbers inside my textbook, the scrawl beneath my pencil—threw me into hysteria. It all looked like the claw marks of unhappy squirrels.

In high school and college, I struggled on, doing well in all subjects except math, which, as Gabriel García Márquez wrote in his autobiography, "not even God could make me understand." I resigned myself to a lifetime of baby math. And now, years later, numbers filled every nook of my skull like swelling marshmallows.

The oppression of detail, the repetition of household chores, grew horrifying. How many times in my life had I put forks, knives, and spoons in a drawer after I'd washed them? I actually tried to add up the total, then calculate the sum in individual utensils—hundreds of spoons, thousands of forks. *Salad or dinner forks?* I screamed silently. Mark hung out his wash to dry on the line and I raced out to count it, to align every T-shirt hem with the ground.

My language and counting problems soon slid into an optical problem, precipitated by my certainty that all surfaces on which I walked had tilted ever so slightly, too little to induce dizziness or loss of balance, but enough to make every inanimate object in my physical environment *crooked.* It became my duty to straighten them.

The human brain weighs slightly more than a pot roast. It lives inside a dark, silent shell of bone, the organizing genius of bursts of electric current in 100 billion neurons. The neuron jungle is densely packed and interconnected—1 million billion possible connections in the cortex alone, estimates say. Several billion of mine were not working. My cortex had the wiring of a 1950s toaster.

Sometimes I felt like a shortwave radio with a rampaging antenna that picked up overlapping stations and a crackle of atmospherics. Sometimes some sort of anorexic cannibal was chewing on my locus coeruleus. My head no longer produced thoughts, only data—not soft, squishy, round clumps, but pointy stabs of noise.

The inherent crookedness of the world drove me to distraction. In the house, I madly straightened rugs, place mats, towels, and books. I whipped out a screwdriver to straighten the cover plates on the electric outlets. Outside, the hems of the sheets drying on the clothesline had to match up—*precisely*. Or the truck was not quite lined up with the walls of its shade house, so I backed it out and parked it straight. Whenever I fixed my stare on the askewness of Mark's bootlaces, he ran for his life.

The brain salad—verbal paralysis, counting, straightening—came in spells, like a tic. I blamed solar flares, bulges in the magnetosphere, drops in barometric pressure, nuclear testing in Pakistan. More likely, nothing was wrong. Quit whining, I told myself. Take a deep breath. Embrace senility. The flaky neurotransmissions were normal for my aging organ, which actually, now that you ask, may have contained just a teensy-weensy bit of the obsessive-compulsive since my birth.

"One of the major hidden manifestations of aging," writes neurobiologist William H. Calvin, "is a decline in many of the neurotransmitter substances used by one nerve cell to signal an adjacent one." My cells were not speaking to one another. Still, most of the brain's parts remain plastic; plasticity, rather than rigidity, leaves nerve cells open to change and learning. As it ages, the brain loses some of its capacity to memorize—its "fluid intelligence"—but compensates with an increase in "crystallized intelligence," the ability to conceptualize and place things in perspective.

They only say this to make us feel better, I told myself after an exhausting binge of lightbulb measuring. I longed for concepts. I craved perspective. All I got were eighty-five rabbitbrush shrubs between the house and the potato patch.

Verbally, I was stuck. Other functions plunged into mental

overdrive, a deluge of completely useless and irrelevant information. One hemisphere had cannibals and fizzling circuitry. In the other hemisphere, darkness swallowed creativity and intuition. "I fear I am not in my perfect mind," Lear cries.

I had a chat with my doctor about neurological disorders. He knew that I was always the complete opposite of a hypochondriac, that I would endure nearly anything before letting out even the most timid peep, something like "Oh, by the way, do you suppose that this severed, blood-spurting arm might be reattached?" Or "Might this entire paralysis of my body from my left temple to my little toe, uh, be a stroke?"

This time, he knew that I was serious, but he was not worried. My age was right there on the chart. Age explained a lot. Age was tilting me toward what a friend called "precocious senility."

I described the symptoms. The postal moment, the Laminates and cannibals, the forebrain hurricanes.

"No matter what, you can't give me a biochemical correction," I insisted vehemently. "I need an edge. I'm an artist. My imagination is my life, my income, the way I make friends. To be creative, I must have many deep-seated pathologies, abysmally low self-esteem." "Selfish steam," my husband calls it. "I must . . . I must *suffer.*"

"You mean you don't want zombie drugs?" the doctor said with a smile, his look suggesting he might have tried a few himself.

I pictured myself in a diagnostic lab, wearing white mummy wrap and head bandages, disappearing into the maw of a gleaming white culvert that would magnetically resonate every last organ underneath my skin. As I rolled out the other end, a sweet nurse would tell me, "Your brain looks just like a toaster."

I liked my doctor. He was neither a pharmacological zealot nor the type to advocate immediate surgery. He didn't drive a BMW. No matter how much I wanted to see a picture of my brain—the

busy little neuron serfs running around in their huaraches, plug-
ging in wires, forgetting to plug in quite a few—he discouraged,
for the time being, a recreational MRI. We decided that I should
have more patience with my unruly mind—try, perhaps, to discern wisdom within the chaos. He thought it might be a good
idea if I took up sea kayaking.

Then, as November ended, the brain fevers subsided.

My brain fevers always calm when I go out to look for the sheep.
I fill my days with copulating ungulates. Cold, sunny afternoons
yield animated maternal bands—ewes and juveniles—each with
a guardian ram in full curl and several younger crazed rams.
Often, I find animals quite close to the same location from day to
day. At other times, they are in one place one day, then far away
the next, as if they have flown there.

Canyon, wide-open desert, distant mesas—the bighorn homeland feels infinite and invulnerable. Is it winter's stillness, where
the loudest sound is silence, that makes it so?

So immense is our space on these winter days, I forget that the
sheep live in a boxed-in fragment of imperiled terrain. Even in
this remote canyon, semiferal dogs once chased a ewe until she
climbed to a safe ledge, where she perched and quivered until the
dogs lost patience and left. There have been sightings of bobcats,
rumors of mountain lions, and a rare but inevitable poacher. The
moat around the band is thin.

On one of my forays far from my usual posts, I spot eight
domestic sheep and goats on the flats behind the canyon rims,
just a few miles from Ram Land, the home range of the Blue
Door Band's males. The rams are not in residence at the moment.
They are downriver, on ewe range, going at it hammer and tongs.
Nevertheless, I become apprehensive.

Desert bighorn sheep are acutely susceptible to bronchial

pneumonia and can pick up the infecting bacteria from domestic sheep. As one wildlife biologist told me, one nose-to-nose contact and the bighorns are toast. A single animal, usually a ram, because rams tend to roam, can carry the disease back to the rest of the herd, where the crisis is known, rather bluntly, as a die-off.

I pace the decks of sandstone along the canyon rim. I change from a mild-mannered voyeur to Bo Peep going berserk with worry. However, after that one day, I do not see the domestic sheep again.

Back with the Blue Door Band, I watch the conception of next year's crop of lambs. So far so good. There are no signs that the rut will be anything but successful—cyclical and certain, as rooted in deep time as the land that shaped them.

Horn clashes, lip curls, chases and courtship, the shiver of attentiveness, the silken grace of flight—the bighorn sheep can do all of this by themselves. I pray there will be no catastrophe, no interference. I watch the sheep for hours, for days. On their tenuous island, their survival means more than a wild animal among us. Their survival, I am convinced, guarantees the tangible truth of our imaginations.

The sheep are bedded down, exhausted from orgies. Their ears twitch and a few let their chins rest on the ground. Others chew and stare at the canyon walls, blinking their pale lashes. I pull from my pack the Book of Common Prayer, a new tack in the strategy to chill the fevers of an aging brain. First prayer, then acupuncture, I think, picturing a forest of tiny needles in my forehead.

The thick book, bound in dark navy cloth with gold letters on its spine, is small enough to fit across the palm of the hand when it is open. Its pages are as thin as tissue. The one I held was a 1945 edition of the 1789 version, an American adaptation of the original text by the sixteenth-century British scholar Thomas Cranmer. In 1979, Cranmer's lineage was replaced by a "simpler" text.

The 1945 edition of the Book of Common Prayer was the prayer book of my childhood, of Sundays in a pew, sitting in my stiff cotton dress and straw hat, reading this small tome not as a canon but as a storybook, a piece of literature, all the while ignoring the minister, a gray-haired Irishman whose name was, confusingly, Lord—"The Reverend *LORD*," one of my brothers boomed in a baritone-in-a-culvert God voice.

The Irish minister's name had a remarkable effect each time a prayer began with "O Lord." "O Lord, we beseech thee, mercifully hear our prayers," we implored over and over, as if he were deaf.

The men in the congregation seemed to need a great deal of help. O Lord was forever beseeching "brethren," and since I wasn't one of them, I took this as a sign for me to tune out and read this exquisite little book, to wander over scourges and plagues, epistles and epiphanies, idols and bleating, bleeding goats.

Something called "alms," a bill from my mother's wallet, went into a collection plate. Over time and remodeling, the church's windows went from clear glass and views of leaves and birds to stained-glass portraits of Saint Francis with pigeons. "The days of man are but as grass," I read.

Today, under a boundless desert sky, I encounter in the prayer book a homeland not of faith but of images. I find movable feasts, holy days gauged by full moons, psalms grounded in an arcane physicality. Pelicans and owls, lions and sheep. The "great and wild sea also; wherein are things creeping innumerable . . ." Rivers swollen with flow, valleys soft with rain, rain greening the hills. "Thou crownest the year with thy goodness; and thy clouds drop fatness."

Nothing fat drops here; no innumerables creep. The lean,

parched desert withers under ten years of drought. The ewes are off their beds, bunched up in a flock, eating sticks and brittle blond grasses. It is a miracle that they are fed.

A ram lifts his head from a bush, then charges the herd, scattering it across the talus. He isolates a ewe and approaches her in a low stretch. Three younger rams form a huddle, heads inside the circle, white rumps facing out. The huddle reminds them of rank without the risk of fights. They are figuring things out with their heads. Theirs is a world beyond me as I sit on my rock with a book of moons and liturgy resting on my palm.

With desert bighorns, as with any other life-form, there is faith in time. From time emerges a more certain yet always elastic portrait of the hooved herbivore that, born in thin glacial air and ice caves, eventually took hold in vertical desert rock.

This is not an animal that eats you. It travels through but won't live in forests or on the flats. It binds its group by matrilineal threads and passes knowledge about home ground from generation to generation. Move a group of bighorns to a place from which their predecessors have been extirpated, and the new ones must draw a map, find the water.

Desert bighorns are gregarious herbivores with clear, predictable, edgy social rituals. Their loyalty to the group into which they were born, and to their natal home range, is extreme. There is even a word for this: *philopatry.*

They are followers. Hours after birth, lambs are followers. Because they are not usually alone or in dense cover, they need not deter predators by hiding or tiptoeing away or looking like a rock or the vegetation. Open terrain lets them see and flee.

By bunching up, herd animals exercise what is called "the selfish effect," using one another as shields and diluting an individual's chances of being eaten. They flee together, as if of one mind.

Wild sheep are superb escape artists. Escape, in fact, can be more important than diet. Insecurity over a predator or other disagreeable surprises, for instance, can induce them to trade good forage for safety. The flight reaction might keep them on the less nutritious range for several seasons. They are habitat specialists. They are particular. This is their salvation and their doom.

While their relatives on flatter lands are lithe and speedy and have powerful lungs, mountain sheep are rock jumpers, muscular, and built to negotiate steep, rugged terrain. Falls, fights, parasites, and avalanches kill them. They can go blind. In homelands of precipices and broken cliffs, of minuscule footholds above hundred-foot drops, a blind sheep faces a serious challenge.

In Darwinian terms, the evolution of wild sheep has been shaped by the selection pressures of food and fear. They must eat. They must escape predators. In order to replicate themselves, they impress or challenge one another with how they look and what they do with their heads. To a mountain lion, they are meat. In a sheepcentric view, they are well designed for *something*: other sheep. And survival means doing their very best to starve a mountain lion.

Out in the far canyon, the air is dry and still. The bighorn rut winds down, an interlude, perhaps, before the mating season's final weeks. Most often, I see maternal bands feeding and resting in an atmosphere devoid of four-legged cantaloupes.

In groups with rams, the rams are frayed and haggard. After copulating, some are listless and vague. All of the rams are thinner, their body weight reduced from its robust prerut condition.

The sheep expend a great deal of energy in chase, courtship, and guarding, while not much time on eating or resting. The rams will enter deep winter with fewer fat reserves and the season's scant vegetation. In some cases, a drastic loss of vigor will compromise survival. A few may return to their home grounds after the rut and die.

Still, there are ewes yet to come into heat. I spend another day at the post with the full view of the boulder cave, where the ewe hid from her five suitors. No sheep in sight. Did I expect to see them in the same place? Taking up where they left off? After so much sheep lust, I expect nothing less.

The boulder reveals nothing but the memory of the chase. I search for sheep upriver and downriver. I walk to other posts, take in broader views. It's sheep nap time, I tell myself. They look like rocks. They look like loaves of bread. I won't be able to spot them until they move or turn a white rump toward me.

A rock falls off the canyon wall with a hollow *ka-chink,* possibly dislodged by a hoof. I scan a broad swathe at the sound's source but see no sheep.

When the bighorns are not here, the canyon feels empty. The emptiness slips down the canyon wall and passes over the river. Thick and heavy, it rises out of the chasm. It spreads across the open desert, combing brittle twigs of saltbush, seeping into cracks in rocks, flowing through ragged arroyos. Emptiness drifts toward a horizon that stretches forever in air so clear, I can see the eroded fissures and ravines in the flanks of a mountain range fifty miles away.

I stay until the sky turns rose under bands of amethyst and Prussian blue. Their faces toward the sunset, the distant mesas flare to the color of embers.

The desert is a place of glimpses, of peripheral movement and not being quite sure whose brushy tail or russet wing you have seen. During the rut, the Blue Door Band has given me so much more than glimpses, and now I wonder if I have suddenly become blind to their world.

A hard wind picks up and sandblasts me from head to toe. I walk and walk and I never see a sheep. Everything looks like rocks.

A day like today would be like the day the wild sheep vanish from the Earth.

"Liturgical time," writes Kathleen Norris in *The Cloister Walk,* "is essentially poetic time, oriented toward process rather than productivity, willing to wait attentively in stillness." I wait in a season of muted color and sound made explicit by cold, cold air. Night pushes at the margins of day. Night's chill robs all warmth from the canyon's mass, and the jade river runs a few degrees warmer than ice.

Late one afternoon, I watch a group of seventeen bighorns as they feed on a talus, heads down, their silhouettes illumined by the day's last angle of the sun. Every filament of their bodies is ignited with golden light. They seem encircled by imploding halos. What strikes me the most about them is the grace of their fit—this animal to this desert, in this light.

All seventeen sheep gather and move off the talus, move as if they hear music. With their muscles, they map the shape of the stone. In single file, they walk slowly up-canyon, bodies still incandescent against gray rock. The lead ewe guides them to an improbable crack. One by one, they enter the crack and vanish.

No matter where I look or how long I wait, I cannot find them again. I cannot find them for the rest of the day or for days afterward. The sheep are gone.

DECEMBER

For years, I have been enchanted by a wild creature that lives in the far south ripples of New Mexico's basin and range province. I follow her life with a manic swing from worry that she has died to news that, despite formidable odds against her, she is still alive on the craggy escarpment that is her home range.

To single out an individual from the herd is a human, rather than a sheep, impulse, for everything about the life of wild sheep is group life. This ewe has no group. This ewe lives by herself on a wildlife refuge that was set aside over sixty years ago specifically to preserve bighorn sheep. Without her, the refuge would be preserving this many bighorn sheep: zero. She is the last remaining native desert bighorn in the Chihuahuan Desert.

On the register at New Mexico's San Andres National Wildlife Refuge, she is San Andres Ewe 067, named for the order of her capture during a refuge operation. I have a photograph taken from a helicopter that found this one elusive animal in a sea of peaks. She hates helicopters and usually walks straight into a wind cave when one arrives. And there she stays. She would likely emerge only after the chopper ran out of fuel, dropped out of the sky, fossilized in the desert sun, the human race expired, and cockroaches took over the world. Then, perhaps, it might be safe.

This time, the camera caught her as she fled. A broken outcrop fills most of the image. On the far left of the frame, the gray-beige bighorn stands against the blue-black rock in side profile, her face turned to the camera.

At thirteen years old when this picture was taken, she is elderly but healthy. A red tag hangs from one of her ears like a Navajo slab dangle earring. Her triangular face tapers to the signature black Y of sheep nostrils set against the pale hairs of nose and chin. Her brow is broad, her eyes two orbs of pooled darkness.

Horns of female bighorns rise from the poll in a short arc, like a bony rebar with torqued ends. Ewe horns lack the mass and curl of ram horns, freeing the females—given all that head bashing—from anxieties over the size of their body parts. As a typical mature desert bighorn female, SAE 067 should have these bony exclamations atop her head. But she does not. Her horns are gone. She looks into the camera with a sleek, smooth head. She is "bald."

For two long years, SAE 067 was alone on over 57,000 acres of wild New Mexico, the only survivor of a herd that died off, one by one, in a tragic crash. She is surrounded by more than two million acres of high-security military bombing range. Below her mountain sprawls one of the largest towns in southern New Mexico.

In the photo, next to SAE 067 is half of a three-month-old lamb. The ewe is in full portrait. The lamb has partly disappeared from the frame, bounding into the photo's blank border. If you look again at the picture—one ewe, solo in a remote mountain range for two years, beside the lamb she gave birth to—you would think that this is the bighorn sheep–equivalent of immaculate conception.

That wild animals have largely moved out of our view is of small note to many of us. We think, abstractly, that they live out there somewhere, browsing or flying or killing or doing whatever it is they do, and we think that we are keeping them among us by the sheer force of our desire, even as we consume, insatiably, the places where they live.

The most adaptable fauna use *Homo sapiens* to full advantage. Canada geese eating entire municipal golf courses, the ravens in the Dumpster, a bison-burger farm outside the van window during a South Dakota vacation—these images may ping a faint nerve somewhere within the daily terrors induced by talk radio or dental work or the imperialistic aggressions of one's government. But the static of artifice soon floods over us again, and any world beyond the human world seems as out of reach as the moon.

The wildest, least tolerant animals edge ever farther away, running desperately out of "farther" itself. The locals, the most rigidly specialized and place-bound, head toward cracks where they will vanish like the Blue Door Band. Occasionally, they are caught in the half-light of glimpses, revealing another visible order, one no longer coexistent, but distant, and we are surprised to see that the abstract wild actually has flesh.

One consequence of distance is acute separation anxiety. I refuse to succumb. Since the Blue Door Band disappeared, I have been desperate for heartbeats other than my own—big mammalian heartbeats. One journey can rescue me from this dire loneliness, from the silence of an empty room in the ark. I am off to visit a bald bighorn in New Mexico.

I leave home after Venus rises above the river bluffs, so big and bright, it casts faint shadows, planet shadows, like a chip of unfinished moon. Thin layers of ice cover scattered pools of standing water left after a snow squall. Dawn washes away Venus, and the crisp winter air washes through my sore brain and cools the static. I feel like my normally abnormal self as I shift into a fifth-gear cruise through Navajo land.

It takes the entire morning to cross the enormous reservation. On the road, pickup trucks and canary yellow school buses sport bright red plastic bows on their front grilles as Christmas approaches. *Késhmish,* the older Navajos call it. At the junction of highway and red-sand feeder roads that disappear into the empty horizon, handmade signs announce SHOE GAME TONITE.

Navajo shoe games, played only in winter, originated as a contest for day and night, with all living creatures participating. Owl never wanted the night to end. Hawk needed the daylight. Gopher chewed a hole in the shoe—back then, a moccasin—so he could see where the stone was hidden and then guess correctly and win. The infamous gambler, Bear, played all day and night, then ran off in haste with his moccasins reversed. The sunlight turned his fur red, and Big Snake, Bear's helper, was given a piece of red stone to wear on his head.

Each creature that crawled, walked, and flew had its own distinct shoe-game song, thus giving the rite its many songs. No one remembers them all, a friend told me. The contest has tipped in favor of night beings, he joked, because, after a marathon shoe game, everyone has to go to work the next day.

Among the most traditional Navajo, songs still frame wealth or poverty. A poor person is the person who does not own a single song. There are personal songs, songs that belong to the whole group, and songs of the chanter—secret and healing, sung only at the proper ceremony and in the proper sequence. Songs lull babies to sleep. They bless new community centers.

When the world began, it was very small. Songs blew the earth up to its present size. Songs turn frustration into power, anxiety into comfort. Like a blanket, they form a zone of protection around the singer. Sing on the way home alone at night in a fearful place and the song will move out into the space around you. Is this not prayer, sounds that come from our breath, lifting the spirit as they meet the air?

On the stretch of interstate north of Albuquerque, hundreds of semitrailers lunge across the desert, knocking SUVs into barrow pits, flattening the Wonder Bread step-van guy, squashing anything on four wheels like pathetic bugs so they might deliver seven hundred cases of room deodorizers to El Paso before dark. Four of them, all double trailers, wheeze past me on a downhill grade, one after another, mere inches between their bumpers. The cloud of grit in their wake peppers my truck. If I take my eyes off the road to read their HOW'S MY DRIVING? stickers, I am dead meat.

I sing a Navajo force field around me. *Thou shalt make me hear of joy and gladness, that the bones which thou hast broken may rejoice.* Adrenaline jolts loose bits of the Book of Common Prayer from the swamps of memory. Another wheeled mastodon screams by, its flanks a hairsbreadth from my side mirror, a minivan plastered to its radiator like toothpaste. *TheLordbewithyouandwiththyspiritletuspray.*

A chain gang of monster trucks blows me off the reservation, then off the highway itself, onto an exit ramp in a valley town below Tso'dził, one of the four sacred peaks that circumscribe Navajo geography. A melting adobe ruin sits in a thatch of blond grass, the weathered walls and rubble of an old stage stop. The interstate-hugging frontage of chain hotels and truck stops, a busy place, offers the newest stage stop. I head for the middle world, the Route 66 stage stop, the old commercial district, which is easily recognized by its universal next West feature: wholesale abandonment.

A battered café hugs the lip of an arroyo choked with dry brush and a shopping cart, upright and loaded with tumbleweed. The arroyo forms an alley between rows of buildings that are boarded up but, if you look closely, still in use for something not easily determined. A tangle of airborne plastic bags rides a gust of wind up the arroyo and snags on a thicket of Russian olive trees.

Winter's bareness does not flatter the place, but the café hints at occupation and hot coffee. When I open the door, four old cowboys on counter stools raise their coffee cups and turn their heads in unison to see what the wind has blown in. In perfect sync, they turn their heads back again, take sips, and lower their cups to their saucers.

The café decor has locked itself into a stretch of years between World War II and a local uranium-mining boom at the peak of the Cold War. "Our food will blow your mine," the menu claims. Black-and-white photos of miners and ore-hauling trucks mix with Jesus posters on the walls. Are any of the miners still alive, I wonder, declining the menu's offer of pancakes called "yellow-cakes," nickname for the radioactive ore.

I order a bowl of chili verde. Somewhere in the Southwest, I dream, is an unsung chef, modest and brilliant, loyal to the simple food of a home village deep in Sinaloa, making diner chili into a work of art waiting to be savored by travelers who yearn for anything original and local, for relief from the monoculture of interstate-exit cuisine. Perhaps this is the place.

Loud clatters of pots and pans emerge from the kitchen. I glimpse a man in a rumpled apron, a pear-shaped man about two shifts away from incarceration. He flips yellowcakes on a sizzling grill. He resembles the cook in a film I once saw. With a cigarette dangling from his lips, the movie cook lined a large pan with a piecrust, plopped a handful of kittens into it, rolled out a top crust, and slapped it over the pie. Lumps of kittens rose and fell under the dough. The cook fired up what looked like a cremation oven. You noticed flour, catsup, and cigarette ash on his apron. From the pie could be heard tiny muffled mews.

Under a slab of glass on the café tabletop lies unavoidable reading material, a collage of graphic antiabortion E-mails. The printouts swallow up faded remnants of Route 66 scenes— cartoon saguaro cactus, road signs, a red Corvette driven by a blonde in white-rimmed sunglasses.

The eating area of the café is a small room with booths of

chipped plastic the color of cheap vampire lipstick. The bench seat is bumpy and uneven, stuffed with the bodies of former diners. Parked in the middle of the room is a 1955 Chevy—half of a Chevy, that is, cut with a blowtorch so that its rear window and boxy rear end stick out from a booth. The cab is cream-colored, the body a frosted gold lamé with chrome bumper and shiny red taillights. This is a clunky Chevy, built when cars had weight. A few models later, they elongated. You could throw your enemy against their sharky fins and impale him.

My food arrives. Bits of canned chopped green chiles float in lukewarm chicken broth. Under my spoon lie the Corvette blonde and a paragraph about screaming fetuses. At the counter, cowboys stir sugar into their refills. They raise their cups and turn their heads as the café door opens.

The last indigenous desert bighorn sheep in the Chihuahuan Desert lives on a long rib of rock beneath a storm-damp sky that shifts from thick slate to open tears of blue. I skirt the mountains' east flank, the Tularosa Basin, but clearly envision its northwest flank, the Jornada del Muerto, a place I once visited. There, in the summer of 1945, the Manhattan Project wizards watched the fruit of their labors rise in a fireball from the Trinity site. Their invention remains loose in the world. No one can stuff it back into its box, and, sadly, no one with any power really tries.

Eighty-five miles long, running north-south in a graceful narrow arc, the San Andres Mountains lie entirely within the 3,500-square-mile White Sands Missile Range. They are one of the West's accidental wildernesses, vast tracts of desert left "pristine" (not counting the waste dumps and bombed sectors) by the military's huge need for huge geography. The San Andres Mountains have been closed to mining and domestic grazing for half a century. Public access is prohibited.

As often as twice a week, the missile range closes the highway across the mountains, from the Tularosa Basin on one side to Las Cruces and the Rio Grande on the other. The lockdowns last about an hour, while the army lobs scary devices across the New Mexico skies. Occasionally, the Border Patrol, also busy around here, throws up roadblocks, and agents check each car.

For illegal aliens, civilians, and sheep, movement across this broad expanse is not easy. The wild bighorns in the Southwest's island ranges live in permanent lockdown. They can no longer easily trot off in a free exchange of populations. Studies have shown that fenced freeways, for example, are influencing gene-flow patterns.

In the valleys between southwestern mountain ranges lies a maze of treacheries. Roads, bombing ranges, fences, cement-lined irrigation canals, four hundred acres of broccoli plants, shopping malls—how does a sheep tiptoe around a Home Depot?—ATV trails, golf courses, subdivisions, RV resorts full of thawing Minnesotans. Entire cities. A few sheep negotiate barriers and cross the basins between mountains, turning up far from their asylums, surprising the hell out of everyone.

I manage to drive through without a lockdown, a roadblock, or screeching overhead rockets. Before I head into Las Cruces, I pull over on a side road to walk and stretch. The road dead-ends at a grim steel gate marked RESTRICTED AREA—DO NOT ENTER. I wonder if the soap-tree yuccas hold surveillance cameras. I face one of the yuccas—green spikes atop a pedestal of brown spikes, a sort of electrocuted palmetto—and I wave, assuring the generals that I am just another harmless patriotic dissident. I take a look at the mountains.

The San Andres fault block rises even as it wears down, filling the surrounding basins with the debris of its past, in alkali flats, *malpais,* beds of quartz sand, and playas of snow-white gypsum. Every mountain range has its own personality. It tells you about

itself when you feel its firm terrain under your feet and ask a
thousand questions. This one, I must explore largely with my
own imagination. I see it as a sky-raking sierra with one of the
world's most social creatures, all by herself. I am not yet sure
what matters here.

Spokes of sunlight stream down from holes in the heavens,
illuminating bands of malachite on flanks of Prussian blue. The
green drifts across the shadowed blue in a net of light, marine in
its motion, as if the mountains were not under a storm, but under
the sea.

A stratum of cloud rings the shoulders of the highest peaks.
Above it, the crests float clear. The escarpment draws rain and
starves the valleys. It rises abruptly from pale green *bajadas* to
ragged precipices, from creosote to bare rock and a bald ewe, all
in a single breath.

She is not a Nelson's bighorn like the sheep in the Blue Door
Band. Her race, *Ovis canadensis mexicana,* is deeply southern,
found in the Sonoran and Chihuahuan deserts of the Mexico–
Arizona–New Mexico borderlands. It is believed that New Mexico, western Texas, and Coahuila may have once marked the
eastern limits of its range. In southern New Mexico, sheep habitat, even without human influences, may have always been sparse,
scattered, marginal. Historically, some of the best of this habitat
lay in the San Andres Mountains.

She is not the only desert bighorn in New Mexico. Small populations of "questionable viability" hang on by a hoof in other
mountain ranges. Some of those herds include stock that was
transplanted from other places in efforts to keep the species in its
historic range.

Ewe 067 lives on the San Andres's southern end in a federal
wildlife refuge that predates the military reserve. The bears and
wolves are long gone. The top predator, not counting the B-52s,
is the mountain lion. When the refuge was established in 1941, it

held thirty-three bighorns. Protection favored recovery, and the herd began to grow.

In the 1960s a San Andres National Wildlife Refuge publication noted, "These shy and majestic mountain bounders are well adapted to their rough mountain habitat. Continued studies are being conducted to better insure that this rare species may never cease to be a part of our North American fauna."

In gross understatement, it has not been easy.

The desert bighorns of New Mexico are cat food. Several hundred pounds of them have passed through the digestive tracts of opportunistic *Puma concolor*. Such a relationship may sound as obvious as roadkills on a Nevada highway.

Mountain lions are exquisitely designed to kill ungulate prey. If lucky in the hunt, they can eat ten pounds of meat at a sitting. Cryptic stalkers, they shape-shift the colors of desert rock and shrub. They travel widely and show up in places where they weren't.

Mountain lions favor mule deer but will take a bighorn incidentally if they encounter sheep while hunting their preferred prey. Mountain lions may run low on deer and hunt more intensively, moving through a broad territory in search of food.

If the bighorns are weakened by disease and drought, if they are isolated remnants with low numbers, or if they are transplants from elsewhere that have yet to map their escape terrain, the big cats may have a profound effect on them. Mountain lions that become frequent killers of endangered bands of bighorn sheep may earn a tracking collar, the tag "habitual offender," relocation to elsewhere, or, in some cases, a death sentence.

Quite successfully, bighorn sheep elude mountain lions due to their acute vision and the pooled vigilance of a large herd. They flee to safe ground on pinnacles, ledges, and fissured cliffs, places that hide them or throw verticality into the path of their pursuer. More commonly, bighorns avoid mountain lion country, a sort of "Let them eat venison" tactic.

In the mountains of southern New Mexico, none of this appears to be working very well. If the design of bighorn sheep aspires to starve mountain lions, here the sheep lost the odds.

More clouds engulf the mountains, draping thin silver veils into the *bajadas* that skirt them. A squall approaches, christening me with wind gusts and the aroma of damp creosote. Using the truck tire as a wind shelter and backrest, I sit on the rough ground and await the rain.

In the morning, I will visit the world of SAE 067 with the refuge manager and hear her radio signal as it blips from the heights. I understand that I may not be able to see her, but I feel sharp pierces of longing to do so. The desire is mine, wholly selfish. In the photograph, she has a helicopter in her face. Is that not enough disturbance?

The camera freeze-frames a hornless gray-colored bighorn sheep against blue-black rock, a red dot of an ear tag, a radio collar around her neck. The lamb leaps beyond the frame, a coil of springing muscles. Considering the noisy steel locust that hovers above her, the ewe looks remarkably still and stoic. Yes, I had this lamb by immaculate sheep conception, she seems to say. The die-off of her herd mates, the aloneness. A broken leg, both horns knocked off. The chopper. And I haven't even begun to tell you about the mountain lions.

The squall delivers weather with muscle, sending me inside the truck for cover. Behind sheets of sleet, the mountains dissolve. The pelting is furious for a while; then I slip over a pass between the San Andres and Organ mountains, underneath the sunlight that reveals itself behind the ice storm.

Only sheep and lions fully understand sheep-lion dynamics. In the past decades, however, the stewards of the San Andres National Wildlife Refuge have had little choice but to try. The lions are intensely studied, as are the bighorns. The efforts to preserve the San Andres herd fall into the category of herculean tasks.

This is how the indigenous Chihuahuan Desert bighorns came down to one ewe.

From the thirty-three animals in residence at the refuge's creation in 1941, the San Andres population began a healthy trend of increase. With this chunk of New Mexican outback closed by the military, mining and grazing ceased, and range for wild sheep improved.

The sheep survived the world's first atomic-bomb blast, less than a hundred miles beyond their mountaintop. They fed and bred beneath rocket tests, sonic booms, screaming jets, and missiles called Patriot and HAWK (Homing All the Way Killer). Their neighbors were a gaggle of accelerators, a fast burst reactor, something freaky called BAT (Brilliant Anti-armor Submunition), and who knows what else that has never emerged from the vaults of military secrecy. What the sheep could not cope with, thrown at them in the years to come, would be bug damage in their ears.

After a setback in the fifties, largely due to drought, the population rose again. From 70 sheep in 1955, it grew in twelve years to 270 sheep. That fat herd of 1967 stands at a high in reliable records. (Some biologists set the number at a more conservative 200. There is speculation that, even in "pristine" times, 150 to 200 animals may be the San Andres's carrying capacity for the species.) On this mountain, the bighorn sheep show patterns of low genetic variation, a sign of inbreeding, and a history of fluctuations: a cycle of crashes to low numbers, followed by gradual increases.

Although wildlife science has made vast leaps forward, population dynamics—the balance of birth and mortality, plus enough complex factors to incite nosebleeds—still evoke guesswork and differences of opinion. In general, herds expand when conditions are favorable. Mortality adjusts the population to a new situation, such as climate changes or food shortages.

When mortality is high, a herd may reach a low point from which it cannot recover. (Although the number is controversial, some biologists set the "minimum viable population" at fifty animals.) Sadly, this may be the story of many of the Southwest's lost sheep. It could leave the Blue Door Band thirty animals away from a similar fate.

In the mid-1970s, counts in the San Andres came in at around two hundred sheep. Ram hunts were allowed, controlled and sparingly, so that some animals could be taken without jeopardizing the herd. The last ram hunt on the refuge took place in 1978.

One of the perils of island life is susceptibility to disease. With its high degree of sociability, a herd can be a petri dish for contagion. Serious disease predisposes animals to predation, to continued and new disease, to poor nutrition and reproduction. Too weak, a population may fall into a downward spiral. Too rare—a species low in density or geographically isolated—they face a thin threshold for collective disaster.

In their holdout enclave, the San Andres bighorns were hit by a virulent outbreak of scabies, a disease caused by ectoparasitic mites. Scabies mites inflict a variety of disorders that can reduce an animal's health and vigor: hair loss, crazed itching, folding of the external ear, plugged ear canals, eardrum damage, loss of hearing, and upset equilibrium. A normally agile sheep with clinical (severe) scabies can lose its muscular coordination and accidentally fall off a cliff and break its legs or crack its skull.

The San Andres scabies-mite infestation was sudden and severe. Sheep counts in 1979 revealed seventy-five to eighty animals, down from two hundred in an alarming crash. Scabies may have predisposed them to another affliction, a virus called contagious ecthyma, which can lead to blindness, lesions, impaired feeding, and starvation. From 1979 into the next decade, 85 percent of the herd died.

Domestic sheep, goats, and cattle, as well as wild ungulates, attract mites; the relationship between mites and host is murky. How *Psoroptes* spp. mites were originally passed to the San Andres ungulates was never clear, either, although many agree that the mites likely came from domestic livestock introduced to the region in the early 1900s. The parasites may have long been present, possibly cyclical, possibly dormant, perhaps residing in a reservoir host such as mule deer, then became manifest in the bighorn epidemic.

In 1979, refuge managers began a salvage operation. They captured forty-nine sheep from the mountain and treated them for scabies. For some, intervention came too late. Accidents and disease-related losses in captivity further reduced their numbers. Only twelve survivors of the roundup would return home, there joining transplants brought in from another area. In 1980, the desert bighorn sheep was listed as an endangered species in New Mexico. In early 1981, the San Andres herd back in the wild numbered about forty sheep.

Over the next fourteen years, annual refuge surveys counted a herd that stayed below forty but above twenty sheep. Disease continued to plague them. The local mule deer population declined and mountain lion predation intensified. Mutton was on the menu. When San Andres bighorns died, mountain lions were the proximate cause.

By 1997, the desert bighorns native to these mountains were extinct, one ewe short of zero.

In the many places across the American and Mexican deserts now empty of their native wild sheep, perhaps that is how the end unfolded, absent of witness: fewer and fewer animals, a dazed gang of old rams in a boneyard of their companions, peering down from their day beds, no future. Five sheep, three sheep, then two, then one, all by itself. Then zero.

On one of the world's most restricted and secretive military reserves, home to earthbound and space technology so sophisticated, it makes your brain itch, the security gate at one of its entries is . . . well, broken. An actual human being replaces the robot box that reads pass cards. The guard is friendly and pleased to see us out in the middle of nowhere with him. After a brief chat, he waves us through.

Kevin Cobble, my escort, is the manager of the San Andres National Wildlife Refuge and a man with a security clearance. He is a tall, slender forty-six-year-old in a brown uniform, with the "untiring efforts" look of someone who works with rare wildlife. Back in his office, I thought I spotted a bulletproof vest stuffed into a pack, but it had a lot of dust on it.

Kevin has spent over two decades with the U.S. Fish and Wildlife Service, working largely with the locals—rare southwestern natives that cling precariously to islands of wild. On another refuge, in the small streams and springs of the Rio Yaqui headwaters in southern Arizona, his wards were fish the size of a half-eaten no. 2 pencil, fish found nowhere else in the world.

Kevin has good-naturedly allowed me to accompany him on a morning in the field. Mere days before my visit, fifty-one wild sheep had arrived from Arizona and southwestern New Mexico, the seeds of a new herd for the mountains that had emptied themselves of bighorns. Kevin and his staff were checking on them nearly every day. SAE 067 now has company.

Yesterday's storm has lifted. The mountains loom closer, one of them bristling with radio towers disguised as yuccas. I am as curious as a crazed coconut to see this accidental wildland. I am in a white pickup truck powered by veggie oil.

"Biodiesel," Kevin explains. "It's a soy-based fuel. We buy bulk gallons of it."

The refuge office and compound are outside the preserve, near town. The staff of four travels a grid of scant dirt roads for their work, skirting the high sheep country at lower elevations and along rough four-wheel-drive drainages. In this vast tract, the refuge has few structures but the sheds and holding paddock at a small encampment called Little San Nicholas Camp. Other structures belong to the missile range, and I am not supposed to ask about them.

The view from the *bajada* across the Tularosa Basin—from here, it is a raptor's panorama—makes a person want to stay and stare for a few months. Fingers of jet black mark the lava beds, or *malpais,* to the north. On the floor of this playa, a valley without river or stream or other drain to the sea, the gypsum dunes of White Sands National Monument glisten snow-white in painful purity.

At the basin's lowest point, water from winter storms pools into the usually dry bed of Lake Lucero and scatters thin sky mirrors across the playa. Blue-violet in the morning light, the Sacramento Mountains line up with the San Andres in classic basin and range parallel. From our raptor's point, the earth's skin is corrugated.

The white dune field below us moves. It is active; it shifts, slumps, and advances. I want to watch the wind push it toward Alamogordo, but we will run out of veggie oil, and lifetimes, before change is evident to the naked eye.

From basin to *bajada,* the San Andres escarpment rises abruptly. We drive through a shrubby green jungle of aromatic creosote, a species with the breadth, across the intermountain West, of a small ocean. Creosote engulfs the remains of wooden observation towers left from the post–World War II days of rocket testing.

The aged timbers gleam silver in the sun, the view still superb but now abandoned.

White panel trucks and semitrailers replace the towers, gleaming like giant kitchen appliances. They are parked on platforms in paranoid circled-wagon clusters, their roofs thatched with satellite dishes and antennae. The trucks are windowless and self-contained, filled, perhaps, with very bored people watching compact video screens, eavesdropping on the Saudi parliament, listening to the universe hum. Maybe they have the refuge truck under X-ray surveillance, like airport luggage, and are observing our skeletons strapped in by seat belts. Maybe the vehicles are empty. What do I know? There is no one in sight.

I look for panic grass, a plant in the desert grasslands community, but we may be too high and on the wrong side of the mountains. Panic grass, I have always thought, should be the official plant of the missile range. I make a note to write the generals about this.

Partway up the *bajada,* here in the heart of New Mexico, USA, we of course spook up a dozen *African* ungulates. They canter away from the vehicle. Kevin puts on the brakes.

"Watch them," he says. "They'll run away from the road. Then they'll stop and turn around broadside and look at us."

On the run, the oryx show us their flashy Serengeti butts. Then they stop, turn around broadside, and look at us.

In the 1960s and 1970s, ninety-three captive-bred oryx were introduced to the White Sands Missile Range. *Oryx gazella,* natives of southeastern Africa that are also known as gemsbok, then hoofed their way into the Chihuahuan Desert, progeny of a state program designed to introduce exotic species for sport hunting. At the time, it seemed like a good idea, if you were a hunter, to transform the "empty wastelands" of New Mexico into an African savanna swarming with shootable horned mammals.

Since the mid-1970s, wildlife management has favored native species, and the oryx are considered pests. They breed, it is said, "like bunnies on speed." Several months after they calve, they are pregnant again.

No one is quite sure how many oryx roam the White Sands Missile Range—perhaps more than four thousand. They have populated the desert well beyond the spacious military reserve and the original confines of their expected habitat. They barely need water, they eat nearly anything with or without leaves, and they have walked to Texas. In Africa, their natural enemies were lions. In New Mexico and Texas, their major predators are human hunters.

No one knows much about oryx population trends or how these exotics affect the natives, such as mule deer, with whom they share a similar range and elevation. In the next basin west of the San Andres, oryx roam the flats with pronghorn antelope. Both the refuge and missile range allow controlled hunts, under escort, to reduce oryx numbers. Apparently, the oryx run, stop, turn broadside, and look at the hunters. Bang.

"What these oryx need is a pack of skinny, highly motivated African lions," I suggest. "Maybe some starving cheetahs." Kevin gives me a look that invites me to pop right on into HQ and run that one by the generals.

To picture an oryx, think of antelope as rather beefy drag queens. The oryx stare at us wide-eyed from underneath lush lashes highlighted by a painterly black eye stripe against geisha-pale cheeks. Black patches adorn brow and nose. Thin horns rise from their pates like ebony scimitars. On sandy-gray bodies of considerable bulk, their black manes run from head to shoulders, and dark markings accent their legs and underbelly. Long tufted tails lie against muscular rumps. One of the staring males could easily weigh five hundred pounds.

The game managers of the late 1960s recognized their substantial investment in imported wildlife and quarantined the exotics before release. It would be neither economical nor wise, they wrote, "to thrust them boldly into the wild, perhaps never to be seen again."

The oryx took one look at the Land of Enchantment and thrust themselves boldly into reproducing. They went from a handful to herds, from quarantine enclosure to open desert like five-hundred-pound locusts. They own the place.

Ecologists, being big-picture nature people, try to get the rest of us, who have the attention spans of caffeinated hamsters, to see landscape in broad reaches of time and change. They would have us look at this piece of Chihuahuan Desert—cholla, mesquite, prickly pear cactus, whitethorn acacia, and, on higher, moister slopes, scattered pinyon and juniper trees—and ask us to see *grass*.

For several thousand years, southern New Mexico's vegetation has moved from grassland to desert scrub, prompted by time, shifts in climate, and, in the short term, domestic grazing. With every organism, from pond scum to seedpod, to charismatic curly-horned ungulate, to smart ape (us), bound in community, ecologists would argue that there could be relationships between the transition from grassland to desert scrub and how mountain lions interact with bighorn sheep.

We drive higher into the mountains. In stands of pinyon and juniper, the climax forest of the high desert, I imagine tawny cats at dusk, slipping behind evergreen boughs like liquid ghosts. Their amber stares—I have seen this gaze in my own encounters with them—penetrate so deeply, you feel as if you have lost the back of your skull. I envision a kill: a brief chase (cats are short-winded and invest much in the stalk), then a leap with a powerful blow, the severing of the spinal cord, a shift of weight to catch breath and adjust grip.

And there are the images of lions themselves as prey, of canned hunts, poisonings, and the spoils of bounty hunters. Photographs of mountain lion skulls stacked like cordwood. A long-lived cultural contempt that holds big cats as varmints or vermin. Hunters who will tell you that mountain lions killed every last deer and elk in three states and then started eating one another.

The mountain lion diet in the San Andres is predominantly and, by biomass, overwhelmingly desert mule deer. Mountain lions also make opportunistic meals of rodents, rabbits, skunks, badgers, ringtail cats, javelinas, birds, and porcupines. They eat bighorn sheep and an occasional pronghorn that leaves its safer open terrain in the nearby basins. They have preyed upon the formidable oryx, taking calves no larger than adult female mule deer, victims that the cats can handle with less risk of injury to themselves. Sometimes they eat odd meals: a box turtle, a golden eagle.

Woody vegetation provides cover for stalking lions. Acutely dependent on eyesight more than on smell or hearing, the victim does not see what is coming and can't get away fast enough. With surprise on its side, a mountain lion can ambush and take down prey two or three times its own body weight.

In the southern San Andres Mountains in the late 1990s, mountain lions were the main cause of bighorn sheep mortality. The cats' major food source, mule deer, had declined rapidly; the cats' numbers had increased in the region. Drought, the bighorns' low and unstable numbers, and other factors also contributed to the band's extinction. From a habitat perspective, too, there are additional insights.

Bighorn bands are known to avoid, and sometimes abandon, habitat where the risk of predation is high. Habitat with obscured long-range visibility makes sheep nervous. For safety, they will go someplace else. In the San Andres, over eighty years of fire suppression left them without much "else." Lacking natural cycles of wildfire, the dense vegetation closed in the sheep view. A concealed feline hunter could get close enough for a successful kill. Disease-weakened sheep made easy prey.

To bring back open-vista habitat lost to bighorn, the refuge staff has been burning the San Andres Mountains. Given New Mexicans' undeserved reputation as pyromaniacs, this is a brave move.

At several burn sites, Kevin stops the truck so we can examine the revegetation—forbs, browse, healthy swathes of black grama grass. Creosote has returned, albeit in fewer numbers. From foot to ridge top, some of the slopes resemble a vertical savanna.

"There aren't many structures in these mountains, no trophy homes," Kevin tells me. "Fire was never much of a threat to property, but the army thought fires sent up enough smoke to interfere with their tests. So they always put them out."

The long-standing national policies of fire suppression, the scolding glare of that mean poster bear in flat-brimmed hat and pants, more or less indoctrinated a public against wildfire. Even as we become smarter about fire's natural role in montane ecology, such enlightenment is often tested, most famously in New Mexico when, in 2000, a prescribed burn near the nuclear-lab town of Los Alamos went out of control.

On the San Andres, lightning fires are now left to burn themselves out. Prescribed burns are planned and watched. Here, the army has come around to support the fire program. Here, by the grace of the generals, go sheep.

"Since we started in 1999, burns have opened up acres and acres of old habitat," says Kevin. "It will be interesting to see what the sheep will do, if they will occupy it now that the vegetation is reduced."

"They" are not the last-stand natives, the locals who might sense that this part of the mountains puts them on big-cat menus. None of those local sheep are left, save one. The fifty-one new arrivals have no imprint of this landscape. They must learn the territory, including the habitat opened by fire.

Near the release sites, to prepare the neighborhood for transplants, refuge managers had killed any mountain lion that was perceived as a threat to sheep. This strategy will continue for a few months now that sheep have been released, change to an offenders policy, removing only the cats that kill sheep, then cease altogether as the herd grows and stabilizes.

Sheep-predator interactions so intensely manipulated by human agent carry contradiction and controversy. Biologists talk endlessly about bighorns and mountain lions, but it seems they cannot easily lift the weight of uncertainty. By comparison, legal pyrotechnics, as long as you don't burn down a nuclear-weapons lab, seem methodically simple.

The sheep people, with their mandate to preserve bighorns, argue that mountain lion predation on small, up-against-the-wall populations of wild sheep will wipe them out. Lion advocates worry about the repercussions on these animals and question the effectiveness of lion control. They rightly argue that wild carnivores are essential to the dynamics of healthy desert ecosystems. Mountain lions eat mutton because they are hungry. They stalk because that is what they are designed to do.

Opponents of predator control think that killing mountain lions to rescue a declining species is a new rationale for an old war on "vermin" predators. They envision cat skulls stacked like cordwood. Purists want nature to "run its course," even if that means the lions consume every last bighorn.

This plodding work of wildlife recovery, this repairing of Eden, why is it so difficult? In a Darwinian view, it may be "natural" to lose local species that cannot adapt to change. We no longer have dodoes, such logic says, because the flightless, bulbous, docile dodoes were such easy pickings for hunters, pigs, monkeys, and other alien invaders. Add to their defenselessness a moral dimension, as people tend to do: The birds died off because they were such *dodoes*.

The exotic African oryx, far more adaptable than the dodo, took on southern New Mexico partly because southern New

Mexico was so perfectly edible. Predators and water were not limiting factors. During a drought, oryx can detect rainfall over great distances. They then move in the direction of new plant growth and find food.

In similar circumstances of drought, desert bighorns have been known to succumb to group death. On the San Andres in 1950, fourteen sheep carcasses were found in close proximity. Bear grass, or sacahuiste, a Nolinaceae-family plant with coarse grass-like leaves, may have poisoned them. The sheep browsed bear grass as a last-resort food; the meal that saved them from starving ended up killing them.

Occasional poisoning would normally not matter. Bighorns and bear grass, as well as bighorns and mountain lions, have evolved with one another, a dance of victims and survivors. For that matter, bighorns coevolved with humans. The difference is the scale and degree of a human reach that now severely compromises the balance.

When a herd is healthy in vigor and numbers, multiple casualties are a misfortune. When the animals are rare, such losses are a collective catastrophe. In this light, the San Andres bighorns find themselves in a sort of dodo position.

The truck wobbles slowly over a rocky two-track. Folds of mountains close in behind us, erasing the vistas back into the Tularosa Basin. Ahead sits a blocky escarpment with a flat crest and a place called Ewe Skull Canyon, one of SAE 067's hangouts. We park and step outside. The winter air is sweet and clean. I want to thank Kevin for the ride, then bolt, and hike around until my feet blister and bits of plants stick to me.

Under the aegis of wildlife management, the oxymoron that is now a fact of life for most North American creatures, spins unbounded tinkering, with further tinkering made necessary by past tinkering, effects of causes, effects of effects—a "cascade of consequences" precipitated by human intervention, well intended though it may be. I cool my itchy feet and stay put. Only with my imagination can I not meddle. I retract my idea of launching African lions at oryx. Let the generals prey-switch and eat them.

The unspoken loss in a highly mediated lion-sheep world is the loss of the two species' own biology—the architecture of precise killers and keen-eyed escape artists, and the fluidity of habitat and climate that pushes their evolution—all of it under the relatively autonomous hand of nature. Here, as in other desert bighorn homelands, the choice against extinction trades wildness for "cultural biology" and the intervention of rescue.

To some degree, one animal in the San Andres Mountains eluded the tinkering and made her own covenant. She is standing on the cliff face about five miles away, bleeping a signal into Kevin's telemetry receiver.

San Andres Ewe 067 was born on the mountain in 1989 to a ewe that likely dropped her lambs in the same site year after year, in terrain more rugged than her usual feeding and resting haunts. For a highly social animal, giving birth was one of her few solitary acts. She chose a cliff shelter with an unobstructed view, perhaps south-facing for its solar advantage.

The ewe lamb born that season did not suffer hypothermia, as newborns can. No golden eagle struck her, as an eagle might when a lamb is a few weeks old and vulnerable. This lamb survived her first round of perils.

A refuge operation in 1993 captured eleven sheep for collaring and tests. Among them was a four-year-old female about to be assigned an identity: SAE 067. With the others, she was treated for scabies mites and fitted with a radio collar. Refuge staff would know where she was on the mountain. They could track her movements. If her radio transmitted a steady stationary blip—a "mort," or mortality signal—they would know that she was dead or had lost her collar.

During the capture operation, she broke her leg. She ran off from the release. Her broken leg mended. She chewed languidly from her day beds and scratched her ears. She may have slipped through pinyon, juniper, and brush, the lair of shadow cats. Or she avoided those places altogether, staying in the limestone ramparts she favored. The other bighorns around her were dropping dead.

Mountain lions, accidents, natural deaths, and unknown causes, but mostly mountain lions, picked off SAE 067's herd mates. With males and females on separate ranges, she likely lost the band of ewes and juveniles that ran and fed with her, but she was oblivious to the end of the rams until none came to impregnate her.

A 1997 capture came up with a ram and SAE 067, another helicopter to chase and net her. She tested positive for scabies and was treated. After the release, the ram disappeared. In aerial and ground surveys, a despairing staff searched the craggy peaks for more than SAE 067. The refuge manager at the time tried to be optimistic. He told me, "They are out there. They're good at hiding."

The staff set up an infrared beam–activated video camera at a guzzler, an artificial water-collection unit for wild sheep. Mule deer put in cameo appearances. Javelina trotted in on high-heeled piglet hooves, grunting through long snouts, their grizzled hairs in stiff bristle.

No bighorns showed up on film. If some were in hiding, they died in their hideouts. Faithful to this rib of rock for centuries, the native San Andres bighorn was essentially extinct.

From 1997 to 1999, SAE 067 lived alone. Her radio collar located her for capture in 1999. She was quarantined in a paddock near the guzzler and came up clean in scabies tests. When she bashed her head against the paddock fence, she broke off one of her horns. After a week, she was released.

Three years later, there she was on her limestone cliff, caught in a snapshot from the helicopter, thirteen years old, bald. A lamb sprang away from her side.

Before my day in the field, I had visited Mara Weisenberger, the refuge biologist. Invested in bighorn recovery in the San Andres Mountains for the past twenty years, she has worked here ten. Both of her two children are younger than SAE 067.

Gently blond and fit, Mara is mostly a big-mammal biologist. She studied under the Southwest's premier desert bighorn biologist, Paul Krausman, at the University of Arizona. With characteristic grace, she once convinced the White Sands generals to reroute a stretch of dirt road out of a streambed so that the riparian area could recover. It did.

Mara knows the San Andres Mountains on foot. She can hang out of a doorless helicopter as it flits about the jagged spaces of sheep country. She works with a species with a proclivity for disaster.

She is also quite ingenious at figuring out the least risk and stress to wild sheep while they are in her custody. Her engineering of holding pens at remote camps and of crates for transplanting sheep reflects an instinct for the animals' well-being and for what can be inadequately described as their dignity, a quintessential bighornness that, in Mara's mind, need not be met with human indifference or arrogance.

For Mara, the recent translocation of sheep to the range marks years of work with an unruly assortment of government agencies. Although she was modest about it, I had the impression that her survival of the politics of wildlife was somewhat analogous to

SAE 067's survival of mountain lions. Now, she and her colleagues had reached a point in which the immediate future was up to the animals.

On her office computer she ran through recent data beamed down, more or less, from bighorns via outer space. Five of the new rams wore satellite collars, a next-generation tracking device. The head count that day was sixty bighorns: fifty-one new arrivals, "the old lady," her lamb (elusive and uncollared, nearly a yearling), and seven more, all rams, alive today to impress us with the ineffability of ram lust.

Before any animals could be reintroduced to the San Andres Mountains, their habitat had to be mite-free. In 1999, the refuge brought in six "sentinel" rams and sprinkled them individually throughout the range. For the next two years, the rams were routinely captured and tested. Over that period, these bulky, four-legged miner's canaries did not contract scabies, and the range was deemed safe for a new herd.

The sentinel rams' other job was to find any sheep from the original herd that had not turned up in two years of searching.

"Sheep can find sheep better than we can find sheep," Mara said.

One would like to think of one cranky recluse from the old herd, butting mountain lions off his horns right and left, hiding in wind caves, never showing his hide—one that tiptoed in and impregnated SAE 067 in 2000 (she bore a lamb that eventually died) and again the following year, his offspring the leaping half a lamb in the photograph.

Plunked down in scattered places, the sentinel rams found no such survivors. However, within two years, and over more than ninety miles, they found the single ewe, and for the first time in about four years, there was a rut in the mountains. A sentinel ram sired the old ewe's offspring. Mara speculates that in a butt with a ram, SAE 067 lost her second horn.

The rams did their work as detectors of disease and lost sheep. Some of the original stock died and were replaced with animals brought in from other areas. Seven of the sentinel rams remain. Three crossed a busy highway into an adjacent range, from which they can peer down at a sprawling facility of the warrior nerds.

On Mara's office shelf, among photos of kids and bighorn sheep, lay a gray horn, a curved sheath of keratin with a rough lined surface. It was smaller and more delicate than I would have imagined. This horn broke off SAE 067's head when she rammed the fence of the holding pen during her brief capture in 1999. In a culture fixated on poster-boy rams, this unassuming crescent of protein carried far more power.

No one had seen SAE 067's surviving lamb in several months. It has never been captured. It was, Mara told me, well past "eagle-bait age" and may have learned a few evasive techniques from its mother. Meanwhile, the old lady stuck like Velcro to her piece of mountain, still an elusive loner.

Mara said, "She survived scabies, she survived mountain lions, and she survived us."

Kevin Cobble raises the antenna of his telemetry gear in one hand and works the receiver with the other. He runs through each sheep's radio-collar frequency and makes notes on his checklist. Today's survey locates twenty-one animals. Others may be tucked into crevices that block the signal. Each day, each signal, is reassuring. Everyone on the refuge wants the new herd to take hold.

I have to wonder if the newcomers are a bit dazed by it all. One minute, they were chewing a jojoba plant in the Kofa Mountains in Arizona; the next, they were in a mesh sling, dangling from a helicopter, then in shipping crates on a truck trailer. Tucson whizzed by. The crate doors opened and they raced off into the bright sunlight of New Mexico.

They are bureaucratic bighorns (years of interagency planning, reams of environmental assessments) with a clean bill of health (vet check, blood tests, ear swabs, inoculations) and a neckload of high-tech sheep jewelry. They must now form a sheep map, become locals, stay out of the maws of *Puma concolor.*

Bennett Mountain fills the horizon, shaped more like a mesa than a peak. Below its steep red-brown face falls a wrinkled skirt of drainages etched deeply in the rock. The mountain spills itself at its own feet. From the heights comes a signal from the collar around the neck of SAE 067.

Kevin and Mara have tracked her movements since the arrival of the transplants. In a very unsheeplike manner, she avoids them and stays alone in her favored terrain, this corner of a craggy mountain. She is off-limits to helicopters and captures. "She is retired," Mara told me.

When I ask Kevin about his last hike deep into the mountains to catch sight of the sheep from the ground, he repeats the mantra of human intent foiled by bighorn invisibility: "I walked and walked and I never saw a sheep."

The contact between humans and the last native bighorn in

the Chihuahuan Desert is this radio bleep, this ripple of invisible waves on the electromagnetic spectrum, waves long enough to bend around the curve of the earth. The waves undulate across five miles of broken winter desert, from one mammal's neck to another mammal's ears. SAE 067's signal comes as a faint blip. I think of it as a heart monitor.

During my sojourn in New Mexico, the globe has spun. Sabers rattle in the Middle East. Ammonium perchlorate, a component of rocket fuel and hand grenades, has turned up in the nation's commercial lettuce at unhealthy levels. A pet-product company has, Frankenstein-like, crossed the genes of a phosphorescent marine plant with those of a sliver-size fish to produce an aquarium fish that glows in the dark. This is said to be the first animal genetically engineered for the sole purpose of human amusement.

In a zoo in Afghanistan, soldiers slash the nose of a bear. A hand grenade destroys the eye of an elderly lion. A zookeeper is murdered, and most of the animals starve to death.

In Washington, D.C., the White House unveils the season's "creatures great and small" Christmas decor: animal ornaments, animal scenes, photos of Woodrow Wilson's sheep (they grazed the White House lawn), sculptures of presidential pets, including LBJ's beagles and an alligator that lived in the East Room's bathroom during the administration of John Quincy Adams.

Down the street, Congress tries to hand Alaska's Arctic National Wildlife Refuge to the oil barons. Politicians jackhammer endangered-species laws, and the Department of Defense may soon be exempt from laws that protect plants and wildlife on military ranges, including default wildlands like the San Andres Mountains. At the whim of a base commander, the aplomado falcon, piping plover, bonita diving beetle, or *Ovis canadensis mexicana* can be declared threats to national security.

There are approximately 68 million owned dogs in the United States. This month, over half of them will receive Christmas presents.

I walk in a moonlike dune field of glistening gypsum crystals. Each crystal scatters cool December light from its minutely fissured surface. Water and ice shape the sand grains. The wind moves them. Beneath the wind, the dunes grow, crest, and slump, fluid in their advance.

The crests of the dunes glow snow-white above flanks that hold every shade of blue, from lapis in the deepest hollows to aquamarine between the delicate ribs of surface ripples. The swales fill the horizon up to the edge of the world: the indigo silhouette of the San Andres.

Anything that hunts or flees the hunter must reckon with white. Over time and adaptation, insects, a few lizards, and a pocket mouse have bleached themselves. The kit fox pales its otherwise earthy grays. The plants—few and stalwart—must resist burial. Their stems or blades check the wind. Behind the slowed runnel of air, the sand tapers into a raised streamer.

White Sands National Monument sprawls below the mountains: ephemeral ground, crumbly and friable beneath my feet. This is not a simple place. The scant rain that gravity collects in this drainless playa has no exiting river, no outlet from basin to sea. The wind flows across the mountains from the Rio Grande Valley. The dunes are creations of aeolian strength, duration, and direction. They are not fixed.

Dune physics slides into the mind with the taste of metaphor: parabolic dunes, star dunes, transverse dunes. Seif, or linear dunes (from *saif,* Arabic for sword), have narrow crests and steep slip faces on both sides. They drift in chains several miles long. *Barkhan,* Kazakh-Russian for ram's horn, gives its name to barchan dunes, which take the shape of crescents with pointed tips, their convex sides to windward.

The slip face of a barchan dune. This is where I am standing. The ambient light above the dazzling white sand has a thin silvery mass to it, untempered and seductive. The dune light induces some sort of craving. It fills a person with ecstasy and appetite, as if beauty were a destiny.

From this ram's horn dune, from so far away, I can barely distinguish the mountain that SAE 067 refuses to leave. It is one of many silken blue layers against a pallid winter sky. I open my silver hip flask and make a toast to her survival.

Up there on that rib of rock, that last-stand bighorn heaven, an extraordinary piece of evolution unraveled: the immemorial habit of society, locked tightly in a native bloodline. For so many months, this most gregarious of animals was alone. She saw no others of her kind, experienced no crashing of horns or lusty coursing, no brushing of blood-warmed shoulders and rumps, no postures of alarm rippling from animal to animal until, as one, they moved to safe ground. No one will know with certainty how her herd mates collapsed beneath the cascade of pressures against them.

The bighorn petroglyph at home, the sheep fed by the spiraling breath of the universe, must be this one. I will make it her, the last native, kept alive all this time by who knows what, some rarefied mystery of instinct and randomness, something purely *wild*. I have not laid my own eyes on her, but I have seen her place, and by this I can imagine how she kept the mountains from emptiness.

A few more hours in the dunes, walking along the slip faces, in love with the white. Dusk turns the blues to oyster gray and milky violet. I am a breeze-blown dot in a petrified sea of polished pearl. Then I drop down the last dune to the parking lot and my truck.

Two people, likely father and son, climb the high mound of sand. We say hello in passing; then they walk on to take their first look across the rippled white playa to the mountains. Until they reach the top the dune, they will be virgins to the view, as I was only hours before.

They stop on the crest of the dune. I sit on the tailgate and empty my shoes of sugary gypsum grains. The man's voice drifts down to me. He sighs and says, "Well, I guess they were right about this place. Just a great big whole lot of nothing."

JANUARY

Shall we be honest about this? The mind needs wild animals. The body needs the trek that takes it looking for them. I am interested both in desert natives and in the places where they live. When I am lucky, desert bighorn geography may actually have sheep in it. More often, there are places where this mammal should be but is no longer, and in this emptiness, too, there is fieldwork to be done.

You know you are in desert bighorn country, sheepless or not, by some of the words tethered to its heart. *Sun, stone, sierra, salt-bush. Arroyo. Acrophobia. Desire* and *desolation. Dust* and *imagination. Absolute clarity, extreme blue.* In a few more lifetimes, you might finish this list, only to discover that most of the words are about yourself.

There are dry mountains and deep canyons where bighorns have died out; places where they persist, tenuously, but may not survive much longer; and places with viable herds, the islanders in habitat scattered across the American and Mexican deserts. And there are places where people will tell you, "Wild sheep live here; we have seen them." You will be skeptical; you will look at those hellish cliffs and think, I'll die, and if you do go, you will never know if the animals you see, or think you see, are phantoms or dreams or flesh, or all three.

In some places, the sheer tenacity of a rare desert creature has given it this chimerical quality. Such a place lies along the cordillera of Baja California, a spine of stark vertical desert that rises between two seas. You cannot come to this country with nothing.

Bring water. Bring that notebook. You will have to stay within the margins of safety, close to your food cache, close to one of those two seas.

It is said that the people of Baja California are the toughest of all Mexicans because of their resourcefulness on land as sere as old bones, surrounded by water that is undrinkable. The Baja California we try to inhabit, as best we can, is this republic of resourcefulness.

During a winter sojourn outside the Colorado Plateau, we trade the high-desert cold for the lowland warmth of Baja California's three deserts—the Sonoran, the Vizcaíno-Magdalena, and the Gulf Coast—during their least fierce season. Mexico is our neighborhood; it feels local. It does not have superpower anxieties. This is a great relief.

Mark, our friend Joe, and I pack fishing and camping gear and head south. For much of the trip, we caravan with friend Katie Lee and her "Pal Joey." Katie's attachment to Baja is four decades deep. The back roads are her songlines, filaments of deep memory stitched up and down the peninsula.

Behind us, the Blue Door Band still had not emerged from its vanishing. I had seen no sheep since the rut ended. When they disappeared forty years ago, they were presumed extinct. To some degree, many of the same threats still hovered: human incursion, predators, poachers, pneumonia, parasites. Had one of the rams wandered about until he met the upriver flock of domestic sheep, then taken fatal microbes back to the herd? Had they all dropped dead like the sheep that ate the poison leaves of the sacahuiste?

I fretted and worried over the Blue Door Band. Then I put my butt in the truck bound for Mexico. I betrayed them for their macho Mexican cousins, for the *borrego cimarrón*—O cheatin' ingrate, for *foreigners*!

To reach the wilder fringes of this country, we plow through the core, the thick gringofied culture that straddles much of northern Baja California and puts Americans on the beaches in barred compounds of second homes and RVs and the Mexicans in the wind-sheared scrub behind them, in shacks, their country by the water lost to them. To the giant columnar *cardón,* the Mexican relative of the saguaro cactus, we announce our arrival in Mexico only after we have driven several hundred miles south of the border.

Then we traverse the desert back roads at a slowed pace, inching closer to the Tropic of Cancer, relishing the feast that our home desert lacks: an ocean lapping its prickly flanks. This seam of land and sea grips us. From it, we make forays outward in a small boat or inland into the sierra, where the phantom *borregos* live.

Underfoot, the Pacific Plate scrapes and rasps against its tectonic opposite, the North American Plate of mainland Mexico. Between peninsula and mainland, the Sea of Cortés—the Gulf of California—floods the cleft above the San Andreas fault. Baja California is, geologically speaking, bound for Alaska, and we are riding the rift.

The main roads of Baja California have been upgraded from bad to less bad. We avoid them and drive the old tracks of rocks and ruts, throwing up plumes of white dust behind us. When these roads are too civilized, we drive the euphemisms.

Once in awhile, to change position and cross to remote camps, we have no choice but to travel a piece of the main transpeninsular highway, the asphalt death ribbon that runs the eight hundred miles from border to tip, bringing most of El Norte, gringos and goods, south in buses, mammoth motor homes, and semitrailers that pass us on one and a half lanes of highway, but only when there is a blind hill or oncoming traffic and the possibility of killing us is high.

For most of these weeks in Mexico, we inhabit the empty quarter of the sea-land seam, the Gulf of California littoral. Our back-road ride spews lug nuts, busts the seal on our truck's differential, and takes us across sand flats and lava beds, past isolated *rancherías* and ephemeral fish camps, around hairpin turns festooned with plaster Holy Virgins in niches and shrines memorializing dead drivers, through miles and miles of *cardonal,* forests of *cardón* cactus so thick you cannot walk between the hulky fifty-foot-high columns without impaling yourself on their thorns.

We are surrounded by bizarre plants, sunburned rock, meager granitic soil, scant water but a sea of salt, and mountains that look like the shaved recumbent bodies of formerly lush ranges. "Everything concerning California is of such little importance that it is hardly worth the trouble to take a pen and write about it," bemoaned an early missionary.

Each night by a campfire, my pen swells field notes into a gnarly bulge. Everything is of such great importance, it is well worth the trouble to note it. At first, I become a list maker, naming plants, trees, fish, mountains, and coves in English, then in Spanish. Soon the names stop and the notes become mostly questions. Then the notes stop and I try to feel rather than think my way through. I try to distill this land. To borrow an image from a writer friend who lives on the peninsula, it ends up as a splintered mirror.

Coyotes yip close to camp, telling us something about our journey. Mark gets up from the bed tarp to a waning crescent moon slung below Venus. He starts a morning fire from the night's coals. Daylight flushes the horizon, then quickly fills the sky with the seductive force of velvet. The sun's great orb rises crimson, sizzling its skirts in the Gulf's calm waters.

The scant desert scrub chatters and cheeps with songbirds, sounds we did not hear at home over the winter. Four vultures roost in a *cardón,* a hulking black bird on the tip of each upraised arm. They stare at us, hopeful at our slowness, thinking that maybe we're dead. They fly off when the caffeine kicks in.

Nearby is a windowless shell of an old bus, stripped to a hollow carcass of sun-blistered metal. The back of the bus holds an erupting biomorph that might have once been an armchair. Around us lie acres of onyx scrapings, the remains of a quarry that was abandoned when plastic eclipsed the use of this crystallized quartz for game pieces, ashtrays, bookends, paperweights, souvenirs. The onyx, with its mottled bands of brown and gold, is lustrous and nearly translucent. We are camped atop four million chess sets.

The sea spreads below us nearly half a mile away, azure and serene, edged by a faint scrim of high tide and dotted with small islands of lava and chalky pumice. The coastline falls to the south in a long, sweeping bay, empty but for a fishing village clustered at its far end.

One year, Mark and I fished this bay with a Mexican friend and his *panga,* a fiberglass skiff, catching yellowtail jack, cabrilla, and an occasional triggerfish. Sleek seals—our friend called them "*lobos*" (wolves)—followed the boat closely. Farther away, California gray whales rolled and showed their flukes.

The islands were covered with blue-footed boobies and preening brown pelicans. I saw one pelican scratch its chin with a foot like an itchy dog. The yellowtail had backs of midnight blue, chrome flanks, and tail fins the color of fresh lemons. The fish fought like crazy on Mark's line and emerged from an emerald sea with a burst of blinding silver in the bright sun.

Instead of fishing, today we turn inland to a jagged coastal sierra with faces of steep broken rock. A narrow canyon cuts through the lowest slopes. Sheep country. I expect to see the *borrego cimarrón* here, a small band perhaps, perched high because we are here and they will be cautious.

Two of the four races of desert bighorns live in lower California. The Weems bighorn (*Ovis canadensis weemsi*) is found in the far-south Sierra de la Giganta and nearby mountains. The larger range of the peninsular bighorn (*Ovis canadensis cremnobates*) runs for much of Baja's length, save the Weems's southern enclave. All together, counting both subspecies, Mexico's conservation groups have roughly two thousand animals to worry about.

At the U.S. border, the peninsular bighorn range spills into the mountains east of San Diego, where some are protected in Anza-Borrego Desert State Park and others stare down from their cliffs at Southern California's perpetual agenda of sprawl. In the United States, at about four hundred animals, the peninsular bighorn is federally listed as an endangered species.

At the onyx camp, we are in the domain of the peninsular bighorn. Their geography, rather than physical features, distinguishes them from the Weems, Mexican, and Nelson's bighorns. In coloring, size, and habits, these races are similar, though Mark and Joe insist that if we find the locals, we shall have to speak Spanish to them.

After breakfast, Mark and Joe hike up-slope and disappear. Scattered *palo blanco* trees gleam white against rust-colored rock. When I rub them, the trees' white trunks leave chalky powder on my hands. I follow one of the arroyos that cut the slope's flank. The arroyo narrows into a rugged canyon. Behind a bend, the walls close in and hide the horizon's band of lapis. Inside this cleft, who would know there is a sea beyond?

I seek *tinajas,* literally translated as "earthen jars" but also known as tanks. Here, rainwater collects in crevices of rock that are often deep and shaded, slowing evaporation. Bighorn ewes

use specific springs and *tinajas* generation after generation, bringing the others, young or old, male or female, to this hardened
fidelity, binding a band to its own geography.

Winter storms refresh the *tinajas.* Leaves on the elephant
trees and ocotillos are signs of recent rains along this stretch of
coast. In this climate of extreme aridity, numerous plants drop
their leaves in dry weather, then leaf out quickly when there is
moisture.

Against one wall of the canyon, a low arch of rock marks a
cave. Although I am pathologically terrified of caves, the mouth
of this one reveals, oddly, a shaft of light behind it. I crawl in. It
is a roofless cave, a kind of chimney in the canyon wall. Inside are
a small chamber and, on the near-vertical back wall, a staircase of
pool-and-drop ledges, each ledge about ten feet above the one
below it.

Joe, who was hiking on the ridge above, drops out of the sky
like Tarzan off a branch and joins me. Nuevo Anasazi, painter,
sculptor, and archaeologist, Joe is also a wizard of southwestern
rock art and, on a certain South Pacific island, a minor deity. He
is a magnet for the signs and remnants of ancient desert cultures.
Whenever we walk with him, it is as if he sees a shadow landscape beneath the real one. Already this morning he has found
shell mounds and lithic scatter—fragments of worked stone—as
well as sheep trails and day beds.

The water pooled on each ledge is neither pocket nor *tinaja,*
which hold water from seasonal rainfall. This water comes from
inside the earth, emerging to the surface like something alive.
The roofless cave holds a rare spring. The pools are shaded from
the sun.

Everywhere we look, we see sheep scat. The blackish brown
pellets have nippled tips and indented bottoms. Some pellets are
old; others are new. We find one the size of a corn kernel, a
lamb's pellet, but it is not fresh.

I am torn, as always, between curiosity and reluctance to intrude, disturb. The spring has but a single route of escape: straight up the "chimney." At water holes, desert bighorns are capable of drinking a considerable amount quite rapidly, a speed that quenches their thirst yet exposes them to predators for only the briefest time. Watering in a group, their muscles ripple with attention. When they drink at this closed-in spring, surely the rock shivers with their wariness. It is a dangerous place.

Joe and I scramble up the wall and out of the spring. In the jumble of pinnacles around the onyx quarry, we find more bighorn day beds. On our hike back to camp, we find Mark.

Over and over, I scan the dry sierra for the sheep. I listen for a faint hoof-loosened rockfall and look among the boulders for bones. I find only a rabbit spine, still attached to the pelvic bone, and pieces of shell brought in from the faraway beach by the onyx miners, who must have known about the spring and just as likely hunted bighorns.

Perhaps water-hole fidelity brought the animals fatally to the spring, there to drink in the crosshairs, an ovid form of sitting duck. Or they stayed away from the danger, found water elsewhere, and then, when the onyx quarry closed, tiptoed back from the margins of disappearance. Resurgence after such peril is not the usual desert bighorn story.

Darkness falls quickly, ushered in by coyote song and an owl's cry from a distant *palo blanco*. The night is so clear, I am convinced that we can see all the way to Isla Tiburón off the coast of Sonora, on the other side of the Gulf, purely by starlight. The island is a cultural protectorate of the indigenous Comcáac (Seri) people and a refuge for introduced bighorn sheep.

From the sierra behind camp, near the arroyo, I hear a faint *baa-a,* sweet and small, like a lamb's bleat, a little *borrego cimarrón* in the dark. The others herd it away from us, using the owl's voice to find their way in the moonless night. Perhaps I imagine this.

I fill a small bowl with camp water for rinsing the day's dust off my face. The Comcáac named the land that surrounds them Conéaax Oacta: the planet Venus reflected on the water and seen when one washes one's hands.

The peninsula's wildness resides largely in its interior, in the bony rib of mountains that separates the Gulf of California from the Pacific Ocean. It is a geometry of jumbled ranges and ridges creased with steep alluvials and of much space between scant settlements of stone and stucco houses, small orchards, water catchments, and goats.

The mountain people seem created by the interior's sheer stamina. They are dignified and direct in manner, traits common to *bajacalifornianos*. Not so very long ago, sewing machines and the seeds of bougainvillea came into their villages on the backs of mules.

For centuries, this land protected itself, "a pile of stones full of thorns . . . a pathless, waterless thornful rock," inviolate by its failure to meet the standard human measures of utility. In the words of one of the Jesuit padre-historians in this desert in the early eighteenth century, Baja California was "destitute." Without asking the natives if they were miserable, he wrote, "The source of all misery in this country is the lack of water."

With greater sympathy, the Jesuits noted the hunger. The sparse bands of natives ate whatever they could pick or catch: cactus fruit, fish, mollusks, birds, grubs, ants, mice, crickets, snakes, small game, and, in the mountains, bighorn sheep and deer. When the *pitahaya* cactus ripened in summer, they gorged on fruit so lush and juicy, it was food and drink at the same time. After this harvest, the larder grew spare again.

For many natives in the Jesuit era, Christianity was not a means by which to give order to mystery. It was food. To come to

the scattered missions was to eat. The fathers may have been trying to find and feed the soul, but another kind of appetite could
lead people there.

Once they came, they were taught that Christian hell looked a
lot like the life they had left, a life of feuds, sorcery, murders, near
starvation. On the other hand, many Indians so hated the cold
that on a chilly day at the mission, a sermon about the fires of
Christian hell delighted them. They wanted to go.

The padres talked of trading the "dark clouds" of heathenism
for the bright light of the holy faith. They also told of an Indian
man who, after eating nearly twenty-four pounds of meat, ate
seventeen watermelons at one sitting. "The hunger," they wrote,
"was continuous."

On his four-thousand-mile journey around the perimeter of the
Sea of Cortés in a sardine boat, chronicled in 1941 as *The Log from
the Sea of Cortez,* John Steinbeck and his companions seldom ventured into Baja's wild interior. The purpose of his trip ("we dignified it by calling it an expedition") was to travel the coastline,
gathering marine specimens with Monterey, California, biologist
Ed Ricketts. The crew's work bound them to tide pools and collections of crabs, cucumbers, eels, annelids, snails, urchins, conchs,
holothurians, anemones, and other Gulf fauna.

During a brief onshore stop on the south coast, at the foot
of the Sierra de la Giganta, Steinbeck by chance encountered a
rancher and his party on their way to hunt *borrego cimarrón* in the
"tremendous and desolate stone mountains." The rancher invited
the Americans to go along.

"We didn't want to kill a big-horn sheep, but we wanted to see
the country," Steinbeck wrote. "As it turned out, none of them . . .
had any intention of killing a big-horn sheep."

From a *ranchería* of gardens and grapevines and houses with walls of woven palms and earth floors neatly swept, the hunters rode into the mountains on mules. Two Indian men went ahead of them on foot, waiting for the riders on the steepest ascents because the pack stock were too slow for them. The party camped on a high ledge with palm trees and a cascading spring.

Of night in camp, Steinbeck wrote, "We have noticed many times how lightly Mexican Indians sleep. Often in the night they awaken to smoke a cigarette and talk softly together for awhile, and then go to sleep again rather like restless birds, which sing a little in the dark, dreaming that it is already day. Half a dozen times a night they must awaken thus, and it is pleasant to hear them, for they talk very quietly as though they were dreaming."

In the morning, the Indians were given a broken rifle and off they went, Steinbeck said, straight up the mountain, while the others lounged by the palm-shaded pool and told stories.

"And we sat in that cool place and looked out over the hot desert country to the blue Gulf. In a couple of hours our Indians came back; they had no *borrego,* but one of them had a pocketful of droppings. It was time by now to start back to the boat. We intend to do all our future hunting in exactly this way."

The party descended the mountain and returned aboard the *Western Flyer,* with Steinbeck proclaiming, "This, our first hunt for the *borrego,* or big-horn sheep, was the nicest hunting we have ever had." They could think of only one way to improve their method. The next time, he vowed, "we shall not take a gun, thereby obviating the last remote possibility of having the hunt cluttered up with game." On a hardwood plaque the crew mounted their trophy: a perfect *borrego* turd.

The crew chugged along the coast in their boat, continuing the quest for marine specimens. The sierra, the difficult interior, was left behind. Offshore from another village, Steinbeck noted, "Food is hard to get, and a man lives inward, closely related to time."

Better roads and bigger tourism, a predatory brand of industrial leisure exemplified by Cabo San Lucas, have changed Baja California. The visitors seem to come as groups defined by their technology: They aren't people; they are four-wheelers, dirt bikers, dune buggers, yachties, anglers, surfers, windsurfers, sea kayakers, the RV crowd, the visored throngs on immortal golf quests.

Perhaps we, too, are a group, a goofy one with animal notes, plant books, and Jesuit literature, casting rods and Montana fly rods, and an old boat with big yellow Colorado River white-water oars, ready to save us if the outboard fails.

The land has always been extraordinarily beautiful, harsh, and agonizingly stubborn, and for a long time hunger and beauty locked it into its own keeping. We, too, reap the aesthetics, nature's scarce and precious beauty. We and so many *norteños* like us can do this because we have the time and the means. We are not hungry.

In one arena, we cling to the delusion of feral self-reliance, to citizenry in the republic of resourcefulness: fishing. Mark declares us protein-dependent. Our daily meat will come from the sea, he says, and he and Joe will catch it.

In a village behind a slip of a bay, we stop for a local fishing report. One family occupies most of the village. The news of the day is that its patriarch has died.

The old papa lived to be over a hundred years old and drove his pickup over the hellish roads until he was ninety-five. One day, he ate a huge breakfast of eggs and tortillas and lay down on his bed. He asked for three *santos* to be brought to him, then "breathed funny" and died.

His son tells us this, although I am unsure if I have correctly translated the part about the funny breathing. Papa's offspring and offspring of offspring surround us, home from a distant town, where they must go to school or work in a wage-driven economy that has eclipsed the small-scale family fishing trades in the remote *campos.*

The family compound is scattered with overturned *pangas,* some functional, others morphed into doghouses. The son shows us a sculpture of a *santo* welded from bits of scrap metal. Someone has colored the saint's face and feet pink. Perched on a fence post is a fat stuffed teddy bear, its body painted to look like a black-and-white Day of the Dead skeleton.

At a junction farther down the road, we stop at a Pemex station and fill the gas tank. On a shelf in the *tienda* is a horn from a bighorn ram. The tip is broomed. A chunk missing from the curved keel marks an old battle. No one at the store remembers where the ram's horn came from, but they have seen *borregos* in the nearby mountains. Rich people come to hunt them, with or without a special permit but always with money, we are told. Occasionally, there is local poaching.

A chain of ridges between a broad llano, or plain, and a small bay, where we hope to fish, slows our progress. The truck crawls over the ruts of a brutal ascent. On the crest, a Mexican rest area: two ten-gallon plastic water jugs by the side of the road, ready for the radiator in need.

The bay yields no fish. We eat rice and beans, tortillas, and nuts from Trader Joe's in Phoenix. Joe says the fishing will not be any good until we rid ourselves of the canned tuna in our cache. "Navajo," he says of our neighbors in Utah, "do not go to the hunt carrying meat from home."

Like so many of our camps, this one lies on a *bajada* above the shore and out of the wind: home on the "thornful rock." The desert is a stage for a hundred-square-mile out-of-control explosion of bristles and wildly gesticulating arms. Backlit by a low sun, every plant glows, creating an aura of needles and spikes.

Ocotillos shoot up from the ground like bouquets of crazy whips, topped with blossoms of flaming red. The *pitahaya,* the organ-pipe cactus with the fruits eaten by the natives in binges, grows in clusters of thick columns. The saguaro cousins, the *cardóns,* raise their massive cylindrical arms skyward, holding a vulture or two on their tops.

On a walk, I discover a fallen *cardón,* its pleated trunk over ten inches thick and showing woody brown ribs beneath a waxy green skin. Under this toppled giant lies the skeleton of a goat. The goat took the blow across its chest.

Pencil-thin stems of *candellila* grow in candelabra clusters. Barrel cacti dot the desert floor. Lomboy ooze a bloodred sap, said to heal wounds. Spiky chollas fling chunks of themselves, which become affixed to my leg. So instant and strong is their grip when they sense a passing host, they seem to fly through the air. Chollas want to go with you. They are best removed with a comb. None of us has a comb. Our hair looks like the ocotillos.

Most of all, I love the boojums. Baja's boojum trees are shaped like upside-down electrocuted carrots. Their ivory trunks, thick at the base, taper at the tip into a pronged fork or a tuft of white blossoms. Their foliage grows in a full-nerd sprout of green body

hair, erect and prickly. Top-heaviness on mature boojums sends
the upright trunk into a swooping bend groundward, then up to
the light again in a crazy loop. On a hot day, don't plan to lounge
in their shade unless you are a caterpillar.

The boojums' winter leafiness, their green spook fur, makes
them quite endearing. I go on a walkabout among them often.
Whenever I feel blue, Mark tells me, "Go hug boojums." I lace up
my boots, grab a water bottle, and go. There is something so . . .
so *vegetablelike* about walking through a forest of looped boojums.
I love boojums. I love them because they are plant geeks.

Recent rains have covered the boojums in leaves that are surprisingly delicate and moist to the touch. In the dead of summer,
when the trees are nearly leafless, their shape reveals their more
botanically dignified Spanish name, *cirio,* or church candle. Endemic to Baja California, with a sprinkle of habitat across the
Gulf, on the coast of Sonora, the *cirio* is in a family of succulents
that includes ocotillos.

Hurricanes blow them over. A complex array of insect species
pollinates them. They grow fifty feet tall and higher, upright or
looped, in the central peninsula, diminutive and lateral on the
windier Pacific side. They grow in Baja California by the millions: Planet of the Hair Carrots. Whenever the warmongering
slugs of the corporate-oil U.S. presidency insult the world with
their appalling hubris, the whole lot of them, I think, should be
taken to the boojums and let loose in their boxer shorts.

In the broken hills beyond camp, near a water hole, we find
bighorn scat. Joe and Mark brave a jungle of cholla to reach a
piece of fishable shore. They return with a halibut the size of a
small air mattress. We wrap the meat in foil and cook it over
coals of dead and fallen *cardón* ribs. We hang the skin and bones
from a paloverde branch for the coyotes, who yip and sing in
ecstasy. On this *bajada* above a darkened sea, the mammals have
full bellies.

Father Francisco María Piccolo, who, in 1702, published one of
the earliest accounts of desert bighorn sheep, was many things,
but this is what I like best about him: He was a gardener. To the
"thornful rock" of Baja California, he introduced maize. With
the help of Father Juan de Ugarte, a fellow gardener, he brought
seed and stock from the mainland and planted olives, figs, avocados, grapevines, pomegranates, and other fruit trees. Piccolo
and Ugarte tested soils and set their workers to build dams and
route scant freshwater into narrow hand-dug canals, or *acequias,*
and then on to water fields and seedlings.

To Baja California's native fan palms, the padres added the
exotic date palm. Coconut palms would come later. When the
mestizos from mainland Mexico showed the local Indians how to
extract and eat the *palmitos,* the tender cores of young palm trees,
the hungry Indians finished off several groves in a short time.

The mission gardens were more oases than Edens, although
water-blessed sites like Loreto, Mulegé, and San Ignacio surely
seemed miracles of greenery, as they do today. Perhaps Piccolo
knew, as most desert gardeners know, that planting edible crops
in a parched land is, more than anything, a gamble, that a crop
can sprout on a promise, then die in a single afternoon. Some
years, the mission villagers ate mangoes; in others, they ate shoe
leather.

The farming of souls, too, was a gamble. Piccolo's laborers in
the garden were the Indians to whom the padres offered shelter
and salvation, Christ and cultivation. When they arrived, the
padres had to know where to find a pool of sinners and how to
assess the obstacles: native customs, traditions, and morals (in
their view, the lack thereof) to be stripped away for the fresh
veneer of a Christian life.

Piccolo had to learn the native languages and dialects quickly.

He needed to know where the water was. Maps to water came through stories, so he had to learn the stories.

Across the Gulf from the mainland, the padres ferried cattle, horses, sheep, goats, and pigs, as well as doors, shoes, bowls, nails, cloth, scissors, chalices, and bells. They tried to discourage their garrison, the soldiers who guarded the holy enterprise, from running off to the godless enterprise of diving for pearls.

For the duration of the Jesuit era, from 1697 to 1768, the changers urged their flock to trade a nomadic life for a sedentary one, a line of social engineering not always acceptable to the changees. All that "lying about in the open air," the padres insisted, could do them no good. They needed houses to sleep in. Still, many of the native converts went back and forth from the new way of life to the old, from mission to desert. Over the years, there were rebellions and bloodshed. At one mission, the locals pierced a priest with "countless arrows" as he walked from house to church.

Many of the natives were endless reciters of prayer and psalm. On and on went their recitations. Many were so zealous about the cross, they erected its likeness on every path, wore it, and painted it on their foreheads or other body parts when they were ill. They embedded wooden crosses with bits of pearled blue shell and polished them to shine like mirrors.

Father Francisco María Piccolo was born in Palermo, Sicily. Like most in the Society of Jesus, he was a learned man, well educated in the humanities, sciences, and philosophy, as well as in theology. He arrived in Mexico at age thirty and spent time among the Tarahumara of Chihuahua. Father Juan María de Salvatierra, another Italian, led the Jesuit *entrada* into Baja California and founded its first mission, which was in Loreto. He was joined by Piccolo, who ended up doing everything. More priests, and nearly twenty mission sites up and down the peninsula, followed, with Piccolo itinerant or gardening at Loreto, Mulegé, and San Javier.

According to one history of the Roman Catholic Church, the early years of the Society of Jesus found them "devoted to the following of Christ, as though there were nothing else in the world to care for." Eventually, members of this religious order mixed their "heroic sanctity" with mundane labor, charity, missionary work, and other needs of the day.

The Jesuits are perhaps best known for their belief that priests can be both holy and brainy. As early as their founding, in the mid-1500s, the Jesuits considered the acquisition of knowledge—empirical, rational, scientific—a spiritually profitable endeavor. By Piccolo's time, the Jesuits had produced a formidable body of writing on every subject from medicine, mathematics, and physics to acoustics, engineering, botany, and zoology.

One treatise on astronomy unfolded as a voyage through outer space. Another told the Pope how to repair the dome of St. Peter's. A political satire on the languages of animals landed its author in prison. Among religious orders, the Jesuits were, in short, the charismatic, pointy-headed intellectuals.

Half a world away from his homeland, the Mexican desert made a scholarly Society of Jesus man like Piccolo into a multilingual horticulturist, ethnographer, hydraulic engineer, and cartographer; explorer of mountains and beggar for mission subsidies; weaver, winemaker, teacher, carpenter; a builder of adobe bricks and stone churches, or at least the supervisor thereof, for the hands that dug the dirt and lifted the stone were native.

Ultimately, the natives would perish not from hard labor, evangelization, or the incessant pressure to emerge from the Stone Age to become full-fledged, tax-paying Spaniards. Instead, within barely a century, disease would decimate them and tip their culture into oblivion.

In the garden of a friend in San Ignacio, I eat a legacy of food brought to the desert by the Jesuit padres. The friend grows grapes, lemons, oranges, bananas, mangoes, papayas, and other fruit, as well as vegetables, herbs, and leafy shrubs I cannot identify. I pick a basil leaf and inhale its spicy scent. I imbibe the bright red, pink, and gold of flowers scattered everywhere. Water runs in rivulets into the garden, lined with cilantro and drawn from the padres' original *acequias.*

The garden and orchard cover a few acres in the town's oldest sector, off the main plaza. The pattern of planting is not in stern gringo monorows, sprayed every four minutes by robotic nozzles dispensing pesticides. The planting is random and somewhat shaggy, like my own garden. It pleases me to discover that I may not be so horticulturally inept after all. This Mexican garden is a model of motley, of devotion and puttering, of rapt attention to the birds it draws.

The proprietor of all this bounty, a San Ignaciano in his sixties, grows food for his extended family and for barter with the townsfolk. When his grapes are harvested and his wine is ready, many neighbors come with bottles and jars.

He also makes toys of sorts. My favorite is a handmade relief model of one of the most treacherous stretches of the transpeninsular highway, the infamous Cuesta del Infiernillo, the Descent of Little Hell: a gauntlet of steep ascents and tight switchbacks, with blind curves and heart-stopping drop-offs mere inches from the edge of the pavement; nonstop Virgin niches; fewer guardrails than is medically advisable; and vehicle carcasses stacked at the foot of the cliffs like dead Japanese beetles.

The gardener-toymaker has re-created in miniature a mountain with a hairpin turn, a blind curve perched high on the *cuesta.* With a minicar in each hand, I make *vrroo-oom* noises and send the cars around the hairpin curve into a head-on collision, screeching their brakes and letting out bloodcurdling pretend screams, wrestling the cars in a wild flurry of my fingers. Off the fake cliff they roll, wheels spinning, another scream, this one with a nice fade at its end.

Everyone laughs. This is what everyone does when they see the *cuesta* miniature: They make the cars crash. Down the center of the black highway, where no driver could possibly see around the bend, runs a single line: broken yellow, indicating it's okay to pass.

Before we leave, our host climbs a ladder and picks an orange for each of us. The fruit has a faintly salty taste. The dates, the famed dates of San Ignacio's many palm trees, are ripe and our pockets bulge with them. The lanky palms tower above town, their topknots bronze in the setting sun. An oasis.

We leave the garden and walk beneath the plaza's laurel trees to the mission church. Our passage to the church is blocked by an albino mastodon of a motor home, whose driver cannot quite park it at an angle without rerouting plaza traffic around the master bedroom (ballroom? maid's quarters? lap pool?), which seems to occupy most of its back end.

The driver parks anyway and emerges with a child-carrier backpack strapped to his shoulders. Inside the backpack, head up to take in the sights along the route directly to the church, is a poodle.

I am too snobby to share a church with a poodle, so we sit in the mission garden for a while, relaxing under a pomegranate tree near beds of white roses. Ancient carved wooden doors lead to clerical offices in the wing off the main church. In places, remnants of blue paint cling to the gray stone, and I wonder if this whole wing was once peacock blue.

Misión San Ignacio itself rises skyward with the palms, its walls of pale rose stone four feet thick, quarried from Baja California's hard-rock heart. The colonial-style facade is busy with stone lions, crowns, castles, and saints in niches, some heads knocked off completely, others eroded to the point that they are just pins.

Padre Piccolo baptized the indigenes on this site in 1716, in a brush shelter, then turned souls and construction over to a colleague. The present edifice, dating from the late eighteenth century, replaced the Jesuits' earlier ones.

When the church is poodle-free, we pass under the pinheaded saints and walk through massive wooden doors. The cruciform floor plan is simple, the stone beneath our feet well worn. It is the smoothness of this stone, I think, that gives the church its calm.

Saint Ignatius of Loyola himself, founder of the Society of Jesus, stands at the center of the *retablo,* the wall behind the altar, in one of several paintings set among ornately gilded pillars and frames. The paintings are dark with age, their saint scenes barely discernible beneath a murky veneer. In a niche along a nave wall, above the pews, stands the statue of a cleaner saint. He holds a real broom. I want this saint, I want him for the dust-bunny war at home. The painted ceiling dances with clouds and putti heads, their baby cheeks rosy and plump. Throughout the church, there is the aroma of roses, candle wax, and fresh tortillas.

The night's camp trades *cardón* and *pitahaya* cactus for palm trees, a forest of them between San Ignacio's spring-fed pond and plaza. Although there are RV parks nearby, we have chosen to enter a chained but unlocked gate, whose sign is too faded to read. The driveway leads to over four acres of uninhabited space.

Lush grass grows beneath the palms. Beyond our bed on this "lawn," water burbles through the *acequia.* In a small pen, two calves appear to be eating palm fronds and dates. No one is about. Other travelers do not know that this is a camping place. We have date-fed beef and a palm grove entirely to ourselves. The proprietor will come in the morning to collect his fee.

In the night breeze, palm leaves rustle gently, like skirts in a ballroom. We are fat with dates and squeaky-clean from two-dollar showers. We are drowning in stars unfazed by the town's dim lights, and we have been to church. After barbed plants and volcanic rock, this not-quite-an-RV park feels like paradise, and yet all three of us ache to be in the desert again.

Beneath the date palms of the Jesuits, I think of the simplicity of Mexican churches as a quiet exaltation, quiet by their poverty, perhaps, but less architecturally furious than churches in the mother country, their tenor calmer than Spain's high pitch toward pious fervor. Here, heathen souls might be soothed not by holy faith but by ancient rose-colored stone, by lemons and pomegranates and bougainvillea, by refuge. The best part of the old missionary life, to me, was the mission garden.

For the natives of central and southern Baja California, for the Cochimí, Pericu, and other groups, the Jesuit mission itself, physically, *was* Christianity. The material things—stone church, fruit, corn, meat, cloth, dams and ditches, beasts of burden—may have drawn them more than the abstractions. Father Piccolo gardened and they came out of the desert to the garden.

Out in the desert, the people lived as close to a true bare-bones wilderness life as most hunter-gatherer cultures have come. The land gave them little but the meager foods of its own marginality. They had tools of stone and a calendar fixed on two measures: the time of hunger and the time of the sweet joys of cactus fruit. The priests believed that such lives needed rescue from the flames of hell.

Three hundred years later, one cannot begin to comprehend the price of "rescue." An entire culture, born of this spare place and woven with story maps to seeps and springs and ways to find roots, seeds, wild sheep, or fish, is gone. Few know how to live anymore without the garden.

The Jesuits of the Mexican deserts were masterful cartographers, and to map their territory, they needed to walk or ride its every detail. Father Francisco María Piccolo was among the most itchy-footed.

Shortly after his arrival in Baja California, Piccolo set off across the peninsula in search of a possible port on the Pacific side. On his travels, he became a naturalist as well as a seeker of potential converts. He described places with Indian names, which he promptly changed to Spanish names. Of Ohobbé, a place with reeds and willows, he wrote, "We called it Santa Rosalía." Kada-kaamán would become San Ignacio. The saints of Europe overlaid the spoken native tongue and went down on the maps in ink.

The padres impressed the locals with their pistols and their horses. When the natives did not understand Roman Catholic heaven, they were told it was a field of *pitahayas* with ripe fruit. Conversions and baptisms were performed en route. Piccolo complained of thorns in his cassock.

Into the sierra west of Loreto, into the wild interior, Piccolo traveled on foot "among horrifying peaks" and later with a party "on good and fat horses and accompanied by Indians." His evangelized territory grew; it was a country filled with potential converts.

In a report to his superiors, he wrote, "Here the good Savior was pleased to open the door of the Gospel for the benefit of so many souls who live under the dark clouds of death, and desire, as they so clearly assured me, to emerge from them into the bright light of our holy faith." *As they so clearly assured me.*

On his explorations into the "horrifying peaks," Piccolo carried hard bread, sugar, and chocolate. He rode barely tamed stallions. Always on his person was an image of the Virgin Mary, perhaps brought from his native Italy, an image that had survived arrows and shipwrecks. In Baja's sierra, it went underwater when his packhorse plunged into a lake of reeds. The men freed the pack and saved the icon. Then they ate the horse.

Piccolo regarded the natives with affection. They were as "precious as pearls" when their souls were saved, but otherwise they were known as "these wretched Indians." He denounced "their infernal priests" (shamans) and "diabolic and deceitful races, wizardry, and all their evil actions"—which included polygamy and practices that the fathers interpreted as infanticide.

The "diabolic and deceitful races" particularly seemed to rankle Piccolo. The Wretcheds, he said, run about in crazed footraces over deer skins, a kind of cape, which they laid out on trails during ritual feasts. Somehow, Piccolo forced them to surrender the "abominable capes." He put the capes under the altar with "other diabolical instruments" and felt better. The Indians then lined their racing paths—obviously places of great meaning—with Christian crosses.

Piccolo's *jornada* brought him in contact with the flora of Baja California, much of it endemic by virtue of its isolation between two seas. He ate the fish of his parishioners—sierra, cabrilla, *pargo*. He noted the wildlife in the eroded peaks and deep canyons: fox, mountain lion, bobcat, gray wolf, and deer, donors of the abominable capes.

High on the cliffs, its hooves resting on vertical air, was a creature unfamiliar to European eyes. Piccolo described it in *Informe de la California,* his 1702 report on the Jesuit mission, as a kind of deer "as large as a Calf of one or two years old: Its Head is much like that of a Stag: and its Horns, which are very large, like those of a Ram: Its Tail and Hair are speckled, and shorter than a Stags: But its Hoof is large, round, and cleft as an Oxes."

A later natural history repeated the description and added an illustration of the "Tayé or California Deer," depicted as a tail-less, barrel-bodied animal with a proportionately undersized head, shaggy neck, dark curled horns, and hooves like a horse's. A hundred years after Piccolo's description, a Canadian specimen of a "tayé" relative would be collected and ultimately classified as *Ovis canadensis,* not a deer but a wild mountain sheep.

Piccolo's sheep description was one of the first to be widely published in the European world. Perhaps he and the Jesuit fathers had seen the bighorn portraiture right in front of their eyes, painted in caves throughout central Baja California by those whose cultures long predated that of the Jesuits' indigenous contemporaries. Here, and on rock faces throughout the American Southwest, were "published" descriptions of wild sheep.

Across the cave murals of central Baja surge figures in red, black, ocher, and white paint: deer, pronghorn antelope, mountain lions, dolphins, manta rays, whales, sea lions, vultures, rabbits; a supernova of A.D. 1054; horned serpents with bulges of food midbody; humans with arms outstretched, their bodies a pincushion of arrows.

Bighorn sheep dominate a number of friezes, drawn in profile, showing both ears and all their dewclaws, mouths open, sometimes pregnant, sometimes impaled by spears, heads turned slightly, no eyes—never shown with eyes.

The Indian groups of the Jesuit era were not, to anyone's knowledge, practitioners of rock art. They did not claim to be descendants of the cave painters. The Jesuits recorded their myths, including oft-repeated stories of giants, perhaps imaginary, perhaps an actual group of men and women of extraordinary stature, who came from the north but later disappeared. The giants, the Indians said, painted the cave murals of the sierra. The giants wore capes.

To Sicily and Spain, Piccolo's birthplace and his country of allegiance, the occupying Moors of the Middle Ages brought the mathematics of the sky and the arts of water in the desert—water, too, for pleasure, run through fountains and courtyard cascades.

To an eighteenth-century priest in the pathless, "thornful rock" of far-west Mexico, such sounds would have been hallucinations. The missions clung to scant springs, largely on the coasts, the high cordillera behind them not to be lived in, only to be crossed on stallions with the protection of chocolate and the Holy Mother. If the land itself fed his imagination, Piccolo was restrained in the telling of it.

Piccolo spent more than half of his life in the deserts of Mexico, held there by his own vow of obedience. Mediterranean Europe was likely an imaginary homeland more than a remembered one, even though bits of it were reproduced in the mission templates of church, pueblo, and garden. He could not allow himself to be homesick; Jesuits don't get homesick. He planted olives and orange trees. He laid his hands on the ebony hair of the Wretcheds, purifying them, he thought, in the fire of divine love lest they burn up in their own metaphors.

The orchards and gardens fed the Indians, but just barely. The adobe shelters and the vaults of stone enclosed their attention and directed it toward the altar, the altar under which this edgeless Jesuit had stuffed the instruments of their animism, taken from the land, their own way of embracing mystery.

After thirty-two years in the Californias, Piccolo died at age seventy-five. The Jesuit fathers continued to cultivate soil and souls in the wildland between two seas. Here is a tally from a report in 1762: infant baptisms, 327; burials, 155; marriages, 112; "couples living in concubinage corrected," 21.

In 1767, the Spanish government expelled the Jesuits from the peninsula. The sixteen fathers then running the missions had to leave or face execution, a decree based on nefarious accusations from distant Madrid.

In a ferry bound for the mainland, then on foot across Mexico to a ship bound for Europe, the Jesuits of the Californias turned their backs to the desert. Each was allowed to carry his cassock, a breviary, and two books, one of theology, one of science.

For a long stretch of days, we leave bighorn terrain to become fish-eaters, affixed to the littoral, to places of lesser hunger. Home is a *casita* beyond the southern city of La Paz, on isolated coastal bluffs (population: us) with a white sliver of a beach and fish that rise to Mark's and Joe's lures and flies, then fall onto a grill or a tostada shell or into a bottomless bowl of ceviche, made on the spot, on the boat, the fish cut up on top of the cooler, then thrown into a marinade of fresh lime juice.

Sierra, bonito, and cabrilla leap into the clear blue air from deep emerald waters. One day, Mark catches a snapper so big, he and Joe stop fishing for a few days until we can finish it: a twelve-tostada fish.

The gulls fuss and shriek over the entrails of the day's catch. Frigate birds move in and make the whole scene edgier. A gull nonchalantly swallows an entire fish head and bulges with meat. Too heavy to get off the ground, it sits on the sand like coyote fodder, shoulders hunched, belly distended, looking as if everything would be fine if it could just belch.

Every evening at the same time, a line of brown pelicans, always in odd numbers—five, seven, nine—glides by us, low on the water, somehow achieving forward motion without a single flap of their wings. If they passed in even numbers or changed their flyby clock, you would worry about the world.

Manta rays leap out of the water and slap down again in noisy belly flops, clearing their gills, tickling off parasites. Mark guts a bonito and finds in its stomach sculpins, a squid, and a mess of shrimp with threadlike limbs intact. Needlefish, as long and slender as shafts of chrome light, have green bones.

At low tide, Sally Lightfoot crabs sidle up the wet rocks. Across their blue carapaces runs a galaxy of white dots. Red-orange legs and claws cling to the slippery rocks even as blasts of roiling surf pound them. The crabs move forward and in reverse, but their sideways scuttle seems the most swift. Their wariness stays true to Steinbeck's description of creatures who know your every move, hurrying or slowing as you hurry or slow, reacting to the direction of every approach. "When you plunge at them," he wrote, "they seem to disappear in little puffs of blue smoke."

Beneath the crab-covered rocks, in pools of clear water, lie dozens of lost spark plugs, the weight of choice for Mexican anglers who line-fish from the shore. Mark tries this spot with his fly rod. Like all Montanans, he held a fly rod in his baby fist soon after birth. In cap and wet shorts, legs planted firmly on the rock as waves curl around him, he casts long arcs of filament over the sea as if he were working a spring slough on the Beaverhead River.

When we have enough to feed us, we stop fishing. We stop fishing when the wind blows, and sometimes it blows all day and night. The boat stays tied up, which does not deter Mark and Joe. They have enough gear to *create* a fish, even if they don't catch one. Eating the lures will be like eating the padres' leather belts and shoes.

On inland walks, I stare up at fat *cardóns* with vultures in them, flush quail and doves from a deserted well, and pick the beadlike sweet ruby fruits of the *mamalita* cactus so we won't get scurvy. On steep slopes, the footing becomes precarious over coarse granules of beige granite that slide like loose marbles. When I accidentally ski downhill, I can feel the heat of friction through the soles of my sandals and hope that I can arrest my slide before I end up planting my face in the thorny trunk of a *cardón*. The walking is easier on the open bluffs above the sea, amid shell middens and soil darkened by ancient cooking fires.

Across the strait lies a piece of drowned coastline, an island of mountainous desert scrub that takes the morning light as thin blue haze, then lets itself be carved into amber ridges and amethyst shadows by the late-afternoon sun. When the sun sets, the desert drains its dusk colors into the sea.

The water around the island turns from a silky sheen of aquamarine to burnished silver, the color of the cuff bracelet of Navajo silver around my wrist, silver made lustrous by the warmth of flesh. In mere seconds, the sea leaches the silver and deepens to vermilion. Its beauty stirs the imagination, and I wonder if the last refuge of all that is truly wild lies not on earth but in light.

Sea level, the weight of the water on our high-desert bones, pushes heavy, heavy dreams into our sleep. None of us can remember so much dreaming, dreaming made thicker, we think, with the night's high tide.

Mark dreams that he throws carrots into the laps of Arabs. We wonder, Are thrown carrots considered insults in Islam? In Joe's dreams: a convertible hearse. In mine: long dives into emerald water, dives to retrieve dozens of hats, except for one with heavy blinders, which I let go in a gust of wind.

For several nights, shrimp trawlers from the mainland work offshore from the bluffs. Their engines grind out our peace. They drop and drag nets with a rakelike dredge that rips up the ocean floor, scraping shrimp, plants, sea fans, anemones, and everything else off the bottom. On trawler nights, my dreams slide into nightmares.

More windstorms come. Where turquoise water lay as glass against white sand, churning, frothy waves now pile up, throwing sea upon land in full force. The ceviche bowl is empty and my dreams spill their darkness into the waking hours.

I read in a Baja California history how the padres scorned the natives for the absence of words in their language—no equivalent for the words *envy, virtue, danger, decency, pious, virgin*. I read about Indian children at the mission schools who could only use two hands for counting material objects because, higher than that, there was not that much of anything.

On a night toward the end of our stay, damp, swollen clouds roll over the Gulf from the Pacific and obliterate Orion, said by southwestern tribes to be the constellation of mountain sheep. In our bed beneath wind-rattled windows, I whisper to Mark, "I need . . ."

"A fish?"

"I want . . ."

"Zombie drugs?"

"I think I must have . . ."

"A glass of water?"

My voice grows raspy and small. "Spooks. I need . . ."

"Sheep? That saint with the broom?"

Like acute sensitivity to changes in light, to an unfamiliar shadow that suddenly hovers in the corner of a familiar room, to a faint slip in the rift that holds this peninsula in paralyzed friction, these things are hard to explain.

What I am trying to say to my beloved, who has fed me from the sea with his own hands, is this: I need *boojums*.

Under a sapphire sky, the inland desert fills a broad valley in all directions, hemmed only by mountains that rise so abruptly from the flats, you would knock your forehead on them if you walked toward them blindfolded. Jagged white veins zigzag through their brown faces, giving them the look of giant chunks of raw agate. A shallow arroyo furrows the valley's lowest point. Haloed by the low sun, *cardón* and cholla cover the land in a swathe of glowing bristles.

This gulf of open desert between ribs of mountains soothes the bone and muscle needed to cross it. There is a balance between sky and terra firma; they are complementary mirrors of infinity. Here, forms and shapes reveal themselves through patient inquiry and the luxury of enough carried water to let you trace them. Beyond the horizon lies the azure sea if we need it.

The truck lurches over a scant track. Near the arroyo, Mark puts it into four-wheel drive to cross the rough and pitted gravel of erosion. Often, Joe and I get out and walk in order to avoid suffering concussions on the truck cab's roof, and to feel the air. In another season, we would be baked to leather, babbling about milk shakes or waterfalls or swimming pools before we dived headfirst into the ground for one last mouthful of sand.

We have seen no one. The valley is uninhabited. The last structure sighted was a roofless cement block sprouting antennae of bare rebar, waiting in forlorn desolation for the construction workers to come back from their ten-year lunch break.

The truck crawls up the valley. I am noticing high, bold faces of rock that are bighorn country. I am not noticing that the valley ends ahead of us, squeezed into a narrow slot in the mountains. The airy dreaminess of open desert pinches into a tight black crack. From where we are, the crack feels like distance, but here, in this valley, distance breeds mirage.

Sixty miles back, before we left the main road, we encountered a man who told us about this arroyo and how it is a watering place for bighorns. He also spoke of a graveyard in the sierra in the opposite direction.

The *borrego cimarrón,* he said, go to that place to die. He pointed to mountains overlaid in blue on blue until the farthest layer was only slightly less pale than air. It is not a watering place, he insisted, but a bone place; scattered skeletons, curled horns, teeth and femurs and spines, rib cages with the wind in them. I cannot tell you more about this graveyard and I am not sure why.

Just short of the black crack, the arroyo is as wide as a riverbed. A narrow ribbon of water meanders down its course but soon disappears into the sand. A snow-white crust of dried salt lines the stream's edges. The water runs clear over settled minerals the color of rust.

We are heading into the crack, into a gorge of jagged night-dark rock. The stream flows there, too, and sheep tracks come to the water from nowhere. Each time we trace the tracks away from the water, they vanish. I do not want to enter the gorge, but Mark and Joe do, and they pull me along the slipstream of their curiosity.

A mile inside the gorge, we park the truck and make camp. Any farther and the road would be nearly impassable, and none of us is fond of pushing vehicles through dry streambeds or streams, even if they are streams of salt and sulfur. Others have driven this way, but their tracks are faint and weathered. There are signs of old mines, of the earth's skin torn off. This reckless exposure may be what gives the gorge its ominous air.

Before dinner, we hike up-canyon to look for signs of bighorn or the bighorns themselves. At one point, the black gorge opens to softer walls of gold and red, and something tight around my chest loosens. Around a bend, we find scattered palm trees, fan palms with stocky trunks, a thatch of wild grasses in their shade, and rustling fronds that hint of paradise.

There is good sheep habitat here: water, food, bedding places, and escape terrain above the canyon and in a far-off spine of mountains turning to indigo in the evening light. Wherever you think the vertical rock is impossible, that is where you may find desert bighorns.

In his natural history of Baja California, written in the mid-1700s, Jesuit missionary Miguel del Barco related the curious acrobatics of the peninsular bighorn. As native hunters pursue a sheep, he wrote, "the sheep approaches the edge of a precipice and jumps off, taking care to land squarely on his head so that his thick horns can absorb the impact of the fall. Once down, he gets up and runs away." From the heights, the hunters look down "without venturing themselves to attempt a similar trick." The horns are so well made, Barco remarked, the sheep's entire head can take the blow of the fall without injury.

I have seen Blue Door Band sheep make extraordinary leaps.

When they slip, they never flatten themselves, legs splayed, and claw for footholds as they slide. Instead, when they lose a foothold, they land on one below it, or the one below that. I have never seen one land on its head. They prefer not to show me this trick.

We leave the fan palms and turn back to camp. Mark and I hike the arroyo. Joe takes the talus above us, looking for signs of sheep until the walls become too steep and he must either descend to join us or be rimrocked.

How much work for all that meat, how difficult it must have been to hunt them, I think. We cannot even *find* them. The most skilled hunters could herd an animal toward their *compadres,* who waited with bows and arrows, only to watch their prey fling itself into thin air, flying into the abyss, horns-first.

Back in camp, the wind begins. Soon it blows with the fury of something trapped, bottlenecked inside this narrow gorge, desperate to get out. The wind tries to blow our dinners off our plates. The wind pushes my discomfort into an ill-tempered gloom.

I do not like this place, I tell Mark, although the reasons elude me. The *banditos* are back in town, drinking tequila. The ax murderer cracked his differential en route. Monsters prefer swamps so that they can drip. In the list of terrors in creepy places, that leaves only the dreaded inner storm known as Self.

The rock is glassy and dark; the walls struggle with the light. Between the canyon walls, the sandy arroyo is hardly two hundred feet wide, and this is the space, so narrow and grim, like an earthquake fault in a primordial schist brain, that we inhabit.

The wild of this desert is a wild held intact by its own raw hostility, a reminder of nature's capacity to awe as well as kill you. Sunsets and bloodred ocotillo flowers and turquoise bays do no harm. I am neither hungry nor thirsty, nor am I punctured with thorns. I have the luxury of attention to insistent beauty. I live in a universe of sensation. But I could not survive here.

The wind cannot find its way out. It tears at our clothes and hair with nothing to temper its howl and grit. A stocky elephant tree barely shelters our bedroll. The night thickens into sepulchral dark. When the full moon rises, it weighs too much. I try to make the canyon into thoughtless space.

After our long sojourn on the sea and wide-open *bajadas,* it seems strange that we have come here. It is a choice that can be undone, I propose, but Mark and Joe want more reasons to change camp than the pathetic assertion that the rock is the wrong color.

Before sleep, we sit together on the sand with boulders for backrests. Joe tells us a bedtime story.

One of the things they did as kids growing up in southern Colorado, he says, was hunt for arrowheads. They searched land as flat as a pancake, chewed and cut and fenced to something entirely different from its original short-grass prairie but still yielding, once in a while, artifacts from its grassland past.

"My brothers and I were pretty young when we went arrowhead hunting," Joe begins, "maybe ranging in age from five to eight years old. Sometimes our sister went, but it usually was just the boys. Our father woke us up early in the morning. He had us dress in jeans and long-sleeved shirts and cowboy hats."

"The felt hats with the white braid looped on the edge of the brim? The cord chin straps with the wooden bead toggle?" I ask.

"Yes, those kids' cowboy hats," Joe replies. His voice is slow and deliberate, careful with this memory.

"We put on our cowboy hats and our dad drove us out to the prairie to look for arrowheads. When we got out of the car, he made us cinch up our chin straps and tie bandannas around our faces, folded into a V over the nose and knotted in the back, like stagecoach bandits. We had to help my littlest brother tie his. Each of us had a pair of goggles. The prairie dust was horrible, so we had to be covered up. Dad made us hold hands so we wouldn't be separated.

"So, in our cowboy hats, kerchiefs, and little goggles, we three boys walked across the prairie, holding hands, following our father, who always walked ahead of us, searching the dirt for worked stone."

It is the Mexican night, not a Colorado prairie, that wraps itself around us, yet the imagination can so easily make this leap. Stories lead the mind to calmer waters.

Natives of the Sonoran Desert who remember hunting bighorn recall that before the hunt they sat quietly in the night, conversing softly, telling stories about fat animals but, out of caution, never mentioning wild sheep.

When they were growing up in Montana, Mark and his siblings had those felt cowboy hats, I think as we slip into our sleeping bags beneath the moon. My brothers and I had those cowboy hats. Otherwise, we would have threatened to hold our breath or choke the family puppy until our parents gave in and bought them for us.

I cannot remember coffee, or putting on my sandals, or hiking down a chasm lined with purple shadows, leaving Mark and Joe to follow later. I only remember passing through the rocky portals and climbing the banks of the arroyo to the valley and the *bajadas,* to the sun.

My company is a scattered thatch of boojum trees and two coyotes. The low morning sun backlights trees and animals. Their auras—one of green leaves, the other of tawny fur—stand out in feline alertness. The coyotes are as lean as sticks. The ragged mountains float hazy blue on the horizons, holding sheep in their heights, occasionally spilling them into the dry washes, where the food grows. I am telling myself my own stories.

Older and beyond the cowboy hat phase, one of my brothers and I went through what I would call our "monk phase." Our family lived in Rome, Italy, at the time. Grant and I often explored the city's lesser-known churches, abbeys, and monasteries. Among our favorites was the eighteenth-century quarters of Jesuit priests, open to the public as a museum.

Off a long corridor of cool stone, each priest had a room nearly as slender as a closet, with whitewashed stucco walls, a narrow bed with a frayed blue cotton coverlet, a bloody crucifix, and a wooden desk by a window overlooking a lush courtyard garden.

This was the life we wanted, we decided; we'd be monks. Each of us would have an elegantly simple room with books and rolls of parchment and lots of paints and delicate sable brushes and a pen for inscribing our knowledge, which, as brainy Jesuits, would be vast and important. Silent brothers in robes and Birkenstocks would bring us goblets of Chianti. The garden would soothe us. We would illuminate manuscripts.

It is this image that I bring to Father Piccolo in Baja California. His room overlooks orange and lemon trees. Its window frame is painted peacock blue. He is seated with his notebook. He writes exhaustive volumes on the local flora and fauna—cactus fifty feet tall, cactus the size of thumbs, bearing beads of sweet red fruit, trees that loop, trees that look dead until rain teases them into full leaf. He writes of pearled shells. He writes of a horizon of azure sea and soil the color of poverty.

His manuscripts are illuminated with fish, fish swimming about the pages like chips of light, fish nosing the gold leaf of decorative script, swirling in schools through the loops of *Benedictus es*. He describes whales in the lagoons and pronghorn antelope on the salt flats. He describes a cow-deer in the mountains. He refers to "precious pearls," never to anyone "wretched." He wears a deerskin cape in the morning chill.

My brother and I never became monks. Father Piccolo of Palermo likely did little of the above. Father Piccolo had an agenda. He had in mind the systematic evangelization of a wilderness people. He believed that lives so brief and full of misery needed the hope of heaven. Any fantasy that we might filter through three centuries obscures the blunt fact that the end result was genocide.

I would like to think that the right way to survive in this harsh desert is on the edge between wilderness and garden. The errant padres lived thus, yet they doomed the very culture that knew how to stay alive here, that knew how places like that black chasm could hold both food and fear.

Streamlining the complexities of history, you could say that, in livable areas, the padres left a legacy of irrigation and horticulture that sustained rural Baja California well into the twentieth century. One had to grow things. One had to be resourceful. The garden did not compromise the wild. This lifeway, too, is now ephemeral.

Today, we will leave the big arroyo and head north to the border, stopping to fish the bay with the yellowtail jack and sunlit islands—the sea, again—and to revisit the onyx spring, where we will find no sheep. We will bear home, triumphantly, not a trophy *borrego* turd but a dog-eared postcard sold by a Mexican conservation group that helped introduce bighorns to Isla Tiburón across the Gulf.

The postcard shows a muscular bighorn ram on a pale granite outcrop, skylining in full profile. The Comcáac (Seri) of Isla Tiburón call the wild sheep "*mojet.*" The Comcáac world is like a planet in a mirror of water, the tall cactus around them an ancient race of cape-wearing giants turned into *cardón.*

My field notes, my splintered mirror of this desert, are full of questions that will draw us back to Baja California to ask them again. My pages bulge with fish and palm trees and pomegranates in mission gardens, with ocotillos and boojums, the goat skeleton beneath the fallen *cardón* cactus. My notes are full of *mojet.*

Desert bighorns may bring you to places where they live, but they may not show themselves to you. This does not matter. What matters is this: Look.

FLYING MESAS

The Hopi Indians of northern Arizona describe dawn, and all stages of creation, in three phases. When I entered one of their villages, an ancient cluster of sturdy brown stone and adobe houses perched atop First Mesa, it was *qöyangnuptu,* the violet darkness that first outlines the shape of a man.

A slice of moon rode the western sky. Venus hovered above the distant "calendar ridge." From this ridge, the Hopi tell time, noting the seasonal movement of sun, moon, and stars against its silhouetted buttes, knobs, and other markers. From stone and stars, the Hopi know when to unfold the year in ritual.

Late winter brings the Powamu, a time of purification and discipline, a consecration of the farming season to come, and one of the great winter ceremonies that mark the arrival of the kachinas, ancestral spirits who come to the mesas from their home in the San Francisco Peaks, far across the brown winter-bare desert to the south, to live among the Hopi until midsummer.

Below sky as dense as ink, the horizon slowly grew yellow, the color of corn pollen: *sikángnuqa,* the dawn light that reveals man's breath of life. Two elderly women wrapped in fringed shawls stood at the sheer edge of the mesa. With gestures made in the air, they scooped the pollen of the horizon toward their mouths in cupped hands and swallowed it. Their thin brown hands waved the invisible yellow across their hearts. Beside them, *pahos,* or prayer feathers tied to wands of willow, whipped in a hard, gusty wind pungent with juniper smoke.

I waited in the rough-hewn doorway of a friend's adobe house, battered by dust and grit, my chin tucked into the wrap of my fleece blanket. When the wind dropped, I opened my eyes to see a kachina walking the passage near my post. This first kachina was, appropriately, Talavai, the Early Morning Singer, clothed in the red sunrise glow of *tálawva,* the third phase of dawn. A stiff fan of eagle feathers framed his head. His cheeks were painted with terraces of white clouds, and a fox skin hung from his white cotton kilt, grazing high-top moccasins of brown suede. He held a bell and a bough of evergreen and walked as if floating. A curtain of raven black hair spilled down his back.

As Talavai floated off, the sounds came: faint bells, the shake of seeds in a gourd, a rattle of deer hooves inside a hollowed tortoise shell. The sounds were made by a throng of masked figures with melon-shaped clay heads or faces painted with lightning, constellations, or bear tracks. Some masks bore halos of eagle down, their tips dyed red. Turquoise hung from ears; ruffs of spruce ringed several necks. Shell anklets gave each step a dry clatter.

A kachina draped in the soft fur of a gray fox climbed the gnarled wooden ladder of a kiva, the circular chamber in which rituals are held. He emerged as if he had just arrived from an underground flight from the San Francisco Peaks. He danced atop the kiva roof, beating the surface as if it were a drum.

The kachinas emerged from the kivas, then passed through the village, handing out gifts to the children who poked their heads out of the doors, watching for these masked men while they gathered their day packs and books for school. Bright sunlight now filled the plaza, where, on narrow ancient streets, a full-size yellow-and-black school bus could not maneuver a tight bend choked with parked cars. The bus was stuck. Inside, some of the kids pressed their faces to the window glass and laughed with delight.

Bordered on the south by the Little Colorado River, surrounded on all sides by the Navajo reservation, most of Hopi country sits atop First, Second, and Third Mesas, the southerly peninsular extensions of Black Mesa. Perched above a gently rolling sea of rock and sand, the villages at first seem naturally hewn from the mesa tops, a crenellated skyline, rather than human architecture, until you spot the spiky mantle of antennas, solar cells, and satellite dishes.

Looking at the high-set Hopi towns from the outlying flats, you have the illusion that it is the mesas, not the clouds of a winter sky, that are moving, as if all the houses and villagers were sailing across the desert floor.

The Hopi claimed their rocky, broken country a thousand years ago, drawing lifeblood from the underlying aquifer that emerges as springs at the bases of the cliffs. Their pueblos are among the continent's oldest continuously inhabited sites; the waters are among the most blessed. This year's Powamu would claim centuries of ceremonial lineage.

Priests and lunar observation, not the Anglo clock and calendar, set the date of the Powamu, or Bean Dance. I did not know I was coming here until friends called to say that it had begun. I drove, because the Hopi mesas are near home. Imagine trying to book a flight on Delta by phases of the moon instead of time set by the Greenwich Meridian. For the Hopi, these days fall in a continuum of religious life deeply embedded in everyday life. The dawn pollen bathes you. Kachinas walk the streets and plazas. The bus gets stuck.

From late winter until summer's Niman, or Home Dance, when the kachinas return to their distant mountain peaks, the Hopi live among a rich pantheon of masked beings. Through the kachinas, the people's prayers are carried. The ceremonies and dances include a kachina in a white shirt and body paint, a neck ruff of Douglas fir, and a black mask with a short snout. This kachina has blossoms for ears and two curving horns: the Pang

Kachina, who leans on a cane. *Pangwú,* the mountain sheep, brings rain and makes the grass grow.

Since December's solstice, the village had been busy with winter rites. The Powamu brings out the So'yokos, powerful ogres who make their rounds in the village to discipline young children. As I watched, they moved down the alley with a retinue of monster assistants. I lowered my eyes as they passed my post.

The ogres stopped at a house off the plaza and grunted, stomped, growled, banged the door, and scraped sticks across rusty crosscut saws. Their terrifying black-and-white heads had bulging eyes, shivering feathers, long snouts, and movable jaws that clacked open and shut over red mouths filled with sharp white teeth.

At the group's periphery stood an ogre with bugged-out eyes, stringy hair, and a red tongue sticking out of beaklike jaws. She was a So'yoko-mana, a woman figure. Deliberately slow-moving in a crow black cape, she needed no gesture to convey her power. She carried a slender white crook for snagging her victims.

The So'yokos scraped and vibrated their saws. They hammered on the doorway of the house. When a woman opened the door, the So'yokos reprimanded the child inside for disobedience. They threatened to haul him away in the baskets on their backs, then eat him alive. His mother offered a meager ransom of food to satisfy these noisy monsters.

She let the ogres clack their jaws awhile, long enough to remind her son of his misdeeds and scare him until he promised to reform. When they upped the ransom, she handed the ogres loaves of bread and fresh-baked sheet cake. This ritual adds a broader social dimension to parental discipline—the Hopi are great seekers of individual and community equilibrium—and helps the children grow up with good hearts.

Heheya kachinas hid among the So'yokos, ever watchful, each carrying a rope lasso. Their bodies were painted red, their shoulders yellow. Tight caps of lambskin topped green masks with a "crooked mouth," a brightly painted oval turned on its side in a wily grimace. Vertical lines zigzagged above and below their eyes. Some Heheyas wore tunics of sheepskin. Others improvised with wraps of thick polyester pile held in place by leather belts.

Heheyas, also known as Crooked Mouths, are said to be good farmers. The Heheya Uncle speaks backward and has a reputation for being somewhat of a lurker. The function of the Heheyas had not been fully explained to me, but I was warned to stay clear of them.

Like many of the infamous Hopi clowns, bane of the nineteenth-century missionaries but persistently keen in their lewd, cathartic humor, Heheyas tend to be mischievous. They help the ogres discipline children and threaten to lasso any unwary bystander. "What do they do if they catch you?" I had asked Hopi friends. "Squish you in their lassos," they replied with a gleam in the eye, implying that there was further but currently unavailable information.

I left my post and walked down the alley, away from the So'yokos. Suddenly, an athletic young Heheya broke away from the group, alive with a feral alertness, his crooked mouth and zigzag eye lines clearly visible. Whirling his lasso above his head, he chased after two teenaged girls who were peeking around the corner of a building. The girls screamed and ran. It seemed a kind of combustible flirtation.

I continued to walk, my back to the Heheya. As a *bahana* (white) and no longer a girl, I could never be prey to a Crooked Mouth, I assumed. I heard a low growl and the whoosh of a rope. Perhaps I should no longer be sauntering down this alley, I thought. I quickened my pace but did not run. Running seemed like a bad idea.

A rope whizzed in my ear, lifted my hair in its whip of air. As I passed a house, a door burst open and a hand grabbed me by the jacket collar and yanked me inside, out from under the lasso's flying loop. The door slammed shut. Curtains were drawn. Outside, the ogres' saws rumbled.

The room was simple, tidy, warm, and fragrant with cooking. Soft-colored woven rugs covered a linoleum floor faded from use. A few house *pahos* were tucked in a ceiling of darkened beams. Hanging from the whitewashed stucco walls were a Pendleton wool blanket with a red-and-gold pattern against royal blue, several carved kachina dolls, ears of dried corn, and sprigs of dried herbs. On the counter, mounds of bread dough rose in bowls covered with tea towels.

A soft-spoken woman offered me a cup of hot coffee and invited me to stay until the Heheyas left. Her husband and two young grandchildren sat at a small table, eating breakfast. The children would soon leave for school, maybe ride the stuck bus. The girl told me the name of her teacher.

"I know her," I said. "She is a friend."

I told them that my teacher friend sometimes received curious notes from absent students, who claimed that their parents had penned their written excuses: "Melissa got the kitchen pox and went to Flagstaff yesterday. Please discuss her." "Jerry had a conviction and the doctor said green liquid came out." "Please excuse Raphael from class yesterday. He fell into the Grand Canyon."

"Are you the one who fell into the Grand Canyon?" I asked the boy. He and his sister fell into a fit of giggles.

Their grandmother was finishing a marathon baking session. She baked for the So'yokos, she explained—"outside bread," cooked in an adobe oven in the plaza, horned bread, or puffy golden loaves with yeasty peaks, moist yellow sheet cakes, and savory corn bread made with blue cornmeal. She had spent much of the night cooking and grinding corn on a metate, or grinding stone, to make the fine meal for her breads, "a corn so sweet," she said, smiling, "the So'yokos like it the best."

Her husband recalled the first ogre kachinas of his youth. "My friends and I were walking around the community center when we saw them. We ran like hell. Later, they came to my house and bargained with my mother."

They told his mother that he should try harder at school. Do more homework. Stop being a bully. I asked if the kids were frightened into good behavior.

"Oh, yes, we were good," he said, laughing. "For about a week."

For most of his adult life, he had worked off the reservation, as most Hopis must do in a wage-driven economy that has largely overshadowed a traditional village life—a life of farming with little water, of teasing corn from the desert with hoe and prayer, of affixing all of one's identity to a stone pueblo in a harsh, arid land. On retirement, he returned to his village to tend small corn-fields off the mesa, to learn again, he said, "one way to be a human being."

"My job is corn," he told me with modest pleasure. "My job is to be Hopi."

I decided to brave the street and make my way off the mesa. I thanked the people who had saved me from who knows what kind of hilariously rude encounter. As I left, I rested my fingers on the metate. It was still warm to the touch.

The So'yokos moved along their way, far up the narrow street, nearly obliterated by windy squalls of dust. A few children cried out in fright—had they been very bad?—and the ogres' jaws clamped open and shut. Saws shrieked and feet pounded the hard-packed dirt. I was chased to my truck by a woolly, fleet-footed Heheya, his lasso so ready, so close, it whipped into a high-pitched scream. I dived into the cab and slammed the door. Safe!

FEBRUARY

Above the river's north bank, the earth layers itself in folios of thin rock, then tilts toward the water in gravity-defying flatiron slabs. Here, all appears to be sliding. On the south side of the river, all is horizontal and as solid as melting red elephants: voluptuous smooth-faced sandstone, a curvaceous massif of petrified sand dunes. The river forms a seam between these two contrasting fabrics.

On the tilted, flaky side, the limestone caprock is as abrasive as sandpaper, rough with sharp granular wrinkles and fossilized marine creatures. I am walking on the melting elephant side. The slickrock feels mammalian, more like my own body. Its warmth is faint, but it bakes up enough scent to arouse flooding blushes of memory, making a person too vulnerable to accomplish anything.

In the desert, February feels like a celestial pause. The troughs of winter silence still run deep. Soon, a more robust sun will dissolve the ambient brittleness, bringing appetite for green, the noise of birds. The morning bears a crisp chill and boneless clouds veil across a cerulean sky. I am in *pangwúvi* again, where the mountain sheep climb.

Every year during this time, I think about driving to the Hopi towns for the Powamu. In the end, I don't go. Science insists that the sun's arc will grow high again and the longer daylight hours will come. But one can never be too sure. On their mesas, the Hopi know what time it is, how nature's power must sometimes be danced and sung. I am relieved to know that, with their solid faith, they are helping the season turn.

Ahead of me, a side canyon interrupts the slickrock massif. Its mouth meets the river here; its headwaters lie miles beyond, in distant pinyon and juniper highlands. In this region, the canyon is one of the river's largest tributaries. It meanders in tight loops, sinuosity encased in salmon red stone. A thin glassy stream flows intermittently along its narrow bottom, framed by a coppery haze of leafless willows. In drier seasons, the wash runs only with blow sand.

For several days, I have taken hikes up this canyon, looking for bighorn rams from the Blue Door Band. Winter still conceals the home sheep inside the crack where they have vanished. I want to see the first nose peek out, the first hoof lifted in tiptoe, moving out into the world again.

After the rut, rams move from ewe range back to their bachelor turf. Although the heart of Ram Land lies a few miles downriver, inside steeper folds of stone, males may roam this way. They come farther afield, sometimes in pairs or trios, sometimes alone, though not for long, since for sheep, terrain without companions is neither "home" nor any fun.

Early on, rams develop home-range fixations, a fidelity broken by occasional idiosyncrasies. Once in a while, weather, food, spooks, a sudden lightbulb over the head, or a hair up the butt—who knows?—will prompt a ram to wander into this fringe country.

A radio-collared ram from the Blue Door Band once broke out of the canyons and headed southeast with a determined gait, as if he was on his way to Texas. He had an abscess on the back of his head, which may have scrambled his radar and propelled him into confusing terrain.

Sickness aside, such excursions may not be entirely erratic. This fringe country, now the outer limits for today's herd, may have once been part of a larger home range. Perhaps the rams are not wandering off, but going back. We do not know if desert bighorns are capable of what wildlife biologist Valerius Geist calls "insights of sobering depth." But as traditionalists, they will, Geist suggests, enter contiguous habitat and, possibly by repeated visits, extend their range.

Enlarging ram range in this upriver direction does not bode well for the Blue Door Band. Farther up the canyon and on the nearby mesas, there are still domestic sheep that can infect a roaming bighorn with pathogens, making him a vector of disease for his herd mates. There are feral dogs, cattle, roads, fences, poachers, impenetrable thickets of politicians.

I tromp up a steep talus near the canyon's mouth, seeking a watching post. Near the top, I scare up a few bighorns and a kestrel. The sheep are not flesh, but petroglyphs etched on a cliff face. The kestrel is real. In midflight, it twitches its wings twice, then speeds up sevenfold, the falcon equivalent of pedal to the metal. A raven passes overhead in a lazy glide, aware that I am not a dead rodent but curious nevertheless. It lets out a gargly chortle. Up-canyon, another raven chortles back.

Everywhere around me, along the river and especially in this canyon, the people of early Pueblo cultures pecked glyphs into the desert varnish, the oxidized minerals that coat weathered sandstone surfaces. Removing this mauve patina reveals the lighter terra-cotta heart rock underneath.

I like to think of petroglyphs simply—as the expression of people's thoughts. Around here, the canyon ancients were thinking a great deal about bighorn sheep. Of all the fauna depicted, sheep images predominate. Follow a canyon wall, pass a boulder, and there they are, trotting across the inert mineral-glazed stone.

The Blue Door Band's ancestors fed the thoughts, art, and bellies of the earliest desert dwellers. Many centuries later, there are more petro portraits than actual sheep.

No one tracked the historic decline with rigorous scientific scrutiny, only with the common litany of loss. Since "pristine" times, and especially from the late 1800s to the early 1900s, the numbers of North American mountain sheep plunged dramatically. Although this desert was (and still is) sparsely populated by humans, its bighorns, too, succumbed to encroachment.

When I sort through the puzzle of recent years—the past half century—I work with scant pieces.

From the 1920s through the 1950s, there were observations of remnant desert bighorns along the river. Most of the sightings came from anecdote. Sophisticated wildlife census methods, on the level of New Mexico's San Andres Wildlife Refuge, were still years in the future.

As the fifties ended, the sightings grew infrequent. Whereas groups of thirty or more animals had once been reported, people were now seeing only singles or pairs, maybe three at the most, usually ewes. Herein lay a blueprint for a local extinction: diminished numbers, habitat fragmentation, isolation, a stubborn tenacity to natal ground. Nowhere else to go.

By 1962, the sightings ceased altogether. The river cliffs appeared to be empty of their native ungulates.

Twenty years passed without a confirmed sighting. In 1983, boaters floated past a sandy alluvial fan deep in the river canyon, the site of a rough-hewn stone shelter with a door frame painted sky blue. On this bottomland, they spotted a ewe and her lamb. The bighorns were back.

The lack of reliable information during those years renders the puzzle unsolvable. What can be assumed, however, is that the locals did not go extinct during that time. Rather, they went missing.

On the back of the elephants, above the canyon, things become a bit dreamy. Ravens chortling softly. Prehistoric thoughts on the rock behind my head like cartoon bubbles. The memory of black-haired children alive with laughter around a table in an adobe house. Air with exquisite taste: clear, chilled, like iced lime. A redrock land that stretches a hundred miles into the sacrament of space. I am not paying attention.

I hear the sound of a waterfall. How nice, I think. A waterfall. Just like Tahiti.

Unmistakable: the splash of liquid on stone. This is most curious. No rain in sight. Not flash-flood season. No water except for scattered frozen puddles in the wash on the flats below. This place is as dry as old sticks. This is not Tahiti.

The water sound comes from a low saddle of slickrock above me, barely seventy yards distant. Atop the rock, in classic position—head erect, hind legs stretched back, back slightly depressed—is a bighorn ram. He is pissing out a thunderous stream on the sandstone.

The ram sees me. There is no doubt that I am a speck caught in his dark amber orbs. He is so impressed, he finishes peeing and yawns. I am accustomed to seeing gray-brown bighorns against gray-brown rock, seeing bighorns that are actually boulders or boulders that are actually sheep. The gray-brown ram against terra-cotta sandstone is startling.

I have not moved.

Run for your life! I scream at the ram without using my voice. *Go back to where it's safe!*

Where did the sheep go for twenty years?

Did their numbers drop so low, they found themselves staring, like the old San Andres ewe and the last of her band, into the tunnel of doom?

There are rumors, words as faint as white ash in white air, that the river band hid its missing generations somewhere in the cracks of this big red side canyon. Another scenario: The river herd died off. Meanwhile, a different group, already in the big red tributary, could have survived in some pocket of safety with permanent water sources. Eventually, it recolonized river habitat. Still another scenario: Bighorns in groups far to the north moved south and did a rare sheep thing: They crossed the river. They established this homeland.

During this time, the area was heavily used by flocks of domestic sheep that were moved seasonally along the rims and into the canyon for forage and water. Fatal encounters would be expected. In the lost-sheep years, the last of a horde of uranium miners scraped the country for ore. Most of the miners were ruthless poachers.

After the miners left and sheep raising diminished, new visitors came to the region for recreation. If there were wild ungulates in this place, there were eyes to spot them. Instead, the bighorns turned into invisible sheep.

It is plausible to think that the Blue Door Band hid nowhere near this canyon, or anywhere else we might imagine. Perhaps they never left the home river corridor at all. Everyone missed them because they were too few in numbers to attract notice. Maybe they looked just like boulders.

If the herd had been reduced to two or three animals, some twist of fate kept it from becoming the dead end of a single gender—one last ewe, for instance, or two old geezer rams. Despite the odds, and the funeral dirges for lost populations elsewhere in the Southwest, this native herd began to rebuild itself, driven by thousands of years of resolute procreation.

The 1983 sighting of ewe and lamb turned into more glimpses of bighorns along the river. Unofficial reports gave counts of about thirty animals by 1995. Last fall (2002), after the addition of the latest lamb crop, the band numbered about eighty sheep.

Perhaps their disappearance for those decades was much like this year's occurrence of vanishing into a crack: wild sheep in the wildest corners of the canyon, slipping up and down cliffs like ghosts. They remained beyond the notice of humans, who tend to think of wildlife in terms of our own desires rather than in terms of the animals' hard truth, their unshakable fidelity to stone. For this truth, we are starved.

The ram remains on his cliff, doing Noble Ram poses. A nonchalant neck stretch. The cover boy, the hood ornament. Some casual skylining to show off his handsome profile. Through my binoculars, I can see up his runny black nose.

I recognize this ram from Ram Land. He is seven or eight years old and has thick-based horns that rise out of his skull, curl and flair around his cheeks like truck tires, then end in splintered tips. He is among the studliest in the herd. He is known as a loner and a roamer, a pioneer of new terrain.

The biologists who are now the band's caretakers say that going upriver from Ram Land and ewe range is going toward civilization—the wrong direction. If by some faint likelihood the big red side canyon was a past hideout, and if the roaming rams "remember" this, it would be much healthier if they were to "forget." The safer habitat lies downriver. In fact, some of the ewes are sneaking downriver, especially as the drought prompts them to seek better food. The band is not only growing; it is stretching.

The ram ambles along the saddle, then stops on a ledge above me and acts like he is peering over my shoulders into my notebook. He shows off his petrified turban. It weighs about twenty-five pounds, nearly 10 percent of his body weight. He tips it toward me. *Don't jump.*

With another ram, the sheer size of his horns would start a conversation. Worn tips and scars on the main horn shaft come from abrasion, rubbing, and butting—butting other rams, butting cactus, trees, fence posts, rocks. The ram aims a vibrato bleat in my direction. For some odd reason, I think of biting, not butting. Bighorns are notoriously inept at biting humans.

The ram moves farther along the ledge, away from me. For a long time, he stares down-canyon. The stare is a fair indication that he is about to embark on a major move. He looks in the direction of his next excursion. Time marches on. I am sore and stiff from sitting. He stares. I think he's stuck. We could be out here a long time.

When bighorns die in the desert, they leave their bones. I decide to spend the remainder of my hiking life on the high river cliffs and in the big red side canyon, searching for a dying place, shelves of cliff strewn with skulls and bleached femurs and rib cages. Bones might shed light on the mystery of twenty years of invisible sheep.

A biologist friend once told me that there are ways to read "genetic signature," to determine the Blue Door Band's founder herd and its relation to other wild sheep in the region. What is apparent now, without such tests, is that this native population recovered itself.

I close my notebook and pack it away. The side canyon whirls its stone meanders across the desert, opens its portal to the river bottom, and spreads a fan of coral dunes below its mouth. In the distance, the tilted slabs of limestone and marlstone mark the river's other bank.

Winter paints its final colors along the river's border: smoky-green greasewood and sage, charcoal black tamarisk branches, the mahogany trunks of Russian olive trees, swathes of bare red-gold willows. At the seam of sandbar and river, snow-white salts frost the rose-colored sand.

The river runs jade when I look at it straight on, cobalt when I look upstream, in the direction of the light. This light is why I stay so long. The telling of it is like talking secondhand blind. Skin knows this beauty better than voice.

On this February day, the bighorns have emerged from their thin air of invisibility. The big ram unlocks his gaze and moves forward. Place-faithful to the core, he heads toward Ram Land. Down-canyon, the ewes are a few months away from lambing season and from teaching me, if I pay attention, the strength of imagination. My job is to be human.

The ram walks over the slickrock, a gray-brown animal against stone the color of a clay pot. The pale bands that run up his hind legs, from fetlock to hock joint and then to rump, are the color of dust. He and his kind deal in certainties that are opaque to us. Theirs is not an ambivalent species. When they go missing, we must simply refuse to turn them into apparitions.

MARCH

The lingering cold, the powder-dry soil, the paucity of green—in early March, the Colorado Plateau is not yet pliant; the earth has no give. This is the month of nature's held breath and, at any moment, an abrupt exhalation. In wetter places, the transition would be described as the thaw, a melting that is fluid, headlong, and muddy. In this desert, the release is felt in rock and air, and you must pay close attention if you are to witness its precise moment.

Mark and I load up the big white-water raft with camping gear and slip down the river on an early-season trip. The sun has grown warm but not quite trustworthy. Along the riverbanks, the cottonwoods still rise as gray lace. The Russian olive trees expect migrating bluebirds in branches still laden with a few pale olives and limp dry leaves.

Beyond the banks, Mormon tea, yucca, and sage hold winter's scant green. On south-facing slopes, there are signs of spring's avant-garde: shoots of cranesbill and a purple mustard plant that emits a faint scent of stale washcloths.

The Canada geese do not fly off as we pass them. They are reluctant to leave their gravel bars, where they show brooding behavior in incessant bassoon honking and fretful struts, necks roped out straight ahead of their bodies. There are pairs; there are threesomes. They are noisy. As the day heats up, they spread their big charcoal wings in the sun. I put on my river sandals and peel off a few layers.

The canyon walls narrow into a hurricane of upriver wind, and we are stuck with it all day. Often the raft comes to a standstill. From blade to grip, the oars carry the tension of opposing forces—downriver current and upriver gale. Sand from the talus dunes blasts us so hard, the grains go into the mouth without the mouth being open. My hair hurts.

My bare toes freeze up and turn ivory and numb, like toes on a wax figure in Madame Tussaud's museum. I leave the boat to walk along the bank and circulate the blood. My toes turn pink again. The wind slams me, but I walk faster than Mark can row against the gale.

We camp across the river from three watchful geese, a male and female and a juvenile from last year's brood who resists long-overdue independence—the goose equivalent of clingy. The sun lingers; the wind leaves calm in its wake. In the quiet, we cook dinner over coals in the fire pan and, because I forgot to pack plates, serve it on a slab of driftwood set between us, like cave people at a banquet.

Before dusk, we spot two bighorns on the canyon ledges across the river. One of the animals is a familiar older ewe, distinct by her nearly white coat and a sagging radio collar. The other ewe has a taupe face that is darker than her body and a blackish spot that looks like a scar on her flank, near the rib cage. The bellies on both ewes are taut and furry. My binoculars are equipped with X-ray vision. I see lambs in utero.

Wherever you are, wherever you go, there are untamed creatures nearby that need your attention. Unplug your modem. Slam shut your self-help books. Quit standing around like a wall trout. Get to work.

Invite warblers to your neighborhood with shaggy plots of greenery. Learn everything you can about the bandit-eyed raccoon that stares at you through your sliding glass door, demanding enchiladas.

Mark the direction of jet black darkling beetles marching up a red dune like a troop of miniature helmets. East? South?

Let black widows live in your soffits.

Lie on your back on a breezy sweep of beach and stare at the undersides of magnificent frigate birds. Master a hyena's laugh and use it when in the presence of politicians.

Admire the male midwife toad, who carries fertilized eggs on his back for a month. Understand that certain species of mollusk can change their gender. Know that from a ball afloat on tiny filaments inside its fanned shell, a sea scallop can tell which way is up.

Crane your neck. Worm your way. Wolf it down. Monkey with things. Outfox your foe. Quit badgering your tax attorney.

Take notes on the deafness of coral, the pea-size heart of a bat. Be meticulous. We will need these things so that we may speak.

The human mind is the child of primate evolution and our complex fluid interactions with environment and one another. Animals have enriched this social intelligence. They give concrete expression to thoughts and images. They carry the outside world to our inner one and back again. They helped language flower into metaphor, symbol, and ritual. We once sang and danced them, made music from their skin, sinew, and bone. Their stories came off our tongues. We ate them. They ate us.

Close attention to mollusks and frigate birds and wolves makes us aware not only of our own human identity but also of how much more there is, an assertion of our imperfect hunger for mystery. "Without mystery life shrinks," wrote biologist Edward O. Wilson. "The completely known is a numbing void to all active minds."

In a small town near an immense expanse of open desert, there is rapt attention to the homeland bestiary. The new season brings it alive again, pitching it toward brazen fecundity.

Migrating white-faced ibis arrive shortly after we return from the river trip. Meadowlarks perch on fence posts, their melodic fluted songs not yet organized. Stalin, a red-shafted flicker with an agenda, returns to the premises. He batters the house's stucco like a schizoid jackhammer, obsessed with opening a passage so that he can personally inspect the roof trusses.

One day, Stalin knocks over a nest on a beam above the deck, a nest left empty for the winter by a pair of Say's phoebes. He does this every year, like clockwork. Between stucco-demolishing sessions, Stalin alights on the beam and shoulders the nest off the edge. The nest drops onto the stone deck and falls apart.

I gather up the wreck of grass, twigs, and fluffy seed-head tufts gathered from nearby rabbitbrush and Apache plume. As the phoebes built the nest last spring, I set out dust bunnies— my house breeds plantations of lint under the furniture—and the birds used them for nest lining.

Inside the nest's downy well is the skeleton of a fledgling phoebe, one of last year's clutch. The bones are pure white and as fine as thread. The skull fits on my fingertip.

River, ibis, bighorns: These are not simple ciphers, but sensations, the season's pulse and call. They deflect a panic and pain at the rush of time. I use their rhythms to keep time in slow epochs rather than headlong years. I self-righteously refuse to be digital. I tell time by the herpetofauna in my friend's closet.

Jackie lives in a stuccoed adobe-brick house on two acres of plant and animal husbandry, a typical mix for many of us in this small desert town. Garden, horse, chickens, dogs, a handsome little grandson on frequent visits, all of this surrounds Jackie in routine motions of hard work and pleasure. I go over there to track one of the markers of spring.

In mid-March, like an eight-pound clock, Elliot, the desert tortoise, rustles inside a burrow beneath a mound of straw in Jackie's yard. All winter, he has hibernated in stillness. Shortly before the equinox, he will sense the warming season and dig his way out into the world again. Jackie listens daily for scrabbling noises.

For most of his ten years, Elliot hibernated in the closet. You would go over to Jackie's old house, have a cup of tea, and think, Oh, there's a desert tortoise in her closet.

When she built her new house, Jackie made him an outdoor home with a clay-packed turtle fun yard surrounded by a curving fence of close-set upright log posts. (Rectangles, she thinks, scream incarceration.) She buried the posts a foot and a half underground so Elliot wouldn't tunnel himself out and lumber toward the horse's corral and, if a hoof didn't squish him or a coyote or gray fox didn't eat him, head on down to Phoenix. Elliot is an expert digger, able to excavate a deep burrow up to thirty feet long with an opening shaped like his own profile: a half-moon.

From March to October, when he is outside, the tortoise follows the track of sun and shade across his yard. He burrows into the soil when temperatures soar—estivation, a summer dormancy. Water from a dripper hose moistens a patch of earth, keeping it cool when he visits it. It's a kind of paradise, this piece of Elliot's desert, although he did not mind his closet days. His burrow there was safe and dark. Shortly before his emergence, Jackie played reggae and other music with a strong beat to mimic the vibrations that springtime might naturally arouse.

Today, the only sign of life in the pen is a border collie puppy sprawled in the sun, warming her belly. The tortoise lies hidden in his winter burrow, his digestive system greatly slowed. Any day now, the metabolism of hibernation will change. He will need to eat, drink, rehydrate himself, and come out into the world.

With a fifty-million-year lineage, desert tortoises have adapted to the extreme aridity of the Sonora and Mojave deserts, displaying variations in each place. Their large bladders store water and convert urinary wastes efficiently, keeping them alive during long periods without rain. They are herbivores that occasionally eat bugs and meat along with grasses, succulents, cactus fruits, and wildflowers—a gluttony of wildflowers, for their moisture.

Desert tortoises can live to be sixty to a hundred years old. They reach sexual maturity somewhere between age fifteen and age twenty. In the wild, they may not run into a mate for several years. Females have adapted to male inactivity and population crashes by retaining sperm for up to two years, ensuring fertilization long after copulation.

A mature tortoise is about fourteen inches long, with a short tail and stocky limbs—sturdy forelegs for digging and strong hind legs, round like an elephant's. The dome-shaped carapace is horn gray, with fine-lined scutes. Underneath, the breastplate, or plastron, is yellowish. A male's plastron is concave at the posterior so he can fit nicely atop the female in his amorous mount. Her plastron is flat, maybe so she won't skid away.

Jackie has watched her box turtles mate. She made them a private semicovered place, but they preferred to do it on the patio, in full view, when she had guests.

On the sex patio, the act took a while, she told me. "I never saw any, uh, thrusting. Just mount and grip." Desert tortoises are known to be a more gregarious species and, in their lovemaking, quite vocal.

Jackie adopted Elliot when he was a hatchling. Half Mojave and half Sonoran, he came from an accidental cross; the two varieties are geographically separate. His wild mother turned up at a house in an Arizona suburb and had to stay because the suburb grew so quickly, she couldn't leave. Tortoises move slowly. In the time it might have taken her to reach the edge of the lot, construction crews could have thrown up six three-bedroom split-levels, a golf course, and a Wal-Mart. How could she have found the open desert again?

Twenty-five years later, she was bred with another adopted tortoise. One day, her people found baby tortoises scrabbling all over the cover on the swimming pool. Jackie ended up with one of them.

"I drove him home. He was in a little box. He was the size of an Oreo. I cried all the way, wondering how I would keep him alive."

Wild desert tortoises are strictly protected; the Mojave population is federally listed as a threatened species. Tortoises captured before the restrictions were in place—over the years, they were plucked off the desert by the hundreds—live a long time, so they and their offspring are still in a cycle of adoption. Jackie has a number for her Elliot so that she won't be charged for illegal possession of a protected chelonian.

In summer, some of Jackie's turtles live on the fat of her garden. Her box turtle rams her tomato plants so the fruit falls off. Later, tomato seedlings sprout up wherever he poops. Bushes give Elliot shade in his fun yard, but he ate the last one she planted.

We sneak over to Elliot's burrow as if we were giants and our insomniac miniature grandmother was finally getting a good night's sleep. Deeper in the burrow lies Elliot's "hot rock." Made of polyresin, with a long cord that plugs into a nearby wall socket, the fake rock stays warm under a layer of dirt and straw. All winter, Elliot puts his belly on his hot rock. This is the Colorado Plateau, not the milder Sonoran or the Mojave. The hot rock is clay red, like the sandstone around us.

Jackie carefully parts the mound of straw until she finds an edge of gray shell and a round mini-elephant leg. She feels movement and knows he is alive. He is much bigger than a cookie. To disturb him too much would provoke a pugnacious hiss and the loss of precious calories. "He has lost a lot of weight," Jackie whispers.

Jackie rescued Sid, her box turtle, from Phoenix, where he was left in a box in the sun and ended up with a fried shell. At the moment, he is in semihibernation in his home by the television. Sid is her rental turtle.

"Kids love him and want him," she explains, "so I give them strict instructions and let them take him home. Then the kids get bored. Maybe Sid gets bored, too. Sid gets overfed. So Sid comes back."

The season begins to turn, and with its turn we are ready to shift our weight, too. The turkey vultures will soon fly back into town from their distant winter quarters, as they do each March, often on the same date each year, give or take a day or two. Our hands harden with calluses from garden work, readying the beds for seed. Soon there will be so much green to soothe our winter eyes, we will forget that we live in a land of stone.

Jackie pulls a few leaves of romaine lettuce out of her refrigerator and feeds them to Cleopatra, her sulcata, or African spur-thighed tortoise, named for the spiny protrusions on her legs. Her yellow-brown carapace is about the size of an inflated sneaker. Full grown (she is barely two years old), she will be twenty-four inches long, nearly as big as a Galápagos turtle.

Because sulcatas do not hibernate, Cleopatra lives in Jackie's living room in the winter. She will eventually move south to a warmer place so she can spend her twenty-five years outside. Sulcatas are common enough to be pets. In Africa, they are raised for their meat and are herded by young boys with sticks.

When Cleopatra sees her lettuce, she sticks out her wrinkly head and stabs, pulls, and crunches with sharp jaws. A muscular tongue pulls the food back so she can swallow it. She is like a blonde at a diner after a long night of wild dancing. I watch and wonder how one herds turtles. In less than a minute, the leaf edge is lacy with turtle bites.

One day, a friend brings us a duck for dinner, a large male mallard with an iridescent emerald head, white neck ring, and a gray-brown chest below a splash of russet. When I gently press my fingers into the mallard's chest, they sink more than an inch through feathers and down before they reach the skin. This is the thickness that pushed against the water of the winter river, insulating the bird's heart.

Mark removes the breast meat with surgical precision. The burgundy flesh comes off thin, delicate ribs. I lay the remains against the far fence for the coyotes, cradling the body in a thatch of dry salt grass. The emerald head flops to one side. The big yellow feet cross demurely. On the tan-and-olive groundscape, the duck stands out like a hill of precious jewels.

By morning, the duck has vanished into coyote possession. Perhaps they wondered why a perfectly good breastless duck was leaning against the fence in the middle of a ranch pasture. Not a feather remained. The coyotes had taken it elsewhere to eat.

When I leave home one morning for a trip to sheep country, two coyotes—the duck-eaters?—cross the driveway as I pull out. They stop and look at the house, don't think much of it, then move on. Their undercoats are winter-thick and reddish, their tails bushy and tipped in black.

Two coyotes in the yard and fresh duck in our bellies, meat made from river plants and proteins: This is a rare food chain for anyone in the lower forty-eight, we factory-chicken hunters, we stalkers in supermarket aisles. Even the coyotes consider trailer-park poodles an easier meal than mobile, living ducks.

No one wants to slit the throat of a hog or clobber weaner calves for dinner. Not many of us want to look into the eyes of animals that are not our pets. A friend says she will stare at an alligator only if it's her purse. I apologize to my cantaloupes when I pick and eat them from the garden. But I, too, am a killer.

In a dream, I sit at a feast, fork poised, linen napkin tucked under my chin, and I eat Stalin, the last red-shafted flicker on earth. He lies belly-up on a plate, his stiff stick feet aimed at the ceiling fixtures, a Russian olive in his mouth.

One way to know for sure that a baby is a human being and not a "noisy pet," someone once said, is by name making, the fundamental human trait of arranging sensory perceptions into thoughts and connecting them with narrative and memory. Very young children name and map the natural world before they organize an abstract one. They build what neurobiologists call a "naïve biology," a domain of knowledge about living things. With animals as helpers, the developing brain orders perception and reality, significance and desire.

Sometimes I remember that animal state, that imagination of such splendid purity. Grown-ups, of course, were pitifully blind to it. "Quit calling us by our names," my brothers and I scolded my mother. "We're not your children; we're *cheetahs*. This oatmeal in our bowls is *cheetah food*." She told us to clean our rooms. Suddenly, we were sloths.

Very early, I inflicted my entire worldview on my teddy bear. Its fur wore thin from being tied to my tricycle and dragged about. It had bite marks in its face. I gave all of my stuffed animals complicated and dramatic lives.

Books, pictures, and zoos fed young minds isolated from the true wild, but for us, as for all children, the animals were nevertheless intensely vivid. Zebras loped through my dreams even though I had never seen a real one. Bombay's elephants slipped their chains and ran home, smashing banyan trees—nothing could dispel my notion that the biggest of animals were the most innocent. At the zoo, the hippos' cavernous pink yawns transfixed me. The birds there bashed their heads against the wire netting

that kept them from flying off. A sign read LOST CHILDREN
WILL BE TAKEN TO THE LION HOUSE.

My older brother filled his sketch pad with race cars and
fighter jets dropping bombs in pellet sprays over a stick figure
labeled MY SISTER, who lay sideways with X's for eyes and a
pool of red crayon blood dripping out of the corner of her
mouth.

On my paper I drew whales, penguins, moose, otters, monkeys, wolves. My kangaroo pictures were upside down. My bears
ate avocados. I could not draw them from life, but I learned
something by working their lines and shapes on paper, something beyond the caricatures and cartoons.

As long as a century ago, the keepers of insane asylums knew
the value of calming their inmates with pets and gardens. My parents calmed their four little inmates with the usual menagerie of
dogs, cats, hamsters, rabbits, goldfish, and parakeets. A maximum
size rule, by parental decree, kept us from keeping tapirs in our
bedrooms.

In the outdoors, beyond the lives of our pets, we witnessed the
lives of animals most adapted to a rural neighborhood: foxes,
squirrels, badgers, frogs, turtles, mice, sparrows, buzzards, ducks,
worms, snails, dragonflies. Road trips brought glimpses of mule
deer, pronghorn antelope, elk, and buffalo in national parks. In
California's Sierra Nevada, we found mountain lion tracks and
bobcat scat. Black bears pawed through an open-pit garbage
dump, eating orange rinds and moldy pinto beans, pooping blobs
of plastic.

One of the wildest animals we saw outside of the zoo lived on
the floor of my great-uncle's study in his house in Sussex, England. My family lived in London at the time and we went from
the city to his house on weekends. Although the house was so
immense that children routinely disappeared in its wings and
hallways, never to be found, we knew where the beast lived.

Between world wars, my great-uncle had shot and killed a Bengal tiger in India. A black-and-white photograph in a scrapbook showed him kneeling in the grass with his rifle, my great-aunt beside him, the dead cat spread below them.

The tiger, minus his innards, now spread across much of the study floor in flying-squirrel position. Backed by soft dark felt, the skin was stretched flat and clawless. The giant stuffed head rose in full dimension, with whiskers, green glass eyes, and a snarling mouth frozen open to reveal ivory fangs and a pink polyresin tongue and throat.

On one Christmas holiday in Sussex, we were snowed in and could not drive back to London. The pack of cousins grew unruly, so my great-aunt told the cook to give us cookie sheets and roasting pans. We took these to a hill near the house and used them as sleds. Afterward, we cleaned up and went to the study, where the family and guests gathered for cocktails before dinner.

People stood on the tiger's orange-and-black pelt and tried not to trip over the big head. The adults sipped warm gin. They restrained my cousins, brothers, and me from rolling around on the tiger in our dressy clothes. The tiger was trophy; it was memory. It was a rug.

The next day, when the study was empty of all but a couple of napping dalmatians, I visited the tiger. The details of its demise were never quite clear, but I had the impression that my great-uncle's Great White Hunter aspirations had halted in the moment captured by the photograph.

He was born into an era and culture that sent young Englishmen to colonial outposts to kill exotic big game as a rite of passage. A tiger hunt, he said, was "something one did." (Given such rites, world tiger numbers plunged dramatically. Three of eight subspecies went extinct.)

I lay down on the rug, using the tiger's head as a pillow. The back of my head rested on the broad shelf between his ears. I stretched out my arms and legs to match the tiger's limbs, but my fingertips and toes fell far short of the paws. *Panthera tigris tigris* was huge. I stroked the crazy black stripes. The dalmatians added crazy black and white dots.

On my belly with chin in hands, at eye level with the canine teeth and frozen stare, I imitated a snarl shaped into ferocity by the taxidermist. In the photograph, the dead tiger seemed but lank folds of stripes with a limp head. The rug had no smell. I had no idea how the tiger's flesh and muscles and bones had once moved.

Of wild animals' true biology, young children have instinct more than knowledge. Their commitment to animal images comes as a devout and ironclad faith. They mean it when they beg you to drop them off in Antarctica to live with penguins. Animals give us voice. They map a world we want to live in. Without them, we are homeless.

Aside from pets and tiger pelts, before agribusiness and Animal Planet, what array of living proteins surrounded us?

As California ranchers, several generations of my family lived alongside cattle, sheep, and other livestock. They cleared out the grizzly bears and wolves. They grazed their sheep in alpine meadows, where bighorn sheep likely suffered the consequences of the incursion.

Shearing crews came from nearby settlements of Yokuts Indians. Hired cowboys came from Mexican labor pools or from town bars, sobered up and got on their horses to drive cattle to backcountry pastures and line camps, where they slept with their heads against saddle leather and carved their initials in aspen trees. Every day, everyone, men, women, children, had contact with horses. Everyone knew how to butcher chickens and goats. The women could kill rattlesnakes, gut trout.

From an older generation still among us come the mantras of ranch and farm life, of households with barnyards and everyone there to watch sex, birth, and death. Kids were not inside reading *Babar and Zephir* or watching Marlin Perkins suck frogs on TV. Children, too, saw the butchering and smelled the blood. Animals were utilitarian and very much present. Placentas steamed on the straw after calving. Stillborn lambs were taken to a grassy foothill for coyote bait. There were tradesmen called "knackers," who bought and slaughtered worn-out horses and sold their flesh for dog food.

"Go out there and whack the heads off those roosters," a neighbor told me when I lived in Montana as a graduate student.

For fresh eggs, I had raised a mixed brood of chicks. I fed them mash and kitchen scraps. I painted the words THE SKY IS FALLING! over the small door of their planked wood coop. I liked to watch the chickens race like bats out of hell into the dark opening under the blue letters, though it was the dusk and cold, not chicken paranoia, that chased them in for the night's roost.

When the chicks matured and it was time to keep the hens and kill all but one uncorked, ambisextrous rooster named Hernando, I went inside the house and took a nap. The smell of terrorized poultry awoke me. I went to the yard and helped the neighbor whack heads and pluck. Scarlet-flecked feathers swirled in the air and stuck to the chopping block. The remaining victims took short, ungainly flights.

Centuries ago, during China's T'ang dynasty, it was taboo to eat any domestic animal that had died facing north. What could that mean? I thought with a mote of superstition. Dead and not-quite-dead chickens were scattered around the block as if they had been strafed by low-flying jets. Since they were headless, I could not tell if they were facing Canada or Wyoming.

Taboos, perhaps, underline the ritual of killing another being. They give ceremony to visceral acts. The most astonishing aspect

of my chicken ritual was *warmth,* body-temperature warmth—
warm air, warm blood, warm feathers, warm steel knife blades,
warm dead roosters. It took forever for things to cool down.

Few of us look our next meal in the eye, there to see all that is
both alien and familiar. The superstore meat department tells us
nothing about throat-slit goats or six thousand chickens raised in
nine hundred cages. Reach into the bin and pull out a shrink-
wrapped packet of skinless chicken breasts. The meat is pallid
and tidy, cool to the touch.

In Montana, my life as a chicken farmer expanded into random
ranch work. On occasion, I helped friends who owned a sheep
and cattle operation on a tributary of the Musselshell River. Mark,
my husband-to-be, and I slept in lofty down sleeping bags on top
of a stack of hay bales set on an ocean of rolling prairie that
ended in the startling snow-capped crest of the Crazy Mountains.
When we stair-stepped off the haystack in the morning, we had
to watch for rattlesnakes on the bales.

At times, I was recruited for herding work. One day, with the
help of Mozart and three dogs, I moved over seven hundred
sheep across the open prairie to a coulee, where they could drink
water. They were not good at doing this by themselves, even
when they were thirsty.

From a different direction, Mark, a more experienced herder,
was pushing another band to the same coulee, but I had the
Walkman, the Mozart tape, the dogs. I yelled, waved, or telepath-
ically transmitted commands to the sheepdog, a border collie that
held the sheep in a compact mass by encircling them entirely,
even as they loped forward. Picture this: a three-thousand-legged
table of wool undulating over treeless hills with a miraculous
unity of motion.

The sheepdog was irrepressible. During off-duty hours, he

herded the ranch kids. The second dog, a Great Pyrenees, stayed with the sheep all her life, day and night. She was their protector, more endearing than carcasses baited with poison. She was also a sky-watcher, bred to survey the heavens for eagles and other aerial predators. She was huge. Her paws were four inches across. She was sweet and she could pulverize a coyote in fourteen seconds. The third dog, my retriever, pulverized tennis balls.

Peering far across the prairie, I spotted the sheep wagon of the neighbor's ranch hand, a man with flawless sheepherder credentials: independent, self-destructively pickled in bars during the off-season, acutely blue-collar. An old fellow, he had a crazed look that might be called "Wobbly nihilist." He lived on coffee and canned chili—"jallypenno," he pronounced it, "not for the timid."

He drove a clunker Bonneville that sounded as if a handful of golf balls had been stuffed into the muffler. Each morning, his hundred-some ewes quietly surrounded his wagon. He threw open the door, rubbed his union suit, and pretended he did not see them. "Where's my girls?" he roared over their heads.

The sheep bands united at the coulee, where I left them and the dogs to Mark. We loaded four hog-tied wethers—castrated males—into the back of a truck bound for the corrals. Slowly, I drove cross-country on dirt clods and wheat stubble, the sheep bouncing around the open pickup bed like piñatas.

I looked at the sheep in the rearview mirror often. They did not appear to be upset. Ultimately, they were bound for the slaughterhouse. They would be packed into a stock truck like smashed Brillo pads and driven to their next incarnation as meat. I thought a lot about vegetarianism. I slipped Mozart into the tape deck so my cargo could hear. It was the least I could do.

Out in the desert of wild sheep, the Blue Door Band's ewes bless me with their company. Closer to lambing time, they will withdraw and scatter. To preclude any possibility of disturbance, I will give them wider berth than they need. What they do during parturition will create a blank in our year together, unwitnessed, as it should be. Until then, I take up the usual posts and spend my days among them.

At home, Stalin, the flicker, has disappeared. The Say's phoebes are building a new nest in the eaves. Out from his winter burrow, Jackie's tortoise blinked in the bright sunlight and ate a tomato. Out in the field, the sheep and I are a bit batty with the warming season. The globe tilts on the spring equinox, tickling the ends of the day with more light, more time for mischief.

A group of nine—ewes and juveniles—works the slopes above the river. They eat the strawlike chaff of old plants. They find tasty new grasses between boulders, where shaded crevices retain moisture. As the vegetation changes with the season, so will their diet. The rumen, one of the great achievements of herbivore evolution, lets them exploit the succulent green as well as dry, abrasive plants covered with grit and dust. They bite, chew, and dump the lot into their fat fermentation vats.

The sheep nap on a canyon wall that is no longer in shadow all day, but sunlit from rim to river. They rise from their day beds and break into random frolics. Even the heavy-bellied older ewes move about with great animation. It is almost as if the whole band had been eating funny plants.

Instigated mostly by the yearlings, the sheep fill their stone world with feisty play. One butts a companion off a shrub and is then butted off the shrub by another sheep. Soon everyone is butting everyone else off their shrubs. A gang of yearlings begins to butt everything in sight. They butt rocks, yucca plants, a prickly pear cactus, the air, one another. Two yearling rams put themselves in reverse, then charge each other with a loud clonk of horns.

A sleek young ewe with a small face and a dark cape jumps

straight up in the air like a piece of toast. Toast pops spread throughout the band like a chain reaction. There are chases and leaps and races along knife-edged ledges above sixty-foot drops.

A chasm of sandstone becomes a game. Several sheep line up and leap across it. One takes a look, then walks around it. The next sheep rushes down one wall and straight up the other.

The last sheep tries the same maneuver but doesn't make the second jump. It leaps upward, misses the wall's lip, and in a split second turns its body in a complete about-face, falls, and rushes back up the first wall. Ricocheting sheep. On a warm spring day in a redrock canyon far from the troubled human world, I am watching ricocheting sheep. For a while, they all race about as if chased by berserk bobcats.

Suddenly, all of the animals stop goofing around and begin to browse and graze like serious grown-ups who have read Valerius Geist's notes about proper sheep behavior: "Adult ewes play rarely," he wrote. "Ewes play less conspicuously than rams." Their tricks fit the cartoon of cows grazing on all four feet as cars full of people pass them. Once the people are gone, the cows stand upright on their hind legs.

In general, today's play fits Geist's description—that is, the occasional behavior of a species that must always weigh the costs of living against reproductive success. Stress, excitement, and aggressive interactions can drain energy needed to find the nutritious forage that supports fetal growth. Thus, Geist observed, ewes are under selection pressure to reduce actions that increase living costs.

Ewes interact less overtly than rams, which are always busy modeling headgear and messing around with flagrant displays of hierarchy. When rams are among females, there is more chasing and harassment, so apart from the rut, ewes avoid them by spatial segregation on their own home range, where there is good forage with less competition. Lamb play is expected, but adult play is "now and then," more likely in spring than in other seasons, and among well-fed, vigorous individuals.

While the ewes cannot afford to lose energy and vigor, they nevertheless need one another. More than one study of bighorn behavior notes the stress of "loneliness." Both genders of this gregarious species, the ewes and subadults in particular, need the group. Alone, a bighorn is more vulnerable to stress. I do not want wild sheep to be lonely.

One ewe raises her head from her shrub and cocks it, as if she had just awakened and found herself in a strange and curious place. She bolts at the group. All nine sheep scatter, rejoin, then flow up to the next tier on the layer-cake canyon wall. Rocks fall noisily as they ascend. They feed, move, feed. Slowly, with more caution than they have shown all day, they descend to the river, cross a sandbar, and drop their heads to the water for a long drink.

As my brothers and I grew up, our childhood menagerie included a little rust-colored teddy bear with a music box in his belly. The music box and windup key did not last long, but one of my brothers lugged threadbare Brownie Singer everywhere, far beyond the average teddy bear life span. Family legend says that he did not plan to give up Brownie Singer—*ever*. We are quite certain that they would have gone off to college together.

Instead, my father removed, shall we say, Brownie Singer from the premises. To this day, my brother remembers being told that Brownie Singer had "gone away," and he retains the image of a little brown bear walking away into the woods.

"It's a jungle out here," I often say as I stare at the parched, rawboned desert and shudder at the idea of similar trauma. One of my shelf dwellers is a honey-colored teddy bear with black bead eyes and a royal-blue T-shirt. I have dressed this teddy bear

in a miniature pair of white jersey-knit Fruit of the Loom briefs—
tightie whities—a doll-size version of the real underpants, complete with thin blue and yellow stripes on the elastic waistband
and the fold-over front fly.

That there is a global shortage of Freudians is a lucky thing.
Otherwise, my possession of this toy (and my brother's fifth
decade of *ardent longing* for Brownie Singer) might evoke disturbing interpretations of guilt, ego defects, repression, and other
psychic wreckage, all of which we would blame on our parents.

With Freud passé, the cognitive sciences now focus on our
identity as *Homo sapiens,* a primate with high-order intelligence,
and on the neurological and evolutionary bases for behavior.
They posit an inherited "innately organized" psyche that has been
shaped by culture and the demands made on our species for survival. They call imagination "cognitive adventuring." *Arrivederci,*
Sigmund. Hello, Charles Darwin.

Among those who study the nature of intelligence, there is fer-
tile dialogue (and healthy doses of disagreement) about early
childhood, imagination, and the developing brain. What makes
us play? Act like brats? Hold funerals for dead birds or talk to
rubber balls? Give animistic powers to bananas, sticks, or the
nothingness of darkness (monsters under the bed)?

Children, the prototypical pretenders, appear to require the
mental stimulation of elaborate make-believe. The links between
pretending and the acquisition of language are complex and not
well understood. The exercise of "fictive acts of perception" may
be aspects of an adult brain in training, a rudimentary but useful
way for people to develop skills that will become entrenched in
their thinking as they mature.

Animals play compelling roles in young imaginations even if
no real ones are available. When children pretend to be animals,
they largely mix fantasy with indirect experience drawn from
pictures, books, and other media. They can transform their bod-

ies into a slithering python or a kangaroo with limp forefeet. They will use a toy alligator to attack your ankles. They would quake in their Goofy slippers if they saw a real one.

Animal role playing reveals more about human identity than that of the alligator. Children often use toys and animals to push the limits of social convention, for by doing so they run less risk of disapproval. That room was never cleaned because sloths were in charge. I'm eating breakfast right out of the dog's dish because I'm a wolf. Something *wild* makes me do what I do. Much of this make-believe fades by the age of six, psychologists say, as children shed their naïve biology and move toward an adult perception of layered reality.

And here we are: grown-up and stodgy. If we are in our fifties and still on all fours eating out of a dog dish, our mommies will call the therapists. Meanwhile, the grown-up, technophilic world is strangely lonely of the flesh-and-blood creatures that spark our brains and tongues and help make us human.

What remains of several million years of coevolution between humans and wild animals has become, in little more than a hundred years, mediated, barely experiential, and marginalized on crowded, surrounded scraps of refugia. The grizzly bears are distant, eating an occasional Canadian. Life with whales comes from whale-noise CDs. Anglers use bait that simulates the taste of hatchery food, since neither fish nor fish food are wild any longer. Unless it's a rug, we are not sure how to behave around a tiger.

As I eat my oatmeal out of the dog dish, I think of T. H. White and his goshawk. The story of his attempt to tame this wild raptor is said to resemble an epic eighteenth-century tale of seduction. Ultimately, White admitted that he would succeed only if he did not, only if he never became the master of his "lunatic bird."

White longed to learn something, but he could do so only through the unrequited love of an imperfectly subdued and seduced wild creature. By remaining itself, the goshawk offered the hope of its own enormous mystery, its own capacity to teach. For White, the loss of such hope was the death of the mind.

With the warming season and longer daylight, I have left behind the worst of the brain fevers of winter, the garbled and temporarily unavailable words, the obsessive counting, the maniacal straightening of every crooked thing. I no longer ponder zombie drugs or feel compelled to subject the gooey mass inside my skull to medical imagery, to peer into its inexhaustible chaos as one would study a weather map, there to discern peculiar atmospheric patterns. So what if a few million of the 100 billion neurons and synapses have been devoured by obnoxious pests. At least I can still button up my own shirt.

Or can I?

As I pack up to go to sheep country, the zipper on my jacket jams. No matter how hard I try, I cannot slip the bottom pin in place and pull the slider up over the teeth. I face Mark, standing very still, arms akimbo but relaxed. He aligns the zipper and zips it right up to my chin. I feel like weeping. Suddenly, I very much want a pair of mittens.

Disguised as an adult, I venture into the out there, as I always do, to get a feel for the world, to learn something, to breathe deep drafts of desert air. Thousands of miles above me in the mesosphere, meteors are burning up. On its tilted axis, the Earth moves at an orbital velocity of 18.5 miles per second. Jacket zipped, I step off the deck and into Earth's hurl through space.

On their home range, the bighorns have returned to their ten-thousand-year-old daily workout: forage, move, stand, recline, ruminate, act vigilant. Biologists call this their "activity budget." If you are wildlife-watching and expect to buff up your karma by bearing witness to the electrifying kinematics of charismatic North American megafauna, you will be bored to death.

The band has abandoned playfulness for the serious business of eating and turning their white butts to the hard gusts of wind. Spring teases green plants from the ground with more vigor. The males travel solo or in bachelor bands. None have ventured upriver to piss on a rock in the big red side canyon. There is a lull in the impromptu walkabout and enough food to keep them in Ram Land.

I spend my days watching matrilineal bands of subadults made conspicuous by the absence of pregnant ewes. The ewes are harder to find because many of them have begun to move to isolated, remembered territory. During lambing season—from April to June for the Nelson's bighorns on the Colorado Plateau—the ewes usually seek the same lambing grounds each year.

Birth sites on the cliffs are chosen for weather protection and security against predators. From my observation post, I see caves, clefts, niches, overhangs, alcoves, and many other possibilities. When the time comes—any day now for the earliest parturition—the ewes will withdraw to their chosen spots.

On the day of the spring equinox, I sit across an arc of blue air from two ewes. They have ditched the juveniles, including their lambs from the previous year. They feed quietly on a talus slope. Both ewes have enlarged udders. Bearing the weight of near-term lambs, their flanks sink in front of their hips, forming dark hollows.

For the equinox, I have brought along the teddy bear in his undies, as well as Nelson, a stuffed toy bighorn ram with soft pile fur the color of a cappuccino. He has a black nose and white muzzle, belly, and rump. Brown velour covers a pair of curled horns. Ever loyal to homeland, his head is cocked in the direction of Vietnam, where he was made. Nelson is smaller than a real ram's testicles. He has none of his own.

I pull the toys out of my pack and set them on the flat boulder beside me, facing the ewes. A side-blotched lizard, about two inches long, with a rosy-beige body and inkblot patches behind its forelegs, emerges from under a blackbrush shrub and spends the morning basking on my thigh, enjoying the warm denim.

The big female has a radio collar and ear tags. The other is the ewe with the scar across her rib cage. These bighorns, like so many in the Blue Door Band, have become familiar.

It is not difficult to recognize individuals, especially adults, by personality traits and distinct physical features. Broomed horns, nicked horns, broken horns, one horn. Gangly, gaunt, sleek, scraggly. Mellow, nervous. Dainty legs, stocky legs. Rangy necks, wiggy topknots. Noses with bumps, bodies with scars. One-eyed sheep. Limping sheep. All shades of pelage from pale gray to tan to dark taupe to mahogany.

Some bear the obvious markings of ear tags and radio collars and a life history recorded by the band's biologist caretakers. From this record, I know that the big collared ewe once broke her leg and stayed in one place for a long time, vulnerable to predators while she recovered. She is known to lamb early. She has in the past produced a rarity among desert bighorns: twins.

On the red-desert equinox, daylight widens and stretches. Life rests on the brink of a potent release of energy—leaves, lizards, lambs, a conflagration of wildflowers, riverbanks and hanging springs fat with food. To feel it, you must slip inside this pause between seasons, ride the current of instinct, notice everything, understand little.

The science of such life is at once complex and easy. So, too, the physical sheep, their sleek bodies, pale lashes over golden eyes, swollen bellies, a healed leg, a day of play. Harder to envision is their ascent through time into form, shape, and breath, the supple flux of an animal with a living tradition of homeland fidelity. To witness this, you must sit on a rock with a few friends and find in yourself an unfamiliar patience.

Stalin, the stucco-punching flicker, is trapped in the screen house. The one-room structure sits in our cottonwood grove, used in the warm months as a guest bedroom and refuge for siestas. The bird got in—somehow—and now he can't get out. Although he has been imprisoned for a while, I have only just discovered him. He seems weak. There are feathers stuck to the screen walls and scattered across the wooden floor. When he sees me, he breaks into panicked flight, raising a swirling cloud of feathers and dust.

Stalin is a powerful chisel-billed bird of the woodpecker family. From close range, I have a good look at his gray-brown back, stiff black tail, and crescent-shaped black chest bib. Near his bill, his "mustache," a streak of bright red feathers, marks him as a male. His underwings, shown when he flies, are salmon red.

I feel wicked. Stalin, you ignorant slut. You are trapped. This bird batters the nest of our resident phoebes. He drills the house as if it were a giant sugar cube. He could peck away until only a roof on sticks remained. Or I could let him die here.

He stops flying and alights on a rafter. We stare at each other.

Stalin drops off the rafter and scrambles up the screen wall in woodpecker position. His toes snag on the tiny squares. He will not leave through the open door even as I circle the outside of the screen house, hoping to reduce his panic by keeping the mesh between us and herding him toward the opening. You simply cannot herd woodpeckers. He crashes from wall to wall in crazed flight.

I go inside. We are close. In slow motion, I pick up a straw broom and use the flat side to guide him out the door. It seems that I will inflict harm this way, so I abandon the broom and pull the cotton coverlet from the bed. I spread the cloth wide between my arms and cover the bird as he thrashes against the screen.

Wrapped and held, wings beating against my palms, Stalin gets a ride to the door.

A ripple of wind combs the cottonwood trees at one end of the grove and moves toward us, bearing the scent of April. Here it is, the exhalation of the season in a single rogue gust. Ahead of the wind, a flock of starlings—hundreds of them—explodes out of a cloud of ranch-bottom dust.

The moment I release the flicker, the wind burst reaches us, pulling him into the air in a hard, high rise to join the starlings overhead. The flocked mass is so dense, their racing motion so strong, I feel as if they are still and I am rushing forward through space.

The sky above the cottonwoods is filled with birds. They blacken the sun as they pass, then let the light through again.

BROOM RIDING

In the painting on the wall, the mountain sheep peered down from an alpine slope flooded in a golden syrup of Bierstadt light. Contemporary western wildlife art seems to require this luridly primeval pigment—arcadian, radiant, as if Eden were not in the Holy Lands but in the Brooks Range.

The animals in the painting were not bighorns. They were Dall's sheep, a thinhorn subspecies found in Alaska and north-western Canada. Cold sheep. Farthest north sheep. Altitudes of heaven sheep. *Ice* sheep.

Dall's sheep like wind because it blows the snow off their forage so they can eat without pawing and wasting calories. Avalanches kill them. Wolves eat the weaker among them. A few sheep lose their footing on icy chutes and cliffs. In one account, a wolf chased a thinhorn into precipitous terrain, where they both fell off a cliff to their deaths.

The painting froze a moment into bovid nirvana: alpine summer, no snow, no lurking wolves, just a fraternal pod of sunlit rams. Wildlife artists seldom waste a gilt frame on anything without testicles and Boone and Crockett curls. Yet the animals appeared petit, more like divine subpolar meat than trophies. One ram lay on a day bed of tawny grass. The others gazed out of the canvas as if they had just caught glimpses of themselves in a mirror.

The painting hung in an art gallery in a sprawling town in Southern California's Coachella Valley, just a ripple of mountains away from Los Angeles. I was far from the red canyons of home. The Dall's sheep were nowhere near Alaska.

Dall's sheep are white and have gold-brown horns. If you stood one next to a dusty gray-brown desert bighorn, the Dall's would look like the desert animal's ghost. In the painting, the Dall's sheep bodies were lunar white, the horns as burnished as a gold-leaf halo on a Byzantine saint. On canvas, wild western ungulates live in perpetual alpenglow, and this artist remained true to style, bathing his slopes in acrylic radiance.

In the art gallery, my friend Nike and I stared at the snow-white creatures with the golden horns. I felt like a Bedouin who had emerged from a remote wadi of squabbling tribes and shabby camels to behold something improbable but familiar.

We studied the painting. "*Sheep angels,*" Nike said. "These must be sheep angels."

The year I went to an annual meeting of the Southwest's desert bighorn managers and advocates, it was held in Palm Springs, California. I left the redrock deserts of home as the river cottonwoods sprouted a green haze of spring leaves. The road slid me off the Colorado Plateau and into the Mojave and Colorado deserts, into warmer air and basins of creosote and sand.

I carved my road trip into what I called a Chemehuevi map.

In historic times, the Chemehuevi Indians lived in the deserts of the lower Colorado River, land that falls on both sides of the California-Arizona border. They were seminomadic people, known to be fast runners and ardent storytellers and singers. One of the best places to sing, they believed, was among the melons in their gardens.

They measured distance by *tiiravi,* or "desert," also the word for homeland and source. From the top of one mountain range across a valley to the top of the next mountain range was a unit known as *cuukutiiravi*: "one desert."

Chemehuevi land ownership matched human territory to the

territory of a herd of bighorn sheep. A particular bighorn sheep song defined this terrain; the song was both deed and map. A person who inherited such a song claimed its myths and stories, its *bajadas,* buttes, water holes, and other landmarks. The words of the hereditary song unfolded a land traversed, the route traveled.

From southern Utah to the California deserts, I dreamed up my own map of animal songlines. Since I cannot carry a tune, I was careful not to sing aloud while driving, lest, Kuwait-invasion style, I left a wake of smoldering minivans, smashed buses, and jackknifed semitrailers, their drivers the victims of my feeble screech.

The spread of land between the Colorado Plateau and the West Coast is a geography of real sheep and sheep ghosts, places where they persist, places where they went extinct—an estimated twenty-seven populations in the twentieth century. My Chemehuevi map was spotty: isolated remnant bands that clung stubbornly to their stone in a few ranges in the basin and range provinces. With land so empty of them, how do we know where to go?

I slept under a tamarisk on the Arizona side of the lower Colorado, where it runs sluggishly between the dams and reservoirs that stair-step the river from southern Nevada to Mexico. Craggy bare mountains held the strip of ultramarine water in an embrace of jumbled chocolate-colored rock.

A band of emerald fringed this once-mighty, muddy river: tamarisk, Russian olive, skinny palm trees with spiky topknots. Behind the riparian thicket, away from the reservoir, all water was concentrated in boat marinas, trailer parks, and RV camps. The pale, scraped-raw desert lay in scattered patches between lawns as green as Ireland.

On the California side of the Colorado River, the road ran well north of the Salton Sea and crossed a space so immense and misunderstood, it felt like home. I crossed a few *cuukutiiravi*. I aimed the truck's nose toward the Pacific and what I knew would be, with each mile, an escalating din of humanity.

When you sang an abbreviated version of your map song, the Chemehuevi said, you knew the right shortcuts from one place to another. The back-road undulations of basin and range were more like long cuts. So much more song was needed to thread together the bighorn's remaining lands.

I stopped for lunch and a walk in Joshua Tree National Park. According to a park employee, Joshua Tree had a chemical problem (smog from nearby Los Angeles was affecting plant ecology). It had a dump problem (Los Angeles was proposing to build The Biggest Dump Ever at a site bordered on three sides by the park.) It looked to me like Joshua Tree had a Los Angeles problem. The park also had desert bighorns. There are two phenotypes, the park ranger said, one of short, stocky, fast animals, the other long, gawky, and "as big as horses."

Over the last pass and into the Coachella Valley, freeway traffic and an exponential increase in people density sucked me up like a flea in a torrent of locusts. I rode the swarm toward Palm Springs, Rancho Mirage, Palm Desert, and other towns strung end to end along the base of the San Jacinto and Santa Rosa mountains, the seam where cordillera met desert floor and the valley's most watered and habitable places.

Then I extricated myself, pulled off the freeway, and found what had to be the last remaining vacant lot in Southern California. (Don't panic. It had a Realtor's billboard.) I wanted to take a long look at the mountains without crashing.

Despite the locust atmosphere, the landscape was stunning. The startling massif loomed above the flats in a serrated curtain of rock that went from 487 feet above sea level to 10,831 feet in a mere two miles, straight up in a neck-arching rise. I stood on the Coachella Valley floor with more than 300,000 people, 600 tennis courts, several thousand swimming pools—some say 30,000 pools—and 100 golf courses.

High above the silvery veil of ambient smoggy haze could be found cliffs, crags, and pinnacles, plenty of stone to eat, and in it an unexpected population of sheep, one of the rarest races of desert sheep outside of Mexico, the peninsular bighorn. The Chemehuevi map had led me straight into the urban vortex.

Each spring, in a different venue, aficionados of the desert big-horn come out of their deserts to share science and talk sheep. The meetings draw wildlife managers, biologists, and academics from northwestern Mexico and every state with desert bighorns: Texas, New Mexico, Arizona, Utah, Colorado, Nevada, Califor-nia. This group exists in addition to the many sportsmen's orga-nizations devoted to North American sheep. The constituency behind the animal is formidable. Few species have so many cham-pions of their welfare.

The host who opened the meeting welcomed us to Palm Springs, where there are "wider freeways but narrower minds" and more golf courses than bighorn sheep. When he encouraged us to enjoy the "village atmosphere," I blinked stupidly. Here, the golf-ball fetchers at a single country club outnumbered my town's entire population. Later, the host showed a slide of a bighorn drinking from a turquoise guzzler: someone's swimming pool.

The conference room held about a hundred attendees for two days of technical papers and presentations. I sat next to a moun-tain lion tracker, a man with such quiet manners, I thought he was nearly invisible, and near a cluster of elders, retired game wardens who spoke of bighorn herds that went extinct in their time. A few wives had come along. They were attractive, neatly coifed grandmothers, whom I liked immediately because each time someone mentioned the Old Woman Mountains, a Mojave Desert range, they winked at one another and laughed.

Men and women, mostly men. A full inventory of Western boots and silver platter belt buckles. Great big veggie-oil pickups parked outside on the hot tarmac. Big-picture people, mentor professors, veterinarians, graduate students who collected sheep turds for studies of diet and genes. The curious-minded, who dug up old papers and challenged old theories, keeping science mobile and dynamic. The room filled with amiable, competent people.

There was a man with a thick curved-down mustache that took the shape of ram horns, and someone in a grand-slam T-shirt: portraits of rams from each North American sub-species—Stone's, Dall's, Rocky Mountain, desert—a grand slam if a hunter took all four. A throng of field geeks, lean and fit from hiking their terrain, proclaimed their horror of paperwork, noting that as soon as you became an administrator, you gained weight and lost your hair. An expert in mountain sheep DNA called himself a "psychogeneticist," a denizen of the laboratory rather than the field, a man, he joked, who had "traded a personal life for data."

It was easy to see how, over the years, these peer exchanges have shaped sheep management in the Southwest. Theirs was the business of tending to wild animals at the fringes of human dominion. They knew so much more than I did. I listened. I had much to learn.

I learned that the proliferation of wind farms, with road building and noise, presented hazards as well as irony: The gains of clean alternative energy could mean the loss of habitat for wild sheep. Wind farms posed questions about how so visual an animal would react to as much as 4,500 acres of whirling blades.

I learned that for transplant stock, animals from Arizona's Kofa National Wildlife Refuge were the most coveted. "Everyone wants Kofa sheep," at least three people told me, widening their eyes with awe. "Big, big horns."

In Texas, where the native desert bighorn went extinct in the early 1960s, the state had worked to rebuild its herds from Kofa and Mexican transplants. Much habitat lay on private land, posing challenges in access and cooperation. The Texas wildlife people reported that they were still beggars, in need of transplants to bolster the Trans-Pecos herds. For a single ram permit, a hunter paid eighty thousand dollars. Two permits drew twenty thousand applicants.

Slides and PowerPoint presentations brought animals into the semidark room. The lion tracker next to me went invisible. In his slides, one of the presenters had put cartoon bubbles over the heads of sheep to show what they were thinking. Pie charts and graphs peppered us with hard-earned data.

Arizona had "the best sheep." Utah had "healthy numbers" as well, along with dizzying growth in off-road-vehicle recreation and oil and gas exploration in critical habitat. The Mexicans expressed the most enthusiasm and optimism, faced the greatest political obstacles, and boasted a giant benefactor in Cemex, the country's largest cement company and the primary underwriter of bighorn sheep recovery in Sonora and other states.

New Mexico reported a grim picture (the mountain lion problem) and some fine but empty sheep habitat. For hope, they had San Andres Ewe 067 (still alive) and habitat improvement from prescribed burns. California seemed to have the largest budget and the coolest outfits for sheep-capture teams: yellow jumpsuits, knee pads, caps with logos.

There was talk of setbacks and progress; of logjams of bureaucratic crud and breakthroughs in research; of tribal herds, managed to benefit native traditions but dependent for funds on hunting permits so pricey, no tribal member could afford them. There was talk of nightmare drought and dried-up water holes and of global warming as a possible factor in extinction risks in low-elevation deserts.

About domestic sheep, I heard of only one crisis. In a northern state, wildlife managers had successfully buffered a population of Rocky Mountain bighorns from contact with domestic sheep and the risk of cross-infection. Suddenly, a flock of woollies appeared near the bighorn range, grazing away like lawn mowers.

On the other side of the mountain, a man had become upset about a neighbor's sheep, a flock that accidentally spent too much time in his backyard. He was at the end of his rope. He loaded up the sheep, drove them across the pass, and dropped them off on the other side of the mountain. In the jargon, this type of wildlife impact agent was known as an "anthropogenic factor."

The litany of mountain lion troubles in New Mexico and California's Sierra Nevada brought my tracker back from the ethos. He gave me a lovely slow-motion Cheshire cat grin. Discussion-wise, in fact, this was the meeting's predominant topic: predation.

"Ten, twelve years ago, we all were talking about disease— scabies, pneumonia, parainfluenza," one of the elders told me. "Now it's all about mountain lions."

Along one of the town's sunny, homeless person–free streets, I found a bench and sat down with my binoculars to scan for sheep. The mountain range loomed above the lanky palm trees, its granite face carved in rough pleats of sun and shade.

The bench sat near a store that sold clothing slightly preowned by Hollywood stars and a design studio with an unadorned, rough-faced concrete wall and a concrete tub planter along its facade. Out of the planter sprung a vigorous thatch of what appeared to be electrocuted grass. In fact, these were horsetails:

tall, hollow, jointed plants that stand erect and "leafless" (the leaves are small sheaths at the joints), somewhat like a reed or a green straw. Two to three feet tall, these plants have an abrasive surface, hence the nickname "scouring brush."

Horsetails grow wild along streams and washes throughout the West, including my home canyon country, creeping from a common rootstock into implacable thickets. They are adaptable, primitive, and remarkably ancient plants with Paleozoic, pre-dinosaur origins. An unlikely but intriguing choice for decorative horticulture, I thought. Le Corbusier meets the Devonian.

My chances of being arrested for voyeurism were greater than my chances of seeing a bighorn with my binoculars as I sat on a bench next to a bunch of hothouse-green arthrophytes. Yet the sheep were up there, hanging above the golf courses.

The sprawl of Coachella Valley towns had sprawled right up into the bighorns' lower-elevation habitat. At the northern end of the Santa Rosa Mountains, the sheep gazed at high-end subdivisions. They trotted through streets and yards tended by fleets of Mexican gardeners. They drank from swimming pools. They became entangled in fences and they ate new, tasty, poisonous plants, the exotic (nonnative) ornamentals around deluxe homes and country clubs.

The sheep were vulnerable to parasites. Parasites persist in watered areas; the golf courses were watered daily. Cars hit and killed lambs or killed the mother ewe, so the orphaned lamb eventually died, as well. Hedges and other dense bands of landscaped greenery soothed desert-baked humans but blocked the bighorns' vision, making them more susceptible to ambush by predators.

No sheep showed up in my binoculars, so I gave the horsetails a good-bye stroke and drove to Rancho Mirage, whose city logo is a ram's head. I waded through streets of chic homes, boutiques selling gold-plated mushroom scrubbers, and golf palaces until everything stopped at an edge of open, raw land, the abrupt rise of the Santa Rosa escarpment. I hiked across stone and dust. I splayed myself against an eight-foot-high fence and silently screamed, *Let me in!*

No, I thought, as four hundred sprinklers hissed onto a swathe of blinding green golf turf behind me. *Let me out!*

The decline of local populations and the 1998 listing of *Ovis canadensis cremnobates,* the peninsular bighorn, as an endangered species triggered studies, especially of the disturbing trends in annual recruitment: Lambs were born each year, but too many died.

In their study of lamb mortality, wildlife managers very, very carefully captured young lambs and placed blindfolds around their eyes to calm them as they fixed special radio collars onto their small necks. As the lamb grew, the collar's cotton threads would break before the collar became too tight.

The study found that "urbanization" was the cause of 43 percent of lamb mortality, both from direct effects (being hit by a car, drowning in a pool, etc.) and from the indirect effects of habitat fragmentation or loss. Bobcats and coyotes killed a number of lambs. Because of weak respiratory systems, the lambs may have been predisposed to predation.

As the valley filled with houses, the sites next prized for upscale real estate lay in fringe areas and higher on the slopes, terrain long used by the bighorns. Some in the neighborhood understood that, on the *bajada* real estate, *Ovis* had preceded *Homo.* Others complained that the sheep were "invading them."

The option to remove million-dollar homes from sheep range did not go over well. Instead, the solution, hard-won by wildlife advocates, was a fence, a "bighorn-proof" camouflaged fence, eight feet high and nearly four miles long.

Ultimately, the community supported the fence and helped raise money for its construction. In one fund-raising effort, the sale of sheep art—sculptures and paintings of the school of the Dall's sheep painting—garnered private funds for land purchases and easements. Angel sheep helped golf sheep.

After the fence went up, the roadkills and pool disasters declined, education efforts continued, and the day I visited, high on a slope, two ewes chewed nonchalantly and stared down at a screaming madwoman plastered to their fence.

Meanwhile, back in the lion's den . . .

Much of the conference's second day was devoted to the dynamics of big cats and wild sheep. Next to me, the molasses-slow gestures of my table partner, the tracker, said more about his vocation than words. He moved with the lithe grace of a cat—or a sloth, the metaphorical antithesis of the suicidal pace of our breakneck world.

"How do you track a cougar?" I whispered, hoping he wouldn't notice the imprints of chain-link fence on my palms. He leaned forward and gave me the precise technique. "Let me walk you through my mountain range," he whispered, "every detail."

Most big-ungulate professionals are also big hunters. Their work reflects the entrenched history of sport-driven management and funding. To some hunters, wildlife-watchers are hopeless weenies. Others hold the conviction that bobcats, coyotes, and mountain lions are unwanted competitors that take prey away from humans who love to hunt them. Of the mountain lion, one presenter said, "We have to educate these animals with lethal means."

Some claimed that mountain lions, or at least the sheep killers, were "out of control." Others believed that wildlife habitat loss and "human meddling" had triggered subtle ecological shifts between predator and prey.

Overall, the discussions evoked a hesitant but honest admission: Biologists' understanding of sheep-lion dynamics was full of uncertainty. The role of *Puma concolor* in today's naturalized ecology of the desert bighorn—small groups on reduced, isolated habitat—remained complex and changeable.

There was mention of adverse conditioning—"teaching" mountain lions to stay out of an area by using shock collars on the lions and sonic collars on the sheep. I imagined a future generation of wildlife managers, very fat, very bald, sitting at remote urban workstations in dim rooms, following satellite-beamed blips on glowing screens. Whenever eater and eatee came within drooling distance of each other, someone pushed the bad-kitty button and zapped the cat.

Such scenarios may seem nuts, but unlike past predator control—that is, wholesale, bounty-crazed wipeout—did they not allow both species to coexist? What would we do if we had to choose between robo-sheep and extinct sheep? Do we extirpate the animal's wildness to keep its flesh?

My head swam. Hell, I was one of those weenies. There was every place in my heart and my life for alpha predators like mountain lions. An ecosystem is neither healthy nor whole without them. Their loss can precipitate a series of disruptions (called "trophic cascades"), including secondary extinctions. Losing big predators may do their prey more harm than good.

Yet when I envisioned feline predators taking out an up-against-the-wall band of bighorns like so many crunchy snacks, I realized, much to my horror, that I, too, might yell for the trappers.

The low background hum of the room's air-cooling system seemed to come from inside my own body. I felt like a humming refrigeration unit. I wanted to go back to cliffrose and yucca, to the dry air of stone. I wanted to shadow the tracker, learn his mountains, read the map of predator and prey, *every detail.*

The conference came to an end. The tracker prepared to morph out of the room and into his pickup. I wanted to say something not completely dumb. So I said something completely dumb. I puffed out my cheeks and crossed my eyes in exaggerated gluttony. I held my head as if it were bloated with giant balls of Styrofoam. "*Science!*" I groaned. "So much science."

The Cheshire cat grin rode slowly up his face. "Nature," he said, as if to gently correct me. "Nature is fluid." Then he told me about a mountain lion in the desert ranges along the California-Mexico border. It was known to have killed and eaten thirteen bighorn sheep, he said. Not long afterward, it died of malnutrition.

Once upon a time, I listened to the spokesman for a coalition of sportsmen's groups as he told an audience about "what works" in wildlife preservation. "Be realistic," he said emphatically; "it's a business."

You raise game animals, you manage them closely, and you shoot some of them. "You think in terms of returns on your investment," Mr. Be Realistic said. "People will not conserve something if it doesn't have use or value."

He showed a video of deer, elk, and mountain sheep running around to a sound track of loud rock music. He told the audience that the sportsman was far more successful with his message than the environmentalist. His comment "No Sierra Clubs ever spent a penny on wildlife" aroused no response from the audience. Perhaps our brainpans were still banging with rock and roll. (Later, when I offered examples to challenge the assertion, one of his cohorts called me a "witch.") A raw dose of economics, however, drew nods.

Get real, the speaker appeared to be telling us. Politicians handle game department budgets and "politicians are not into [here, a fake flaky gesture of fluttery, unmanly hands] the magical, mystical, 'sacred animal' value of wildlife. They are into cost-benefit ratios. I tell legislators the red-meat value."

Better habitat means more rams and bull elk, means more hunter tags, means more revenue, he said. "If it comes down to four bucks a pound for red meat, then that's a pretty good return on investment."

There is not a shred of doubt about it: The sportsman's dollar helps wildlife. Every government wildlife agency in the West depends hugely on financial and political support from hunters. This partnership has a long and intricate history. Even as the public increases its support of wildlife for other values, the hunter– game department partnership will continue.

When state budgets waver and shrink, sportsmen's groups often step in to restore or supplement funds. They underwrite permits and habitat preservation. The Foundation for North American Wild Sheep, for example, has brokered the retirement of numerous domestic-sheep allotments on public lands, paying the sheep rancher for a buyout that no government could afford. The buyouts add safe habitat for bighorns.

Much is rooted in the unsentimental premise that exploiting wildlife at sustainable levels saves them from doom. To *have* wild sheep, deer, elk, antelope, moose, and bears, you have to kill them. The people who kill them are their greatest funders. To sustain a game species, this view asserts, it must be harvested. Call it "conservation by trophy."

Those with less banged brainpans will have to address the complexities of hunting as "good biology." Meanwhile, an implicit goal in the work of bringing desert bighorns to healthy levels is the goal of hunting them.

State wildlife agencies are addicted to hunter money. From the millions of dollars generated from sportsmen over the years come budgets for monitoring, translocation, restoration, and other programs. The relationship is tight: The bedfellows seem married for life. A few would argue, like Mr. Be Realistic, that the bighorns' *non*game value—as an ecological mystery, as an embodiment of wilderness, as an ancient, intimate relationship between human and creature—is irrelevant.

From attending the California conference, I had sensed a more broad-minded view. Capable, devoted, underpraised people were working hard to keep this species on the planet. The deepest truths emerged in the field and through the vision of biologists like the University of Arizona's Paul Krausman.

Over a professional lifetime as a field biologist and teacher, Paul Krausman has remained a staunch advocate of the desert bighorn's inherent wildness. The key, he insists, is habitat— spacious, far-flung, unbroken homeland, where nature's hand is relatively autonomous and vital.

With sheep confined to cliffy atolls in a sea of human activity, management of these animals has a tendency, and often an urgency, to intensify. Given this trend, Krausman fears that cultural selection will wholly displace natural selection, that wild will give way to something else: sheep behind really long fences, sheep altered genetically, like soybeans, to adapt to "humanized" landscapes, to stay out of swimming pools or taste awful to mountain lions. Animals will be ear-tagged, collared, tattooed, and trucked, mined and modeled for data, tracked from outer space, their lives lived under surveillance: a captivity based on the best intentions of those who wish to rescue and protect them.

"How soon before the habitat available for wildlife is so limited that the degree of management intensity becomes identical to farm management? Every bit of domestication takes a little away from the wild side of wildlife," Krausman writes. "Is that choice more desirable than extinction?"

It seemed to me that Krausman and others believe in conservation biology in its richest sense: Wildlife is best served when humans honor the full spectrum of its worth, be it economic, biological, moral, aesthetic, and even spiritual, the miracle of a species's evolution and remarkable adaptations, its place in our imaginations.

And the stories they weave are a vital part of this: a canyon hiker's glimpse, the hunter's chase, futile or full of meat, days of intimacy with mammalian blood that is not our own, creatures *who know the earth is steep in every direction,* who, like snow-white angels, fly off the cliffs with wolves.

Given time, you will eventually match your own habits, at home and afield, to the habits of the animal you study. Bird-watchers rise at dawn, peck at little plates of seeds and raisins, do their errands in eager swoops. Crepuscular in hot weather, diurnal and on the move when it's cool, desert tortoise people lumber up and over speed bumps, wondering if they will meet someone of the opposite sex sometime in the next two years. Desert bighorn people eat, move, stand, ruminate. They are vigilant. They nap.

On my last morning in the Palm Springs area, I roamed a quiet neighborhood on the people side of the four-mile fence, eating carrots, moving, standing, ruminating. Legal issues did not allow me to dip my lips into someone's swimming pool or take a nap on an agave and flagstone terrace. My vigilance turned up a random poodle with a friendly man on the end of her leash.

My internal refrigeration-unit hum had been replaced by a blood thrumming that matched the susurrations of lawn sprinklers. Inside, I hissed. Where the steep mountains and washes butted up against the neighborhoods, acres of mesh wire caged cobbles and boulders, keeping them from avalanching into streets, pools, and horsetail boutiques. A palm frond crashed down onto the roof of a parked Lexus.

After all was said and done, anyone in this community who was not a golf palace developer would likely admit a fondness for their local bighorn sheep. Many had rallied to offer their support during the study of the dying lambs; the "cute" factor played hard. This was a nature-conscious place. According to literature about the local zoo–botanical garden, visitors could see "exotic African wildlife that exist peacefully with native plants."

When I asked the poodle walker about the bighorns, he beamed with an unabashed thrill at their presence, at their tenacity. "Our mountains should have them," he told me. "They belong here."

At the café where, after my amble, I bought coffee for the road, I asked the young java maker the same question. "What sheep?" he said.

I nosed the truck around vegemorphic lawns and links and through fleets of big shiny cars. I found the freeway, then left it for a back road aimed at the Colorado River side of the Chemehuevi map. The Mojave's basin and range rhythm, the very curvature of the Earth, soothed me.

In the sheep-habitable mountains and canyons between the Coachella Valley and home, some places have sheep, and some do not. The Chemehuevi map is patchy, and there are long interludes between songs, despite herculean efforts to bring bighorns back to their home deserts.

According to a reliable count, 50 percent of all populations of desert bighorns alive in 1990 were from translocations, defined as releases of animals into areas where no other bighorns are present. Rigorous research and preparation precede each such action. Wildlife biologists, including Paul Krausman, widely agree that reintroducing animals to their historic range is a vital tool of restoration ecology. Many restoration efforts have been successful. Some have failed. In one study, a map shows points of sheep reintroduction. The graphic for a successful translocation is the black silhouette of a right-side-up ram; for a failure, it's an upside-down ram.

At the Nevada-Arizona border, I approached a thin ribbon of highway atop 6.6 million tons of concrete wedged between the walls of Black Canyon like a giant gray Pringle: Hoover Dam.

Hoover Dam holds back the Colorado River into the fjords of Lake Mead. Where there were once canyons, there are now coves. Charcoal and brown mountains, Gothic chunks of volcanics and andesite breccia, jut above reservoir waters of man-made, unsouled green. The mountains hold cliffs, cracks, ledges, and unobscured views, all within reach of water. The mountains hold bighorn sheep. Here, one would think, Chemehuevi operas might be sung.

Overall, the Lake Mead bighorns have been a healthy lot; wildlife managers take good care of them. Without risk to the nucleus herd, they have transplanted animals to other parts of Nevada as starter stock in ancestral terrain. Lake Mead sheep provided founder herds in Zion National Park and in southwestern Colorado. At home above the reservoir, in the arid, ragged peaks and ravines, they struggle to eat and reproduce. They struggle through dreadful droughts. They struggle with terrorism.

Steep-graded switchbacks led me to the dam crossing. The crest of the venerable arch-gravity dam, completed in 1935, doubled as the highway bridge, the design of innocent, slower, less crowded times.

For the past twenty years, highway planners had charted an alternative to this crossing. The old route was strained by a delirious population boom in nearby Las Vegas, streams of through-traffic between Las Vegas and Phoenix and along what was now a North American Free Trade Agreement (NAFTA) route for commercial truckers, and by cars and buses spewing hordes for tours into the dam's bowels.

In a post–September 11 world, the place became simply too

bombable. Here lay security hell and gridlock on the hair-thin rim of a giant potato chip.

Traffic was heavy. I killed my engine and waited for an hour in a line of vehicles behind the highway checkpoint. Under the restrictions, trailers, RVs, and motor homes were inspected—armadas of them flooded this recreation vortex. Heavy trucks and commercial vehicles, anything large and enclosed, were prohibited. Their drivers took a route seventy miles to the south. If you were driving a rental truck packed to the rafters, you had to go the long way around, too, because inspection was so difficult.

Except for the threat of death by carbon monoxide, by electromagnetic radiation from the spiderweb of transmission lines, by the postal move of an overzealous security guard, I did not mind the bumper-to-bumper wait. It gave me a chance to scan the cliffs for bighorns.

When I whipped out my binoculars, a state trooper whipped out his scowl. I whirled my fingers around my ears in curling motions, the universal sign for a lunatic, although I intended to mime ram curls and my search for sheep. So I sat, squinted at the cliffs, and gagged on fumes, thinking, *O. bin laden* meets *O. c. nelsoni*. Indeed, it was a new world for the bighorns at the dam end of Lake Mead.

Not far from the dam, contractors were engineering the Hoover Dam Bypass, a freeway and bridge across the 840-foot-deep chasm of the Colorado River. The bypass would eliminate "numerous substandard geometric elements"—that is, it would have none of the old road's looping switchbacks, horseshoe and hairpin turns, its slowdowns, blind curves, and turnarounds designed for nothing larger than a golf cart.

The new route would shoot straight across a formidable medium of tumultuous rock with a high-speed four-lane road. Truckers would fly by. Trade would flow. Terrorists would curse and look at the dam in their rearview mirrors.

In its environmental review, the Federal Highway Administration said it had chosen the alternative with the least harm to wildlife, one close to developed areas rather than through undisturbed terrain. Nevertheless, the bypass sliced through routes of traditional sheep movement and twenty acres of lambing habitat. The road might isolate small groups from one another, the review stated. If a local sewage-evaporation pond, used by wildlife as a watering place, had to be fenced, the animals would need a replacement.

At the checkpoint, the exhaust fumes induced hallucinations. I laid my head back, closed my eyes, and counted sheep. Single file, they followed their ancient internal map. One by one, semis and trailers loaded with slick candy red 290-horsepower jet boats smashed them.

Against the monster trio of corporate commerce, the military, and national security, against the public's numb fear, against a million Las Vegans who never drove their stretch SUVs under eighty miles per hour, protests about harm to wild creatures that no one saw were but pitiful peeps. The strategy was to protect the local flora and fauna, not by biology but by mitigation.

The Hoover Dam Bypass design would put high fences on both sides of the new highway. The fence would run along its full length, plus extra on both the Nevada and Arizona ends for good measure. "Out-jumps" provided escape for any sheep accidentally trapped inside the fenced right-of-way. In their movement corridors, sheep would find safe crossings: structures that directed them into at least ten wildlife overpasses and underpasses. A new artificial water source would replace any lost ones.

Was it my imagination, or were things around here a bit Wizard of Oz, backroom console, pay no attention to the man behind the curtain?

On the Arizona side of Black Canyon, construction crews gnawed away at the chocolate brown rock. The government had required that they take "desert tortoise education courses." Somewhere out there were a stack of gila monster documentation and biologists who monitored bicolored penstemons, peregrine falcons, and any freak-out bleats from bighorn ewes trying to give birth during dynamite blasts. Threatened cactus and other native plants were plucked from the bulldozers' path and taken to a nursery, to be replanted when the bypass was completed.

In seventy years at this crack of Black Canyon, we had become a sensitive lot.

At the roadblock, I ended my sensitivityfest and started the engine. The line moved forward; the guards became more selective with their random inspections. The scowling state trooper signaled me to stop. He tried to look officious, but I think he was bored and his feet hurt.

What was I carrying under the topper shell at the back of the truck? he asked. *Brooms.* The congestion was making me edgy. But he was tired and cranky, too, and had to stand in a shroud of exhaust fumes, listening to his chromosomes snap. Camping and other personal gear, I told him, and he waved me through. Without being blown up, I crossed the crest of the dam and drove up the switchbacks on the Arizona side.

The spring sun heated the stone. A thermal on the canyon flanks carried a hawk on its rise. In Chemeheuvi myth, Red-Tailed Hawk hunts bighorn sheep and puts their eyes into the empty eye sockets of his wives. In this, there is both an appreciation of keen vision and a heart-deep craving.

In a Chemehuevi story, Deer, Chuckwalla, and Mountain Sheep traveled together. At the lowlands and foothills, Deer remained. At the foot of the rocky desert mountains, Chuckwalla said, "I'm cold." Mountain Sheep cracked a rock with his horns. "This will be your house," he said. "What will you do?" asked Chuckwalla. Mountain Sheep said, "I am going to live in those mountains."

A shadowed slice of river trickled out from under Hoover's massive wedge, limpid and clear from the slack water backed up behind the next dam downstream. Upstream, on the cliffs above the reservoir, amid clumps of silver bursage, the Lake Mead bovids perched on their day-bed ledges like knickknacks, chewing their cuds and watching the Jet Skis and powerboats crisscross the bottle green water.

Red meat. Four bucks a pound.

APRIL

～

Let me say this before rain becomes a utility that they can plan
and distribute for money. By "they" I mean the people who cannot understand that rain is a festival, who do not appreciate its
gratuity, who think that what has no price has no value, that what
cannot be sold is not real, so that the only way to make something *actual* is to place it on the market. The time will come when
they will sell you even your rain. At the moment it is still free, and
I am in it. I celebrate its gratuity and its meaninglessness.

—Thomas Merton, from *Raids on the Unspeakable*

The talus slope is a landslide in stasis, fractured black rock spilled
from rim to base. Nearly every outcrop and boulder on the talus
bears an incised drawing of bighorn sheep.

The sheep lope across the mineral-varnished surfaces. One
emerges from a crack into daylight. Some leap; some leave tracks.
Their horns curve like rainbows. They have little ears. Heads lift.
Necks turn. Legs stretch upward in a vertical climb.

The instinct is to study each rock panel, each petroglyph individually, to aim interest at the details, to sort the details into order
or category, to count them. Stop counting. Shut down that part of
your brain. Look at the talus again.

There is astounding perspective in the whole of the slope, in
its vertical rise and all four hundred feet of its breadth: tiny sheep
at the top, midsize sheep in the middle distance, big sheep at the
base—this pair, for example, near your feet.

They show their bodies in profile, straight backs and curved bellies. Their slender legs extend as if in motion. The horns are front-facing arcs with an implied flair. The smaller ram stands above the larger ram as if behind him and more distant from the viewer.

The larger ram seems frozen in place, his neck erect beneath the sweeping double curves. From nose to tail the ram petroglyph is seven feet long: as large as life—larger, in fact. He stands not far from you, as rams have stood before me in the canyon of the Blue Door Band.

Beyond him, the rock drawings form a band of desert bighorns scattered on the ledges. Perhaps you notice, too, the line of etched footprints that "hike" rock to rock up the slope as if following a precipitous path. Perhaps you have heard that when the quartz stone that chiseled these images struck the rock surface, it released sparks of cold, jagged light.

The entire cliff itself is the artist's canvas, you think. A frieze or mural on the broken wall of basaltic lava, a single narrative of what people dreamed or did, or needed to do.

Like flesh-and-blood animals, the stone-carved bighorns array themselves on a steep, perfect sheep cliff with plants to eat, escape terrain, and good views. The highest petroglyphs, the smallest figures, nearly reach the rim. Above them, snowy tufts of clouds float across an ultramarine sky. The animals' legs bend in an upward run toward the blue, off the stone.

We meet for the first time, shortly after sunrise, in a parking lot in a town in California's northern Mojave Desert. The initial impression is mutual but cordial panic.

For an all-day trek on a hot spring day into a remote desert region used daily by the United States Navy for the rehearsals of war, my guide is a dignified septuagenarian in a tan shirt, navy blue slacks with suspenders, and a straw Stetson. I am wild-haired and squinty from a grueling road trip, wearing shorts, hiking boots, and a loose white cotton shirt that I have buttoned up funny, although I won't notice the mismatched closure until later.

I see a stranger who may or may not be prone to cardiac arrest on this hike. He sees a disheveled woman who limps and winces because of a hip joint worn down by excess mileage. A third observer might wonder, Will they make it out of the wilderness alive?

I cannot find my notebook and pen. I cannot find my water bottle. Behind the truck's open topper, a plasmic blob of gear lies on the tarmac, as if dropped from above by a passing F-14. Again, I have driven from home in Utah to California. It is beginning to feel like a commute, a westerner's commute, a slide across the earth's curvature from the Rockies nearly to the Pacific, as if I were off to visit a neighbor.

From the road-trip heap, I extract what I need and shove the rest of the wad back into the truck. My day pack is loaded and cinched up.

Because my guide is such a gentleman, I sense humor rather than dread in his skepticism about my preparedness. He has an air of reserved affection and an unspoken curiosity about what, exactly, today's adventure might turn out to be. We size each other up and decide that we are healthy desert curmudgeons who will, today at least, survive a trek in the wilderness. It is implicit: We shall take good care of each other.

I close up the truck—we will drive his vehicle to the trailhead—and reattach to my pocket the clip-on plastic card that identifies me as a visitor to a military preserve that is grimly paranoid about terrorist attacks. I have passed the security check at base headquarters. I am here to see an improbable canyon with several thousand petroglyphs of bighorn sheep. The canyon is off-limits to the public and accessible only with an official escort. Kenneth Pringle straightens his straw hat and asks, "Ready?"

If you want to study lakes, go to the desert. Here, in this far-flung reach of the Great Basin, lie the ghosts of Ice Age water. All waters flow inward. All waters—they come from scant precipitation—drain into closed valleys, where, for the most part, they vanish.

Bone white playas in the surrounding terrain—the Owens, Indian Wells, and Panamint valleys, and a deep valley named Death—form the arid sinks between mountain ranges. The rhythm names the province: basin (alluvium-filled depressions bound by deep faults) and range (ragged, sky-scraping escarpments). The mountains' granitic ribs run with a north-south grain, pulled apart by an east-west stretch across the basins.

Marooned above the dry valleys, the Coso Range rises dark brown and bald in the morning light. The Cosos are mostly granite, with the added spice of earthquakes and volcanic ruptures, of basalt flows and domes of lumpy rhyolite. The canyons that finger their west flank hold one of the largest concentrations of rock art in the hemisphere.

We head into the shimmering silver-and-white expanse of China Lake, one in the region's chain of Pleistocene lakes, then follow a causeway on its edge. As Ken drives, I rivet my gaze on the ibis and avocets that feed in several acres of shallow water, an evaporating puddle of spring rains and all that is "lake" about China Lake. Ahead lies a low-slung ridge of intrusive igneous rock known as pluton.

As a guest of the military, I think it best to watch birds and ponder the pluton and lumpy rhyolite. Off to the west, obscured by the nervous mirages that hover above the alkali flats, lie things I am not supposed to see. Cruisers? Aircraft carriers? Submarines? The day grows hotter under a sun that tilts the desert toward its fiery summer. A rogue wind lifts diaphanous veils of alkali dust above the playa. Turkey vultures circle a gypsum mound.

"Ken," I ask, "what the hell is the U.S. Navy doing in the middle of the Mojave?"

In 1943, the Navy set aside more than a thousand square miles of this California desert for ordnance research and testing. Although smaller than White Sands Missile Range in New Mexico, the Naval Air Weapons Center has the same character: a clear-sky, airspace-safe, wide-open expanse of the arid West, ideal habitat for lobbing missiles and rockets. By virtue of its closure to other uses, it forms a huge buffer of accidental wilderness around and beyond the bombed bits. It also presents the full irony of cultural treasures saved from vandals by the secrecy and restrictions of America's war industry.

For nearly forty years, Kenneth Pringle, a physicist, helped blow stuff up. His career postdated the Manhattan Project but fully straddled the Cold War. While nothing nuclear was exploded here (but what do we know?), some bombs need triggers that ignite their core and, as Ken puts it, send the device "into high order." As a civilian scientist for the navy, he specialized in weapons materials. He is now retired.

Ken has clearance to escort nonmilitary visitors to the rock-art sites in the Coso Range, sites protected by the Naval Air Weapons Station as a national landmark. One of the rock-art canyons is open to the public for escorted, tightly controlled weekend tours. All other sites are closed. In a rare exception, the navy has agreed to let me into one of the closed sites, with Ken as my guide.

I am no stranger to petroglyphs. The abundant engravings of ancient Puebloans surround my home. A panel of flute players, spirals, atlatls, cornstalks, a scorpion, and smatterings of three-inch-high sheep lies a quarter mile from my door. Here, I want to see what is unique about the motif of wild sheep in the Cosos, something I do not see in the redrock canyons of home: life-size bighorns carved into the face of the rock.

Ken has been instructed to keep me in the far end of the Cosos until late afternoon. "Today," they told us at the base, "will be hot." The forecast for temperatures in the high eighties does not bother me. I have hiked in more brutal temperatures and know the required cautions.

"Heat? No problem," I spout to Ken with desert-girl swagger.

"It's a hot day on the base."

Oh. *That* hot. A firing day. Behind us, on the flats, planes will be dropping scary plasmatic blobs. We cannot cross back to town until the all clear comes over Ken's radio.

Ken strikes me as someone who truly wants to know where he lives, to understand its bedrock and biology, its deep and its recent past. His official science often involved geology fieldwork in the military reserve's remote quarters. Unofficially, he was intrigued by artifacts, lithic sites, "house rings," and other traces of native cultures, but especially by the astounding profusion of figures engraved on the Cosos' basaltic rubble. The rock art drew him into a parallel avocation, archaeology.

He studied the Coso petroglyphs on weekends for over twenty years. In the sixties, he and two colleagues, Campbell Grant and James Baird, made the first systematic survey of the area, one that sited, recorded, and tallied by motif over fourteen thousand petroglyphs in thirty miles of canyons. Later studies suggest that, regionwide, this might be a considerable undercount. Although the theoretical bases of their work have evolved into other hypotheses (rock-art interpretation remains ground for what has been described as "academic tribal warfare"), the 1968 Grant-Baird-Pringle book about the survey, *Rock Drawings of the Coso Range,* remains seminal and invaluable.

From the salt flats, the road winds through a deep cleft in the mountains. Before reaching the canyon, we pass through a forest of Joshua trees. Almost to a fault, these tall, spiky yuccas prefer the gravelly slopes of specific moisture, a middle world between chaparral and colder altitudes. Each tree grows from a single yellow-brown trunk into multiple branches with bayonet-shaped green leaves. Above the treetops looms an unusually tall Joshua tree that did not fork. It consists of a single trunk and topknot, like a giant electrocuted flagpole.

The Joshua tree woodland gives way to a high tableland with views of the snow-crowned Sierra Nevada on one side and the indigo ridges that enfold Death Valley on the other. The dirt road roughens to a two-track lane, then nothing. We park and start hiking cross-country toward a slash of jagged black rock in the distance: one of the petroglyph canyons.

Our pace is steady, unhurried. There is no shade, not even a disobedient Joshua tree. A low-growing cover of hopsage, saltbush, blackbrush, and other drought-tolerant shrubs blankets the land's gentle roll. In their midst grows a splendor of late-spring wildflowers. Most startling are red mariposa lilies, delicate cups of fire-engine red on slender stems, and the royal blue flowers of chia, a sagelike shrub.

Far above the Mojave pastorale, a jet climbs, banks in a hard turn, then roars back toward the playa to send some scary plasmatic blobs into high order. The rumbling sound of the jet engine reaches us long behind the plane's trajectory. Ken is not worried. I am looking for rocket carcasses amid the saltbush. I am not looking for bighorns. The Coso Range bears thousands of their images but not a single living sheep.

We enter the canyon in its upper reaches, a shadowy fissure in the rolling green, buttressed by low cliffs of broken, tumbled boulders and lined with pale ecru sand along the dry streambed. Whereas red dominates the sedimentary sandstone of my home canyons, here the rock is volcanic, ranging from chocolate brown to black to a glossy purple-black where it is heavily patinated, a color like the skin of an eggplant. As soon as you describe the rock's color, the light changes and it is something else.

Even though I have never been in the Coso Range before, this land is familiar land, desert that reveals water by its lack of water, a hand shown by the erosional force of ephemeral rainfall and runoff cutting through the bedrock. Nevertheless, I am unaccustomed to a canyon of volcanics, to wandering a gorge of fire rock. The black-wall, beige-sand palette stuns, then soothes me. It turns the bright magenta spark of a hedgehog cactus flower into a miracle.

The swathe of pale sand in the canyon bottom makes the easiest passage. Against several boulders in the wash, where runoff accumulated, then evaporated from the surface, feral burros or wild horses, maybe even coyotes, have dug pits in the sand in search of water. We see quail, hear chukars, and glimpse a towhee that is believed to be endemic to these lava gorges. The backs of the spiny lizards are the color of charcoal; the reptile makes itself local by matching the rock.

For nearly two miles, the jumble of rock on both sides of the canyon forms a long gallery of figures. Figures on outcrops, on flat slabs, in the cracks, beneath overhangs, on water-smoothed stones along the streambed, on the countless boulders of all sizes, from toaster to boxcar, that fall from rim to floor: a continuum of human imagination, etched into the skin of the Cosos.

More than half the region's rock-art motifs are bighorn sheep, overwhelmingly adult males. There are also dogs, lizards, snakes, mountain lions, birds, deer. Paw prints, hoofprints, handprints, footprints. Humanlike figures: clothespins with horns, stick figures with bows and arrows, elongated anthropomorphs with elaborately patterned torsos, ear bobs, pin-size heads, bird-claw feet, headdresses of quail feathers.

A procession of figures emerges from (enters?) a natural crack in the rock, a theme that is uncannily similar to an ancient Puebloan panel in my neighborhood, nearly seven hundred miles away. Dogs surround sheep. Hunters impale sheep. Two archers aim their arrows at each other.

Atlatls, projectile points, bag shapes, "shields," or polygons with interior designs. Grids, spirals, chevrons, checkerboards, rakes, dots, meandering lines, curves that nest in one another, and grooves, sometimes a groove low on the canyon wall, up to thirty feet long. What is missing or rarely depicted: plants, baskets, home tools, shelters, women, rabbits, dead people, mountains, the moon.

The artists' medium was the broken *malpais* itself. Pecking the basalt with a stone tool removed the patina of age and weathering, a natural varnish of iron and manganese oxides bound with clay minerals. The chipping away revealed the pale rock beneath the surface—a negative of light against dark. Newer etchings overlie older ones. On north-facing surfaces in particular, chartreuse, yellow, red, and orange lichens edge toward a group of sheep and hunters, obscure the upraised tail of a canid.

Despite his long acquaintance with Coso archaeology, my guide is not a loquacious one. He does not stuff my head with theories and chronologies. I hear no lectures about the complex cultural dynamics of Great Basin aboriginals. He rarely points out a specific figure or panel. I am left to find my own. I do not wonder what the images mean. Instead, I ask myself, Why are these thoughts in *this* place?

No one has visited this canyon in a long time. The sole sign of human presence is a bucket-shaped carapace of thick rusted metal lying in our sandy path, a chunk of missile dropped from the heavens. The rock art remains untouched—no initials, no scratch-over markings, no bubba glyphs (bullet holes). The metaphor of our millennium, the rare modern glyph inserted among the graffiti of antiquity, can be found in an adjacent canyon, where someone has pecked $E = mc^2$.

The canyon widens to a broad amphitheater. The sky is more open here, a perfect spot for lunch once I am assured that large metal objects won't drop onto our heads. I am alert for jets but pretend that I am not. My visitor badge is a kind of pledge to refrain from memorizing the behavior of contemporary naval aircraft.

We sit against boulders in the warm sun. Above us stretches a landslide of boulders covered with images of sheep, some of them life-size. The slope holds a band of bighorns on ledges of black rock.

Clayton Eshleman is a poet who, for various reasons, some of them wounded and dark, wanted to learn something. *Learn something:* In this regard, he quotes poet and polymath Charles Olson: "'It doesn't matter whether it's Barbed Wire or Pemmican or Paterson or Iowa.'"

Eshleman chose to learn as much as he could about the Paleolithic cave art of Lascaux, Combarelles, Chauvet, Pech Merle, and other sites in southwestern Europe, underground chambers of polychrome frescoes associated with human existence from 9,000 to 35,000 years ago.

Eshleman believes that the birth of metaphor, the seed of narrative, came when "people began to separate the animal out of their about-to-be-human heads and project it onto cave walls." Held in the hand of our species, tool and pigment created a line on stone. The hand curved the line into a horn or head or rump, the shape of the creature itself. Shading hinted at volume. Energy came from a thrust of neck, motion from the stretch of limbs.

Each stroke fit the perception of an animal form, the *memory* of a form. The forms were of those with whom these people had an unbearably deep bond. Was there not also aesthetic pleasure in this? The art was anything but clumsy. With stunning grace, the full bestiary of the Paleolithic was rendered: bison, horses, panthers, ibex, bears, reindeer, and other creatures. The art came out of the stone, Eshleman writes, "as if the earth was seen as a ripe pelt of animals."

What I will give you, of course, are merely brushstrokes, the woe-fully incomplete distillation of others' hard-won research, a bag-lunch lecture, let us say, heard while the boulder backrest roughs up your shoulder blades, prickles of saltbush stab you, and sharp pebbles pierce your butt.

Erudite perspectives have been brought to southwestern rock art, even to this slope of life-size sheep and processions of horned archers, the set of footprints leading up-slope. These drawings are by no means meaningless. They represent high metaphor and deliberate investment in the supernatural. With a kind of barmy delight in the idea that the drawings are ultimately indecipher-able, I believe that the best experts on meaning are the experts who say, "We don't know." On safer ground, however, context for the rock art can be described.

Here, as in the caves of Europe and the alcoves of Baja Cali-fornia, stone was a medium for thought. The earliest Coso images, including a motif of bighorn sheep, may be more than sixteen thousand years old, dating from the Ice Age. People had been in the region a long, long time, with changes in subsistence and culture as the climate changed, in a general trend, from wet to drier.

Rock engraving as a native idiom continued in and around the Coso Range throughout the millennia, then flourished in a con-centration of canyons roughly from one thousand to fifteen hun-dred years ago. That the bulk of the petroglyphs are believed to fall within this span makes them comparatively recent, the work of the late prehistoric and the early historic periods.

Inhabitants of the Great Basin during these two periods are loosely defined as pre-Numic and Numic, respectively, not for a "tribal" nomenclature but for a common language stock. These hunter-gatherers spoke related languages, shared cultural similar-ities, and interacted with one another in this expansive region, including the deserts and valleys of eastern California, where their descendants still reside.

Studies of regional native groups, as well as sophisticated dating techniques, tell us the who of Coso rock art and edge toward the why.

One school of interpretation falls along the lines of "hunting magic": The people brought their desire to kill, eat, and wear animals, especially bighorn sheep, onto the rock. Weapons, hunters, dogs driving game to ambush—such motifs formed a literal reading of the hunt. They recalled, or urged, the procurement of food. In some eyes, the obsession with the desert ungulate, not an easy or frequent meat source, constituted a "sheep cult," which (a long stretch here) contributed to the decline of the species.

Other theorists suggest that something beyond menu might be embedded in this extraordinary art. The animals depicted were not the animals that people often ate. The mainstay of the European Paleolithic diet, for instance, was red deer, yet artists covered the caves with bison. The Numic groups covered the stone with bighorns, but they ate seeds, pinyon nuts, and rabbit, so much rabbit that the middens around habitation sites are thick with their bones. Bighorn, antelope, and mule deer provided occasional additions to these staples.

A different interpretation of Coso rock art decontrusts the theory of hunting magic and links ethnography—accounts that describe native beliefs and practices from the past century—with the archaeological data. Drawing largely from the work of archaeologist David Whitley, this angle of study speculates that Numic artists used the stone for drama, for dreams, for the animals' source of vitality. Nearly all of this effort was directed at the weather.

The ethnographic record, Whitley tells us, supports the idea that the motifs of Coso rock art were the expression of shamanistic beliefs and visions. As a powerful functionary in Numic society, the shaman treated illnesses, cured rattlesnake bites, and found lost objects. He (shamans were invariably male) was well practiced in the arts of augury and was sometimes called upon to change the direction of the wind.

In order to influence physical events like wind and sickness and social disharmony, a shaman had to tap other levels of reality, a world not overtly visible yet rich in dreamlike imagery. He put himself into trances, met and used spirit animal helpers, tapped their power. The shaman, Clayton Eshleman writes, acts as "a kind of magnetized psychic quagmire for his group."

The bighorn sheep served a shaman with a specialty: "rain doctor." Widespread native belief linked this animal with rain. When a sheep was killed, it was said, rain fell. Those who dreamed of killing bighorn sheep were particularly adept at affecting weather.

Rock-art dating suggests that the engravings intensified during a severe drought across the Great Basin and Southwest. A collective pull on rain, and its symbolic association with bighorn sheep, found its locus in the mountains of fire (*Coso* from a Shoshonean word for fire). The Coso Range became renowned as a center of rain shamanism. Whitley writes, "Not only did surrounding groups seek out shamans from the Coso region for rain-making ceremonies, but the last living Numic rain shaman travelled specifically to the Cosos to make rain."

Narrative and symbolism, repeated endlessly on the basalt fissures of the Cosos, gave entry to the supernatural world, wherein lay powers over the natural. The record on the rock face invested the visions with great potency. A weather doctor dreams. A spirit helper dies. The rain comes.

Near the base of the cliff, a rock artist laboriously etched two rams in side profile. Instead of curling back from the forehead as real horns do, the rams' horns face front, forming the stylized double arc of a bird in flight. It looks as if the rams are wearing their horns sideways. From nose to tail, the boat-shaped body of the larger ram is longer than my outstretched arms. His rack could fit on my head and break my skinny little neck with its weight.

In these canyons, the sheep-figure styles bear iconic similarities, but the details never seem to repeat themselves. A ram is drawn with reversed horns, as if a strong tailwind had blown his coiffure forward over his eyes. Several sheep have inner sheep: a smaller figure incised inside their bodies. One sheep mounts another. A herd of rams runs across an outcrop, their legs as long and gangly as a giraffe's. An anthropomorph with ear pendants faces a ram that appears to be decapitated.

Among the figures at our lunch spot are sheep with two heads, one on each end of a single body, so that the direction of the run could be either way, to the left or right, like a Chinese pull toy. A fat sheep on its hind legs leaps up toward a deep crack that is guarded by one of those wily black lizards.

At the top of the cliff, four bighorns are tiered on a stand-alone frieze with breathtaking grace. The next thing above them is the vast Mojave Desert sky, and that is where they seem to be headed: up and over the rim, out of sight. Near this cliff, I feel as if I am animal-watching, an ever imperfect witness to expressions of unfathomable imaginative depth.

We hike out of the black rock narrows and into the green swales of treeless uplands. A few Numic meals—black-tailed jackrabbits—hop away from our path. The sun has grown hotter.

The jets have returned to their lairs and it is safe for Ken to let me out of here. We might just make it out of the wilderness alive.

On the crown of a rise, we stop for a rest and a knee-buckling view. The day feels fluid, the season on the cusp of summer's scorching. What more could a person want than a spring day in the desert with red mariposas, petroglyphs, and a physicist?

To the north lies the glorious valley of the Owens and the smooth blond backs of the Inyo Mountains. To the south, the creosote flats and gypsum basin, where inward-flowing waters vanish. To the west, the silvery blue granite scarp of the Sierra Nevada.

To the east recede pale, silky cutout layers of basin and range, no end to the rhythm, the burnt-salt hole of Death Valley hidden amid the folds, lower than the sea. The mountains above Death Valley hold the region's scant remaining red-blooded desert big-horns, bands that survive the fiercest heat, living on ghost water.

Around here, the locals say that the wind begins at the foot of the Cosos. As everyone knows, weather comes from the west and southwest. The storms that build behind the Sierra carry weight and intent. The storms need to be lured over the dry basins, tricked out of the rain shadow. What better place to call them than from these heights?

THE LOCALS

I put the Cosos behind me and head east toward southern Utah, driving across space that all but the most dust-gagged grouch would call a void. It is space so immense, you cannot actually *see* it, at least not with the part of your brain that copes by dwelling in the middle distance, the safest mental quarter for surviving the everyday crush of towns and cities. Out here in the Great Basin, there is no middle, only the farthest horizon and the minute details of a sagebrush leaf or a grain of sand a few inches from your eyes.

Before I crossed the California-Nevada border, I had taken a rough back road to a rib of wrinkled mountains near Death Valley National Park. Death Valley's herd of about three hundred desert bighorns uses both flanks of this range, oblivious to the political differences in their terrain: protected habitat on the national park side, greater perils of human incursion on the other. I entered as one of the invasive projectiles. In the seven hundred miles between the Sierra and home, there were not many places with bighorn sheep. In the millions of acres around me, the locals could be anywhere.

I chose one drainage among dozens and drove partway up the *bajada* that skirted the base of the mountains, stopped, and parked. I walked for five minutes, glassed a cliff, spotted nine ewes. What was I, some kind of sheep magnet?

The ewes had stocky bodies and thick necks. They looked as pale as ghosts. Compared to that of the sheep of home, their pelage was a lighter gray, the rump patch less distinct. Appearance varies by geographical area and the homeland gene pool.

These ewes showed me features that seemed to arise from their place. I watched them for a while. And what they did, mostly, was bury their noses in wildflowers.

Back on the highway, heading east, the windshield reverie turns to the biology of local adaptations and a less esoteric sub-tickle about the need to find a telephone somewhere after the next hundred empty miles.

Take, for example, local color. At home in the redrock canyons of the Colorado Plateau, the side-blotched lizards have buff-colored backs with a hint of rose. They live in a buff-rose world. The charcoal-colored lizards that I saw in the Cosos camouflaged themselves against the dark basalt. In the white sand playas of New Mexico, the bleached earless lizard evolved a white col-oration to blend with the snow-white gypsum crystals beneath its feet.

In their dry, unpredictable environment, the four subspecies of desert bighorn favor a metabolism that accommodates drought. They have smaller bodies and shorter legs than their northern cousins. Their horns are larger, a feature that is believed to per-form a thermoregulatory function in extreme heat.

These creatures become who they are by adapting to a partic-ular geography and biotic condition. They are idiosyncratic and local. They are nature's specialists. If their populations are small or confined to remnant habitat, or if they depend on a precarious niche or food source, the risk of extinction can intensify.

A changing world has instead favored the generalists, the animals that adapt, often aggressively (think of coyotes and cat-fish), to the presence and behavior of millions of human beings. As robust competitors, the generalists often displace the native species, which shrink in numbers, lose genetic vigor, and become more or less captive on small refugia. The generalists use us, live at our fringes, or move in among us. *Wild*life is gone, a cynic might say. We now live amid the feral.

The desert bighorns' intractable faith to their homelands seems both to save and to doom them. Perhaps they would fare better if they were not so quirky and perishable, if they were not so bloody local, if they were not so "inconveniently" themselves.

I carry my shrieky sarcasm down the Nevada highway, aiming the truck east at a cross-grain to the north-south basin and range rhythm. Somewhere out there is a telephone.

In a press of culture that lurches toward the numbing conformity of a universal (call it the species *Homo sapiens consumerii*), there is less room for local peculiarities and colors. Weather becomes not an adventure but an impertinence. You no longer know where the rain comes from. Everything looks the same. You lose the safe places and the foreboding niches. A Petco now sits over the lip of the arroyo where, according to the old folks, the spooks and skinwalkers lived. The diner with that edgy menu now has an espresso machine from Italy.

Airtight allegiance to place could make you a loser, left behind by the great sweep of a monochromatic, generalist world.

There comes a time in a woman's life when she is quite relieved not to be smart anymore, when she surrenders a certain cognitive alertness and leaves life's irksome details to others. She conveys an aura of lofty preoccupation, as if she were on the brink of solving the world's most profound philosophical dilemma. Meanwhile, she is actually . . . well, she is not wise, or cosmic, or visionary. She is simply *spaced-out*. Such absentmindedness does not lend itself to trouble unless one happens to be driving across Nevada.

The long, lonely road rises and falls in a breathing rhythm of block faults, of dark mountains and pale valleys. Ascent, summit, descent. The bright sun floods the highway with a fierce gold light. For miles and miles, I encounter no other vehicles. Each empty valley gives way to seductive fantasy: Maybe I'll live here, I think. Or there. Maybe here.

Somewhere in a glorious eternity of sky and sagebrush, I pull over at a lone roadside outpost to make my phone call at last. Either there is no sign at the store or, daydreaming and road-numb, I miss it. The blockish red building is obviously commercial. It is a place that reeks of copper-wire communications technology—a *pay phone,* maybe a pay phone that has yet to be gut-shot or ripped out of the wall by angry losers like me who don't own cell phones.

The door sticks. I push hard and it flings open with a loud crash, my body a backlit spaghetti-Western silhouette standing beneath the transom.

There is a bar. There are women who are not dressed for cool weather. They glare at me as if I were about the twenty-eighth extraterrestrial to drop by that day, like when was it ever going to end, Nevada being a state that could really grow sick and tired of space aliens. I wonder if there is a phone. I wonder why six blondes would sit around in a bar in their underwear in the middle of the day.

The bartender speaks with courteous indifference. "We won't sell you a drink," she announces. "And you're not looking for work, right?"

"I'm looking for a phone," I say to a wave of eye rolling by my hosts. Business is slow—not exactly rush hour. Lipstick is re-applied. Satin camisoles are flounced with yawny tedium. Everyone is wearing dangerous shoes.

The bartender's bangs are moussed into a stiff crest. She is very athletic-looking in a red kimono the size of a cocktail napkin. It *is* a cocktail napkin. She figures I am so clueless, so pathetically uncellular, she will, this once, help me out. "Use our phone," she offers. When she walks over to the end of the bar to pick up a cordless telephone off its cradle, her bangs precede her by three inches.

If a man walks in, I tell myself, I will just pretend I'm the accountant.

When I finish my call, I thank the bartender. A million questions swell inside my head like aerosol foam. I envision a session of candid shoptalk over cups of herbal tea, secrets of the trade revealed, perhaps a comparison of the sexual fetishes of ranch hands versus those of the local road crews. Maybe they could do something with my hair. But I inquire only about the next town.

"Fifty miles up the road," the bartender replies. "It's flat broke and leaking people. At the rate of one or two families a month, they pack up and move to Vegas."

With this mantra of the rural desert West, I can commiserate. I know what heat and isolation and wind can do to plans to lead Normal Lives. I know about feuds and how people get cheesed off at each other for about thirty-five years but never remember what the fight was about. How everyone starts to look like the country around them, squinty and restless and wily. Maybe they eat rabbits. Maybe some simply pack up and move away.

The only certainty is the certainty of what they leave behind: thunder in August, heart-crushing love affairs with the light, no money. How warm air rises from the valleys at noon and comes down cool from the high country as the sun goes down. How the ground beneath your feet shapes your muscles. How where you live—the locale—makes you who you are.

I say good-bye to the blondes and I am back on the highway, riding the Great Basin's wide-open swells. I gas up in the leaky town. Not many live here in the first place, and now they are exiting like tumbleweeds with a marketing plan. Las Vegas booms, the fastest-growing city in the West. The more you fill it, the emptier it gets.

Everyone has work to do, I think. Everyone needs a job. If I had been less spaced-out, less enamored of the landscape outside my truck window, I would have missed the one and only time in my roaming life to ever wash up at a bordello. I would have had a lesser picture of Nevada's fluid employment opportunities.

Tough women in charge of details. Women making a living and treating a traveler like a human being.

I drive on. The wind picks up a tumbleweed and blows it straight at me. It bounces off the wheel well and rolls over the hood, on its way to Las Vegas. This broad shelf of broken country from the Sierra to the Colorado Plateau: it feels like one piece. One piece of home.

MAY

In May, you fix the flat side of your feet to a patch of desert and rejoice in the revelation that nothing is under your control. The intensity of colors is hallucinatory and the weather can be trusted. The air feels like velvet but tastes of the coming summer heat. Arms want to be bare, hair left to the breeze. It is impossible to go indoors before dark. I feel the momentum of new life in the desert as a mass rather than time, something held in the rock itself, the way it takes the light.

May's ambitions yearn for pure motion. The river offers balance between the languid and the reckless, and I travel it often. Before the searing heat comes, there is time, too, to move about the canyon country on foot, looking for bighorns, looking for crowns of magenta blooms atop burly barrels of hedgehog cactus, looking for something within myself in a place too deep to identify. May is *añoranza,* a longing, as in "to fill one's heart with."

For what the sun does this time of year, words from Pierre Teilhard de Chardin come to mind: *lucid intoxication.* Light dazzles every surface, bends the heart. Red cliffs, khaki river, coral sand dunes. Celadon lichen on upsweeps of beige sandstone. Silver ganglia-rooted cottonwood trunks half-exposed in the river's cut banks. Blue-black junipers that lean out over the mesa, telling you the shape of the wind.

On a rise of sand and slickrock we call Wild Onion Mesa, I seek green-topped pearlescent bulbs with hints of pink. But there are no wild onions to be found this year. The drought leaves them dormant. Instead, yellow flax, a variation of blue flax, is in flower amid the ephedra, bearing diminutive cups in Tibetan colors: orange, saffron, gold.

The lower elevations display a sweeping purple sea of scorpionweed flowers—acre after acre, growing as thick as a wheat field. By itself, scattered on the gravelly pediment it prefers, scorpionweed, a phacelia named for flower heads that coil like a scorpion's tail, is relatively nondescript. In the billions this year, its explosion is a mystery. Not even the longtime locals remember anything like it. Where did all their seeds come from? How many years had they stayed dormant, banking their bloom until this one year, this one week in May, even as the drought still plagues us?

On a windy day, I walk a high rim above sheep country and find acres of mariposa lilies among the scorpionweed. Their goblet-shaped flowers range from the palest pink to shades of lavender. Milky green stems, as slender as twine, raise them to the sun. The strongest wind gusts flatten them to the ground. Why does the wind not shred them? What binding agent holds paper-thin petals to stem? When will they end their pollinator seduction and release a blizzard of pink?

As I hike, I cannot find a stepping place without scorpionweed or mariposa lilies underfoot, so thickly do they cover the ground. At my watching post, I carefully place my feet on two flat rocks and sit on a third rock so I do not crush any flowers.

Below the rims, along the river, the wind turns canopies of emerald cottonwood leaves inside out, revealing their silvery undersides. The wind sends clouds of sand so high into the air, a rosy haze blocks the sun. The hurricane of sand through the canyon nearly obscures the sheep. They turn away from it and nonchalantly chew the new greenery. Purple blooms stick out from the corners of their mouths.

At home, we fill the garden beds with seeds and seedlings, the promise of summer food. Stalin has disappeared, gone to some flicker gulag, and the Say's phoebes rebuild their nest in the eaves and raise a brood in peace. A bull snake slithers through one of the flower beds, its body a racy pattern of brown and yellow beneath blue flax and golden California poppies. It sips water from the dripper hose, then coils up under the chili plants.

Down the road, my neighbor tries to cultivate a plot next to her house. The soil is good, but not even burdock, knapweed, or goatheads, everyone's favorite weeds by virtue of having no choice but to surrender to them, grow with their customary vehemence. The plot sprouts a motley scratch of choky-looking things. On this spot, the previous owner of the place penned the coyotes he caught as pups, after he killed the adults. The coyotes gnawed the wire and paced the dirt into shallow trenches. There were faint rumors of caged bobcats, too. Nothing will grow there now. My friend gives up on a garden bed and proclaims, "This will be the coyote sorrow place."

Along with the phacelia explosion, moths explode. They morph from larvae hidden in the vegetation to thousands of winged bits of dull gray flannel, bashing against every surface. They are noctuid moths, a large family of common nocturnal moths. They find their way into the house, live by day on bookshelves or up the sleeves of clothes hanging in the closet, so that when I put a shirt on in the morning, five moths fly out from the cuff. At night, the moths careen around the insides of lamp shades. When the house is pitch-dark—we live far from any artificial light—they strain against the skylight above the bed, pulled to the glass by the stars.

Our screen house fills with moths and the riddle of how they get in but cannot get out. Hundreds cover the screen walls. Bodies fall to the floor. It is both B movie and a bother. Before a guest sleeps there, I must sweep up dead moths and the film of powder they leave from their papery wings.

At the door, I flick on a camp flashlight. Like a magnet, the fat beam lures the live ones away from the screens. I walk away into the night, followed by an undulating Pied Piper wave of flying noctuids. The guest sleeps in the screen house without moths in his face. By the next day, a hundred more moths are inside again. The phoebes feed them to their chicks. The chicks hulk up and spill out of the nest, moth-fattened, glowering down at us like tiny vultures.

On the river sandbars inside the canyon, Canada geese lead troops of olive-green goslings with robust bodies and wings so stubby, you wonder at the force that will, in a matter of weeks, extend them to nearly three feet across. When the goslings tire of their march, they plop down in little puddles of fluff.

Ravens stuff a mess of branches and twigs into a notch high in a cliff, filling it with their raucous charcoal offspring. The raven-itos glare at their parents, who cannot resist playing with a piece of windblown bubble wrap. They stab and pop the plastic. When they see that I am watching, they stop and try to look deeply mysterious. The sun crawls up the canyon rims, warming the walls, but the ravens' nest remains shaded all day.

Mark returns from the river to report six bighorn rams across from one of his camps. They fed safely in the heart of Ram Land, a group of males aged four and older, with at least a hundred pounds of headgear among them.

They acted as if their horns itched, Mark said. One of the rams furiously rubbed his rack on a juniper. The other five rams sought bushes and swept their curls back and forth on sturdy branches. The contagious horn rubbing turned into lackluster posturing—extended necks, flared nostrils, bulging eyes—then a keen interest in filling their bellies.

Compared to the ewes, few of the Blue Door rams are marked, but one in this group wore an ear tag and radio collar: Ram 930. He limped badly and would not put weight on one of his front legs, Mark said. If most of your movement is vertical, as if you must move up and down skyscrapers made of loose, hanging boulders, the loss of agility can be catastrophic. Time after time, the other rams butted him off his bed.

By the river, in camp, I sit in the shade of a willow, waiting for the heat to break. I feed my head with an Italian opera and as I listen to the tape, I catch myself making Pavarotti eyebrows. Whenever he hits a high note, I see those black brows slant in darts of winsome precision.

He inflates his barrel chest and sings until you think your heart will crack open like a hopeless coconut. Verdi, only Verdi, the tenor's native tongue. The river swirls by as if orchestrated to the same music. Tanagers migrate upriver through the willows. Claret cup cacti bloom in midlife-crisis red, and three bighorn sheep stand on the opposite side of the river, insanely jealous of my camp opera across from them.

Both ewes wear radio collars. One has a red ear tag. The third sheep, a yearling ram, still has a babyish face, but his horns are popping boldly out of his skull, growing from thick blue-gray bases. Horns and skull bones grow rapidly for the first three years; then serious butting begins. In the meantime, he takes the company of the older ewes and lurks in the willows, trying to spy on me.

Early May marks the peak of lambing season for the Blue Door Band. Those born earliest are now a month old. The last of the lambs will come by mid-June. Boulders and willow thickets hide the ewes' rear ends, so I cannot see if their bags are swollen, a sign of one of three possibilities: imminent birth, a lamb born and suckling (current whereabouts unknown), a lamb lost so recently the mother's milk has yet to dry up. The absence of a lamb on each ewe is worrisome. To keep the band going, it should have healthy lamb recruitment: productive ewes and a high rate of survival among the year's crop.

Lactating ewes need water and nutritious green food for their milk supply. As long as food and water—potholes, springs—are available in the cliffs above us, the ewes tend to keep their newborns near the secluded lambing grounds. As the spring annuals and perennials dry up, summer temperatures rise, and the lambs grow stronger, lambs and ewes move to slopes where more food and other sheep are found. Then, for much of the summer, the ewe bands and nurseries stay closer to the river. Perhaps these ewes lost their lambs and came off the canyon walls.

Their curiosity is their own doing. They have wandered into view, unfazed by a human and her raft, whereas I fret into hysteria about disturbing the band during lambing season. Slowly, I raise my binoculars to my eyes. They bat their long lashes. The river between us, slow and tawny, crisscrossed with orange dragonflies, says everything about their sense of security. The river is a firm boundary. The ewes won't cross it. They hate to get their feet wet.

The sun's ferocity peaks and we grow sleepy on this riverbank. I unfurl my Thermarest pad under the willows. Four moths fly out from the rolled nylon. The bighorns amble along the talus, dropping their noses to sniff the ground, scraping here and there with a hoof, ready to bed down. The yearling ram and one ewe drop to their bellies, stare at me, and strain to hear Luciano's boundless canto.

The ewe with the red ear tag walks up the slope to the seam between talus and cliff face. The high, narrow ledge holds a crescent of shade, a blue-violet lens in the ambient red-gold sun. For a moment, she stands in a posture of caution. She burps a froggy-sounding bleat, then finishes her climb to the ledge. Up from the rock pops a lamb, a spindly fur-ball lamb.

The lamb is less than two weeks old, a leggy nine-pound mouse-colored package of hope. She has a small hornless head, concave face, big ears, huge dark eyes, and animated ears. Her hind legs seem disproportionately husky for the rest of her body, an exaggeration, perhaps, of the haunch muscle that will be needed to push her up and down cliffs.

Since birth, her pointed hooves have darkened and hardened. Their tips came out soft and white through the tender birth canal, then held her in a wobbly upright stance within minutes. The hours after birth coalesce all instinct of sheep as a follower species: The lambs will go where their dams go—anywhere.

The ewe has parked her lamb within hearing distance, possibly within sight as well, while she grazes along the talus slope. The arrangement accommodates the lamb's rest and the ewe's need to eat, as all the while both stay near escape routes. Freezing in position, hiding, and camouflage protect the fawns of deer and antelope. The adaptive strategy for bighorns is to be born well developed, agile, and speedy in precipitous terrain. This female lamb can jump, bolt, and judge distances, making instantaneous decisions about running around a crevice that its larger mother would leap over. The lamb reads the rock with her genes.

The lamb stops the ewe in a frontal block, then sidles up to her flank, her stubby dark tail quivering and twirling against her pale rump like a propeller. She drops her head under the mother's belly, whomps her snout against the udder a few times, then suckles eagerly. The ewe stands briefly, looking indifferent, then drifts off and beds down on the ledge.

The lamb tucks herself against her mother's uphill flank, away from the sheer drop. When they are very young, it seems that the lambs rest and move on the uphill side of adults. Older and in nurseries, they run with a particularly fast ewe or bunch up with other lambs, scattering, then gathering in ebbs and flows of energy.

The second ewe is off her bed and showing me her hindquarters. Her bag is shrunken and dry. Either she is barren or she lost her lamb some time ago. In this rugged country, lamb remains cannot be easily found. Causes of death—predation, poor mother-lamb bonds, respiratory illness, overall puniness—remain uncertain.

The balance between natality and mortality, the stability of the population and its growth since its bottleneck years, pose complexities that underscore my ignorance. Will the band have enough progeny to keep it viable? Will the canyon always have native desert bighorns? We locals need one another.

What is born with the lamb across the river is more than a nine-pound neonate ungulate. A living tradition, too, comes with each birth: overt and subtle social behaviors, with much significance—the equivalent of language?—invested in horns, heads, rump colors, and other physical features. Each lamb possesses the tenacity, albeit often challenged, of what biologist Valerius Geist calls "a particularly durable ice age creature." This ice-age ancestry encoded desert into its genes: smaller body, shorter hair, paler pelage than northern counterparts; a flair for sedimentary rock, a fondness for cactus.

The lamb I am watching is philopatric, an instant homebody, faithful to her natal ground and to matrilineal groups that endow her with the homeland map. This fidelity inclines her species to sedentariness, a biological term for creatures restricted to limited areas. These sheep are like mollusks attached to an entire canyon.

The lamb's heart rate will rise as distance separates her from cliffs and escape terrain. Unless the nature of predation on this range changes dramatically, a mountain lion will not likely eat her. She will run for her life when she hears a helicopter. She won't cross the river. She will hate to get her feet wet.

All four sheep have risen from their day beds. The adults graze as if they have not eaten since the Holocene. To reach some of the greenery, the sheep must act like giraffes. The young ram stands atop a boulder and stretches his neck to mouth a cliffrose. The lamb stares at me and wonders what else the cat dragged in.

Eventually, these animals will join larger groups of ewes and lively playmate lambs. It will be bedlam. For now, though, there is a quiet concentration on grass, leaves, and wildflowers.

Despite the drought, the sheep find adequate forage and maintain their vigor. They eat all my beloved familiars, the blazing miracle of spring growth in harsh, arid country: ricegrass, galleta, blackbrush. They devour the sticklike stems of Mormon tea—sheep asparagus—and the succulent young shoots of Russian thistle. These baby tumbleweeds are such a favorite among bighorns, some biologists call Russian thistle their "ice-cream plant." In dry spells and hot weather, the sheep eagerly seek the dry stalks of sego lilies and dig up the bulbs of mariposa lilies. They eat the scarlet blossoms of Indian paintbrush, the fruits of prickly pear cactus.

I, too, would eat a mariposa lily, a million petals of paintbrush and cliffrose. When one of the ewes across the river lips the pure, creamy velvet cups that crown a yucca plant, I can feel the silken petals on my own tongue. The bankside willows are all musky sweetness, the pale rose sand warm on my bare feet.

Pavarotti slides his fearless voice, so full of grief and yearning, into the cool river under a burning sun. I want to rise up and bite the desert to bits. I want to understand what these wild creatures, this canyon and river, this spring day in the high-crowned desert, flooded with peach-colored light, are trying to express, for surely it is in some way akin to what we long to say in our own singing.

The biologists who study this band of bighorns divide their time between the desert and their home in Montana. As keepers of knowledge about the group, they are drawn by the critical time of lambing season into weeks of observation. They track radio signals and record details of physical condition and social behavior.

They know what everyone is eating. They map movements and grow uneasy about roaming rams. They note missing individuals and tally the year's lamb crop. They count sheep.

When the biologists arrive in early spring, I am at first reluctant to share the band. For so long I have been in deep sheep shadow, this uncommon refuge of sanctified thought. I watch them, and when I sometimes get bored, I read books in their presence. I amble around their terrain as if the canyon holds nothing but us and a rare contentment in a difficult world. I have become proprietary.

This selfishness evaporates the moment I see Dave Stevens and Nike Goodson Stevens at work. While I may be an anthropomorphizing, limpet-brained mote, these two are the true shepherds of this native flock.

On a rim above the river, Nike holds her antenna high in the air. She slowly sweeps it in all directions until her receiver picks up a signal bleeped from a collared bighorn. She runs through each assigned frequency and comes up with six bleeps—six sheep accounted for.

Taking into consideration signal direction and strength and other nuances of radio telemetry—it takes practice to read them— she can pinpoint an animal's whereabouts. The topography below us is rough: tiered stacks of jagged rock, carved arroyos, shallow, hanging canyons, walls that break into cliffs and debris fans. If a sheep is in an alcove or behind a rock, its battery-powered collar may send a weak or uncertain signal. Time and patience refine the bearings. Notes are taken. The antenna turns.

Having noted today's clearest bleeps, Nike sets us the task of making visual locations. Even with binoculars, I cannot find a single animal. They are doing their rock imitations. Dave is a master at sightings even with unaided eyes. Eventually, we have several live sheep in view and under the scrutiny of binoculars and spotting scope.

All but one of the ewes have lambs. Only a few days before, Dave and Nike spotted the now lambless ewe with her offspring. They must now presume that her lamb has died. When you see a ewe band, the nursery seems abundant—lambs everywhere, scrambling up and down the rocks. Yet seldom is survival 100 percent, a lamb for every ewe. For the first two weeks of their lives, the young are vulnerable.

Another worry: Thirteen or more unmarked ewes are missing. Nike can estimate this number based on the ratio of collared to uncollared females. Out of the herd total of about eighty sheep, thirteen is a significant blank. Poachers prefer rams. Extraterrestrials prefer Nevada. That leaves rustlers or another vanishing act.

"Do you think they crossed the river?" I ask.

"Ewes hate to get their feet wet," Nike says.

Jokingly, she tells me that the ewes were plucked out of the canyon by other desert bighorn biologists, rustled as illegal transplants by states that want to increase their sheep numbers and reap revenue from trophy ram hunts. But clearly she is worried. Nike frets over missing sheep, lost lambs, walkabout rams venturing too close to domestic sheep. She worries about poachers, bobcats, mountain lions, disease, die-offs, any of the numerous threats to a relict population.

Using binoculars, she once watched dogs wildly chase a young bighorn ewe. "The chase was serious," she told me. "The dogs cornered the ewe on a ledge. She shook and shivered, obviously terrified. Dave and I were a half a mile away and couldn't do a thing about it." The dogs slunk off, and Dave and Nike are still trying to determine if they were feral or wandered far into wild country from a human settlement.

The cadence of Nike's voice hints at her roots in Virginia and Louisiana, not the most likely places to spawn a lifelong devotion to western megafauna. Yet she had the kind of childhood intimacy with nature that seems almost storybook these days, one that was possible before asphalt and minimalls devoured open lands and the media stream devoured young minds.

"From the time I was six until I was thirteen years old, we lived at the edge of Williamsburg and had woods and a field near our lot," she said. "I used to ramble in the woods and field daily. I was a real bookworm and especially enjoyed books about animals, wild and domestic. When I learned, at an early age, that there were people who actually studied animals for a living, that sounded like an ideal job."

Nike earned her own way to the West and a doctorate in wildlife biology. She worked on several studies with Dave, who at the time was the chief research biologist at Colorado's Rocky Mountain National Park. Eventually, they married. After working together in Alaska, they made Montana the base of various research activities.

Early in her career, Nike spent a number of years studying the effects of domestic sheep on bighorn sheep. She is not shy about telling anyone and everyone just how bad it is to have the species in near proximity. She can make killer shrimp gumbo. She is allergic to deer. When she travels around the Southwest's canyons and mountains, she sees the land not so much as scenery, but as habitat. If places are empty of bighorns, she says, "This place feels so empty."

Looking through my binoculars, I have in view a distinctive five-year-old female. "That's our weird ewe," Nike tells me. "She has never had a lamb. She's probably barren, maybe a result of inbreeding."

We are grateful for a day without wind. The spotting scope stays steady on its tripod. We gather information for each animal: age, condition, daily patterns (feed, rest, feed, move, rest, feed). We note whether a ewe is approaching parturition, if she has a lamb at her side, if a lamb is missing, or if the ewe is too young to lamb. Maternal behavior, group size, age-sex composition. Each observation—Dave and Nike are out in the study area every day—adds up to a dynamic portrait of the band.

Against a trend in recent years from generalist field biologists to those with narrower specialties in a single species—the grizzly expert, the wolf-study woman, the person who spent forty years with sucker-bearing cephalopods—Dave's generation is at the tail end of the generalists. He worked in Rocky Mountain National Park for twenty-four years, keeping a broad array of fauna healthy, everything from mule deer and Rocky Mountain bighorns to greenback cutthroat trout.

His grandfather was a Forest Service ranger and his father was career National Park Service, as well. Dave grew up in Yellowstone, his front and back yards a multimillion-acre volcanic plateau with a hefty portion of the lower forty-eight's wild mammal biomass. His toys were elk teeth. His father did what rangers used to do before they became prisoners inside their pickups: He ranged. He made his backcountry winter patrols on skis, spent summers deep in the park, and then, when the school year began, moved his family to the small community of Mammoth, on the park's northwest border.

Dave is a hunter: a stoic, patient, nongadget kind of hunter, possessing what Mark, also a Montanan, calls "Buddhist stealth." He has eaten the heart of a bear. He told us that he once found the carcass of a bull elk and, underneath it, the remains of a mountain lion. The lion had successfully killed the elk, probably by a neck grip and snap of vertebrae, but was pinned by the elk's huge bulk as it fell. In every death in the wild, there is a story.

After Rocky Mountain National Park and his stint in Alaska, Dave retired from the Park Service. To continue a life in the field, he and Nike took on a part-time study of the band of bighorns on this big desert river. Their office is the size of half a Middle Eastern country, remote and not easily accessible, a Chemehuevi-style geography defined by sheep rather than by human use.

The day's work is done. I open my pack to put away my binoculars. Two moths fly out. We load up and hike across the open desert to the kidney-smashing excuse for a road out. Dave and Nike will search again for the unmarked ewes, trying to establish, before summer's heat slows down all local mammals, a profile of the year's reproduction. They will also venture up-canyon to Ram Land to check on the boys.

This month, most of the rams appear healthy. They decorate the cliffs with their bachelor bands, woefully irrelevant this time of year, as the ewes do the work of bringing young into the world. But there is the limping ram that Mark observed. And another unmarked ram has made an unusual move: He has crossed the river. On separate occasions, Dave and Nike, then Mark and I spotted him near the banks, looking as if he were the only bighorn left in the universe.

The ram has but one horn, a curl so heavy on one side, you would think his head would tip over with the weight. Dave and Nike speculate that he lost a horn in battle. Ram horns catch and neutralize blows from opponents. One-horned, he is less shielded from butts to head and body and clearly at a disadvantage.

Perhaps the other rams harassed him until he packed up and left. He is fattening up on riparian vegetation that he has all to himself. We think of him as the sheep version of Ferdinand, the pacifist, matador-adverse bull in the children's tale, his nose full of wildflowers, a dreamy, far-off look in his eyes. Testosterone and the rut, however, may bring the errant ram back among the clashes.

"Rams," Nike has told me, "have a rough life."

On the riverbank, a dense thicket of camelthorn blocks my passage, and I must decide whether to lunge through or walk around it. The detour option means that I will miss a stretch of our search area. A lunge through the thicket will expose me to sixty seconds of leg plague. With its inch-long needle-sharp thorns—thorns from root to tip on pliant, lashing stems—camelthorn will shred my bare skin.

River people, a scantily clad lot, do not like scratchy plants to inhibit their carefree flits along gorgeously bare and pure sandbars. What irks them more are *exotic* scratchy plants that inhibit their carefree flits along gorgeously bare and pure sandbars. If there is flesh to be lacerated, let native plants draw the blood.

Camelthorn was one among many nonnative, crazed colonizers to quickly occupy riparian habitat after dams no longer allowed the river to sweep and scour during floods. The plant spreads rapidly by underground rootstock. It is strong enough to push up through asphalt. It is in the pea family and appears on lists of noxious weeds in at least five states. Desert bighorns find this scourge to be quite tasty.

Camelthorn grows in brakes of togetherness rather than as scattered, loner shrubs, so you must find a way to walk and swim around a field of it. My choice at the moment is through or around: blood or beach.

Mark, Dave, and Nike spread out along the riverbank beyond me. We have spaced ourselves so that we can cover a broad swathe in our search. The clues we were given indicated we should comb only a half-mile stretch between a certain rapid and a bend in the canyon. In the earth-toned blend of rock and sand, Dave has told us to look for the orange plastic ear tag.

Snowy tufts of evening primrose dot the upper decks of the sandbar, and the jumbled talus holds rock gardens of prince's plume with swords of yellow blooms and the distinctive fanned gray-green rosettes of narrow-leaf yuccas. The river flows by in a sheet of tawny water, sunlit and dreamy. Far upriver, the raft rocks gently on its tether. Dave stops hiking and appears frustrated. He wonders if we should take our sweep formation away from the river, higher on the talus.

I think about dropping down to the river. Rising thermals carry the spiced honey scent of wet sand along the scrim of water and sandbar. I wasn't going to cross the wretched camelthorn, but I do. And there it is, our quarry, in a spread of brush. I call to the others.

The dead ram lies on his flank, his neck braced back and his nose partly buried in the sand, as if he had slid a few feet on his side. It is neither the repose of violence nor of a go-to-sleep death. Skin, limbs, radio collar, ear tag—all are intact. No sign of bobcat, mountain lion, coyote. No blood, no puncture wounds. The cliff is set too far back from the sandbar for a free fall and crash landing.

Above the body—it is too fresh to call it a carcass—and higher on the sandbar, where the camelthorn thins, there are two bedlike depressions and a faint fretwork of what appear to be the tracks of a gray fox, a visitor rather than the perpetrator. In this dry air, there is not yet rot, not even a cloud of flies. The ram has not been dead for long. On cue, two ravens ride the air to a nearby outcrop and perch quietly, as if three pounds of ebony birds against red rock were invisible.

Sand covers the ram's nose. Eyes normally amber and having dark horizontal pupils have turned black and dull. The horns flare back in a swoop of rough, hardened keratin, their tips broomed and splintered. One horn has lost an inch-wide chunk of outer sheath, probably a battle scar. An uneven patch of fur on the forehead may also be an old abrasion from head bashing.

The ram is about nine years old, caught and collared when he was three, according to Dave and Nike's records. He is Ram 930, seen with a bachelor band along the river not long ago. He was limping, Mark said. Mark had watched the other rams pick on him. They butted him off his food and bed. One ram pressed against him and raised a front leg in a series of powerful ventral kicks.

Nike is surprised that despite what might have been a fractured or broken leg, the ram stayed with the boys rather than sequestering himself. "An injured sheep usually goes off alone or to the periphery of the group. They don't intermingle as often. It's a protective instinct."

The one-horned ram that resembled Ferdinand apparently crossed the river for this reason—to avoid harassment. (We had not seen him for some time.) But Ram 930 remained with the group. His bum leg might have resulted from a blow or a fall, but when Mark saw him, he was not removing himself from the aggressive rams. Judging from his age and horn size, 930 was likely a dominant ram himself.

We stand beside the dead animal. Dave is getting his knife, his very big knife, ready. He and Nike are edging toward a hypothesis that no predator was involved. Nor had the ram lost his balance on a cliff above us and fallen out of the sky to the camelthorn patch. The bad leg did not overtly kill him. Mark had seen him mobile, butting off the big rams that were butting him.

Nike looks down at the ram in the sand and camelthorn and pronounces her verdict: "Ram murder."

I have never seen a knife as sharp as the one Dave holds in his hands, poised to begin the necropsy. If you put yourself within an inch of that blade, flesh would part by sheer entry into its force field. I kneel down and wrap a hand around each of the ram's horns to help Dave lift the head. This is the first time in my life I have touched a desert bighorn sheep. A teaspoon of blood spills from the ram's mouth, blood the color of fresh raspberries.

Dave removes the radio collar and ear tag. Nike works her hands up and down the injured leg from hock to shoulder. "No sign of fracture, no break," she tells us. Dave examines the leg and agrees. They wonder if the injury is high in the shoulder instead, damage serious enough to cripple the ram.

I am astounded at how petit he is. This is a trick that bighorn sheep play on the human mind: not that large an animal, actually, standing on its wild heights, apart, aloof, noble, looking as huge as an elk.

Dave wears rubber gloves. The hunter's knife touches the skin, and before I can breathe, the ram's belly and shoulder are open.

The ram's lungs are full of blood, his heart bloodshot. The front chamber of the sheep's chest is filled with red fluid. Internal bleeding was likely the direct cause of death, but what caused the bleeding in the first place? A blood vessel broken by a blow? A pierced lung? Did he injure his leg in a fall, then, weakened and less nimble, take a death blow to the shoulder?

When he watched Ram 930 with the other males, Mark was close enough to see that his breathing was not labored. With slow internal hemorrhaging, Nike says, the death might have taken time. Whether the two scraped depressions above the dead ram were beds of bachelor companions or beds of his own making cannot be known, but their position seems to indicate a place for dying more than a day bed close to escape terrain.

Dave's long experience as a hunter is apparent in his skilled surgery. The ram's heart is small and dark, once a fleshy pump of eighty beats a minute. His kidneys and other organs show the desert bighorn's adaptations to aridity, a physiology that takes moisture from the vegetation the animal eats and eliminates waste with relatively small water loss. Of course, this ram also quenched his life's thirst with the big sandy river.

The ravens remain like statues until Dave pulls aside a few coils of intestine and opens the gut, which is a swollen army green mass of rumen covered by a thin membrane. The fermentation vat. The desert eaten. The organ that transforms everything from creamy yucca flowers to camelthorn into bone and blood, flesh and sinew, the sustenance of keen vision and a complexity of aggressions with one's head.

The ravens hop off their outcrop and move closer with a guarded impatience. They have waited for something—I guess it's us—to open the carcass for them. They are looking at what could easily be a week's menu of raw meat and guts. There is no frenzy, no circle of turkey vultures. We are surprised to note how little scavenging has occurred since the ram died. The canyon's food is lean, slow food.

After what seem to be but a few cuts, Dave says, "My knife is dull." To me, it looks like it could lop off your entire forearm as if it were a hunk of Gouda cheese.

Dave bags up body tissue to be taken off the river to a veterinarian for analysis. Clues may shed light on the death of the ram and also on his life, his physical condition and signs of respiratory ailments, parasites, sinusitis, or other afflictions, all of which will give Dave and Nike more insight into the herd's health. The one thing that Dave must do for a complete study of Ram 930 is this: cut off his head and take it in.

Dave is so clean and deferential in his work. We know this must happen. We are not queasy. Yet there is in this act something that demands that we behave in a manner that eludes us. Perhaps our distress comes because Mark and I are not hunters. Until this day in May on a remote stretch of river, I have only caressed bones. I was a virgin to the touch of creatures that I had watched for months, alive and animated in their chasm of sun-drenched stone.

Dave and Nike tell me that despite their long experience they, too, feel this way. Nothing can be taken lightly, no gesture made without respect and reciprocity. An elk's body across a dead lion. Hunters who believe that to bring the horns of a wild sheep out of the desert is to invite wind and torment. Long hours of minding this herd, worry over missing ewes, lambs that die. All of the disheartening and exalting turns of creation ingrained in a deep-time bond between place and animal. "Live in Nature," wrote Henry Beston, "and you will soon see that for all its non-human rhythm, it is no cave of pain."

Mark walks to the river, fills his cupped hands with water, and comes back to the ram. He sprinkles it over the flank, the muscles that moved the ram through the canyon.

Downstream, afloat again, we tiptoe the raft past a feisty nursery. Several ewes have brought their lambs down to the banks. With six lambs are adult ewes and juveniles, a flock of fifteen sheep. Nike is adept at counting and recording them even as the sheep bunch up, spread out, then bunch together again like a puzzle in motion.

The lambs buddy up with one another when the group pauses. On the move, they take the flank of a galloping ewe, any ewe, then find playmates again and practice flawless leaps up and down ten-foot-high pinnacles. The commotion seems a combination of play and wariness. The ewes are alert because their lambs are so young. Later, they will act as if their own young bore them to tears.

Among the group are enough unmarked ewes to make Nike feel less apprehensive about her lost sheep. The ewes will be accounted for as ewe-lamb seclusion ends and the birthing season gives way to group life and a settling in for the hot summer. Nike estimates the year's crop at about fifteen to seventeen lambs.

On the mortality side, they can confirm one dead ewe, who likely fell or was caught in a rockfall loosened by last year's monsoons. Below a cliff, they found her radio collar and bones scattered by scavengers. None of us has seen the one-horned Ferdinand ram that crossed the river to sniff wildflowers. His fate may remain unknown. Ram 930, the "murder" victim, died of ritual.

Dave and Nike's published research shows that annual adult ram deaths in this population are four times higher than ewe deaths. Exhaustion and injuries from the rut predispose the rams to accidents. Dave and Nike once watched dominant rams kick a young ram in the testicles. The ram withdrew from his assailants and died shortly after from an infection.

Rams use less secure terrain than do homebody ewes. They often travel solo and without the pooled vigilance of companions. Such trouble befell a ram that wandered near the open country of the canyon rim. Tracks near his carcass implied that a mountain lion, likely a transient and obviously an opportunist, had attacked him from above. At the site of another ram kill, much less of a carcass was left by his human poacher: a gut pile with a radio collar on top of it.

And there are what might be called "foolish sheep moves." When the veterinarian examined the remains of a four-year-old ram, he found signs of a skull injury from fighting. However, the head wound was not the cause of death.

The year the ram died, the spring growth of cheatgrass was especially virulent. Cheatgrass fits the mantra of noxiousness: exotic, scratchy, an aggressive invader of disturbed (overgrazed) land. Cheatgrass bears supple stems and awns when it first sprouts. Bighorns eat cheatgrass while the plant is young and green, then shun it as the awns quickly dry into stiff quarter-inch quills with barbed tips.

The ram may have waited one day too long in the life of hardening cheatgrass awns. During the spring's unusually lush growth, perhaps he ate one mouthful too many. The vet found that a cheatgrass awn had lodged in the ram's throat, opening a window for bacterial infection. Swelling from the infection blocked the ram's throat and he starved to death.

"Number Nine-Three-Oh was a good ram," Dave says as we float between the canyon walls. "I liked that ram."

Dave often talks of individual sheep with the interest of someone who has read and remembered a remarkable biography. "One of our handsome rams" or "one with lots of personality," he will comment. He recognizes sheep in the bloodline of the band's big chocolate-colored ram, a ram notable not only for his color but also for his mature age and size.

There is no easy ticket to longevity. Some large-bodied, big-horned rams burn out early, while shrimpier rams in the same age class may last longer. "Number Nine-Three-Oh was a small ram but a top guy," Dave says, grinning. "I watched him go through puberty."

I am not the first to imagine a retirement home for old rams, a sunny ledge in the canyon ramparts with a decent view of the river and its ridiculous humans, a creaky-boned pod of toothless old geezers with a cloud of indolent flies orbiting their chipped but still operatic curls. Not exactly your hood ornaments.

Rams live by their heads. Horns are weapons, shields, and rank symbols. Combat is not intended to kill or injure, though harm can be done. Rams fight in a long, tedious sequence of blows and counterblows that take on impact like a shock-absorbing wall. Even if it must be determined by combat, rank lets males live in a society with a predictable vocabulary of aggression aimed at breeding success.

Bighorn rams ignore or occasionally charge a disabled animal. Persecution of injured dominants is a moment of directed motion, mixed with the motions of walking, grazing, resting. Mark saw limping Ram 930 among rams of equal size and age, the ones who so often challenge one another. We found his body not long afterward. In animal lives that unfold according to their own instinctive choreography, well beyond human view, this is more of a story than the bighorns usually tell.

The raft rides the slick caps and troughs of a wave train in a rapid. Tied at my feet, resting on the raft floor, is a heavy canvas duffel bag. The boat's motion presses the bag against my leg, and I can feel hard ridged horns through the fabric.

Once off the river, Dave and Nike will take Ram 930's remains to the vet. After the lab work is done, pieces of bone and horn will be given to Navajo medicine men. They will use *tsétah dibé,* the mountain sheep, in ritual and healing.

We have heard from Navajo that bighorns carry clouds on their backs. In the clouds are seeds for corn and other plants. It is also said that when people hunted bighorns in the old days, the hunters slapped the sheep's butchered paunch against a stone. The sound would bring rain. In this association of animal and weather, there is an echo of the faraway Cosos.

Any day now, the canyon will gain the thick summer heat and we will live in an oven of bare, baking rock, the air vibrating with ripples of cicada song. In this desert, you must drink the last of May's ephemeral coolness as if it were a tonic. For a split second, you think of bolting for cooler ground—a high mountain, the breezy seaside—but if, on the other side of that fantasy, you are still here, you will stay for the duration, living close to the river, the only habitable place for miles and miles.

The raft slips downriver, below the heartland of ewe range. As the sun angles its way to the horizon, it leaves blue velvet shade in the cusp of each bend. Beyond the curves, we slip into the red-gold light again.

JUNE

⟑

Binoculars. Notebook, pen, camera. A stash of nuts and yak butter. Mud and plant bits stuck to disheveled clothing: woolly and tweedy, handy for sleeping in. Hair that smells like swamp turf. Calf muscles as hard as cast-iron frying pans from brisk hikes across one mountain drainage and over a pass to another. Senses sharp, vision keen. Could spot the copulation of deranged pygmy badgers from several hundred yards away.

A ride in a skull-rattling Soviet-era helicopter the color of clothes dryer lint, the one and only map of the area sucked out of the open door during a nasty patch of turbulence hit shortly before the chopper sets down on a sodden patch of tundra that is featureless but for the steaming-fresh tracks of a giant but underfed bear. The chopper flies off, will not be back for days—make that weeks—because blizzards will ground it. You figure what the hell, set up your forty-pound canvas pup tent, kill the nearest marmot with your bare hands, skin it, and cook it over a Sterno can.

Time for science.

The image of the wildlife biologist and naturalist a generation or two ago remains iconic, especially from those who chronicled their studies on the page—Murie, Mowat, Mech, Schaller, Matthiessen—and worked when the Earth still offered up vast tracts of wilderness and a bounty of creatures to observe. Even though that bounty has diminished to marginal numbers and desperate listings, and wilderness has shrunk to nature preserves within commuting distance, who would not trade their left kidney for time in spectacular country with intriguing animals?

"I built and furnished a small log cabin close to a nameless little lake near timberline in the virgin wilderness," wrote Valerius Geist as, in 1961, he began his study of Stone's sheep in northern British Columbia.

The neighborhood offered a rich menagerie of far-north fauna: moose, mountain goats, caribou, black bears, grizzly bears, wolves, lynx, waterfowl, grouse, "clouds of willow ptarmigan," and handsome black to silver-gray thinhorn sheep with white bellies and amber horns. Because there had been no grazing by domestic livestock in the study area, Geist said, no introduced species, no mining, roads, or towns, the animals interacted under the relatively autonomous hand of nature.

In subzero weather, when the bitter cold slowed his note-taking hand and his binoculars and scope froze or fogged up, Geist observed the sheep from the warmth of his cabin. For filming, he put on white overalls and a white towel around his head and moved closer. Sometimes he simply placed himself in full view of the sheep and waited until they grew bored with him and resumed their routines.

He watched the Stone's sheep rut, raise young, eat, move about their range, and die. In winter, they foraged on south-facing slopes. In spring, he saw green patches on the mountainsides, where vigorous thatches of new grass sprouted around the edges of long-used sheep beds that were well fertilized by defecations. He noted kills (most by wolves) and shot a few rams of his own, studying their body conformation, beheading them, weighing their horns.

In the Yukon Territory in 1965, Geist fluttered up to sub-Arctic heaven to live with angel sheep—Dall's sheep, in habitat they had likely occupied since the Pleistocene. Research on Rocky Mountain bighorns in Banff National Park in Alberta, Canada, gave him more years in the field.

The Banff sheep did not live in a virgin wilderness, he said, but in country that had seen more than a century of human influences. Elk had plunged to near extinction. Replenished with transplants from Yellowstone National Park, they promptly over-populated and mowed down valley flora.

Wolves were poisoned out—twice—and bison went locally extinct. Bears lived in the garbage dumps. Moose hung out in parking lots, listening to tourists' car radios. The gregarious mountain sheep, too, had the part wild, part zoo, part fashion model peculiarities of park inmates: not hunted, habituated to the proximity of humans, some nearly tame, others a nuisance.

Geist considered the tameness of the Banff sheep an asset. In his 1971 classic, *Mountain Sheep,* he claimed that a "close associa-tion between the investigator and his study animals is, during at least part of the study, a most desirable situation, as it allows him to gain insights unobtainable in any other way."

He seduced the Banff bighorns through their craving for salt. He brought salt to them as if it were candy. The sheep came to recognize him, follow, pester, and butt him. The rams broke out in "slugging matches" in their eagerness to reach the salt he carried. The sheep looked all over the place for him when he climbed a tree to load a camera. They used him as a snowplow, taking the path where he had broken trail.

"It is hard to imagine a wild animal more readily tamed than mountain sheep," he wrote. "They habituate readily to man if not hunted and will accept him as a two-legged salt lick if he so wishes."

Today's field researchers, in minimal-contact style, go to great lengths to avoid disturbing their subjects. They lurk in blinds or behind rocks or on distant rims, using powerful optical devices. They try to catch the animals doing something *wild.* In this light, Geist's style seems extraordinarily intimate.

Distracted by his salt offerings, the sheep let him run his hand along their heads and open their furry ears so that he could read the marking tags inside. From up close, he noted scars, broomed horn tips, bits of an opponent's hair stuck to horns, eyes with cataracts, swellings of preorbital glands. He discovered that some had black tongues and some had pink tongues. The mucous linings of nose and palate could be black, pink, or piebald. The ewes were bigger pests than rams. The lambs were shy.

"They did not mind if I touched their bodies, parted the hair, and extracted ticks from their backs. Most sheep are extremely sensitive to being touched anywhere except their head. One could make most sheep bound up straight by sticking one's finger gently into their ribs just behind the front leg."

Since Geist's work in Canada in the sixties, the basic techniques of fieldwork have not changed dramatically. Grunt hikes, wretched weather, hard boulders for seating. Boundless reservoirs of patience. Scorn cast upon sheep tickling. Less than charismatic note taking. (Day 1: eat, move, rest, eat. Number of lip curls and rear-end sniffs per Class III ram. Calcium content per dry weight of two leaves of *Encelia farinosa*. Day 2: eat, move, rest, eat.) In the past twenty years, however, sheep-watching has been joined by the business of sheep *moving* and the rapidly evolving technology that supports capture and translocation.

Sheep capture in the fifties and early sixties usually involved an elaborate corral or gate-and-panel trap baited with salt, sheep-food pellets, apple pulp, hay, or cabbage (they loved the cabbage), and a burly but quiet team to restrain the animals physically for tagging and treatment. ("A group of noisy, arm-waving men running up is sure to cause undue fright," one wildlife manager wrote.)

Before plastic ear tags came into use, wild sheep wore aluminum livestock tags, plastic streamers, or tape. Handlers experimented with heat brands on horns and freeze branding that turned body hair white with a contrasting symbol or number. Odd bands of red-rumped sheep were sighted after they had been sprayed with dye from an electronically triggered nozzle set up at a water hole.

On many ranges, helicopters and nets replaced corrals and bait, with a gunner aiming a projectile syringe gun to zap drugs into a galloping animal's hip or rump. Immobilizers and neuroleptic tranquilizers (followed by drugs that reversed the effects) numbed the sheep for the handlers, who noted that the drug etorphine often induced the munchies, an uncontrollable urge to eat, when the animal came around.

Today's capture method of choice is more often drug-free. The animals are restrained in soft mesh slings and hobbles. Blindfolds calm them. Small but efficient crews work quickly, among them a veterinarian to watch for signs of stress.

No animal has asked for his ears to be punched or his neck to carry a radio, for dye on his derriere, or for a juicy mouthful of galleta grass to be interrupted by a chase over a havoc of boulders, splitting him off from his companions.

The intervention is skilled, short in duration, and infrequent in the lifetime of these animals. It is, we believe, in their best interest. It is, as long as we refuse to relinquish our occupation of habitat or to curb our monstrous appetite for more, a strategy of island management. But it is not wildness.

Perhaps this is one reason the work of field research invokes such wraiths of nostalgia. Time with his wild Canadian sheep seemed for Valerius Geist such a pool of quiet, as much self-education as a documentation of mountain sheep biology. *A nameless little lake. The virgin wilderness.* The yearlings put their soft noses in your pocket, looking for salt. Your hand froze when you took notes. The mountain was not only a place but a process.

Thousands of years of evolution unfolded in a stage play of neck stretches and rump dances, dwarf birch and willow ptarmigan. Notes ranged from minute descriptions of horn growth to broad insights into postglacial dispersal. There was, too, the great, sweeping whole of the world.

"Clouds lay several layers deep over the valley and ice crystals shimmered in the air if the sun broke through during the short winter day," Geist wrote about his Canadian wilderness. "Snow drizzled down, winds scattered it over the slopes, and packed it hard in hollows. On sunny days standing on the mountains, I could see the sun reflected in the valley. It was cold, bitter cold."

Binoculars. Notebook, pen, spotting scope. A stash of dried mangoes and gallon jugs of water, slugged down at frequent intervals. Sand and dry plant bits stuck to disheveled clothing: a swimsuit and sarong, a birthday suit to sleep in. Calf muscles sore from hiking, brain the consistency of polenta left in the microwave oven too long. Hair that smells like sun and river—Silt de Triassic mousse—from repeated swims and sixty-second styling under the cosmic blow-dryer, a finger-in-the-socket look that chic Manhattan salons would die for.

The raft brought me here, there was bear shit upriver and I ignored it, and the thought of a tent in this heat would incline me to strangle a bighorn sheep if I could get close enough to it. Screw the Endangered Species Act. It is bloody hot. I kill a cucumber with my bare hands and drink more water.

Time for science.

In a canyon heated to 105 degrees, I conjure Geist's words: "Snow." "Ice crystals." "It was cold, bitter cold." Summer in the desert is a good time to read about arctic ecology, about Scott, Shackleton, Freuchen, about the explorers who froze to death or ate their dogs.

If field biologists in the desert tell you that they have on a single hike discovered half a dozen seeps in several side canyons, five new species of *Eriogonum,* and a rare hermaphroditic vegan pupfish, don't believe them. In truth, they have been sitting under the same juniper tree for three days, staring at a rock.

I am out here sacrificing my golden years for science. Camp lies on the beach below, a sweep of pale rose sand shelving into

milky jade water—cool water, swimmable water. My tongue
hangs out. I have dragged my polenta brain to the shade of an
alcove, shade that is 103 instead of 105 degrees, but without the
sun's ferocious burn on the skin.

Despite the lure of the river and a cooldown, I do not want to
leave this perch, for fear that my movement will alarm the sheep
that feed across the wash—nine adults and juveniles, five lambs.
By holding their ground in the cooler shade cast by a high wall,
they are somewhat active. A few of the ewes know I am here, I
think. They stare in my direction without alarm. These days, the
lambs are older and more robust. They have crossed the threshold from shaky little toddlers to naughty little sheep.

One ram lamb mounts another ram lamb in what may be his
first impulse of spontaneous mounting. (Among adults sorting
out ritualistic aggressions, a dominant ram will act the role of a
courting male and the subordinate will let him do so.) A third
lamb mounts the other two in a triple hump. Already, along with
the mounting, there are pretend charges with small hornless
heads turned sideways, awkward rushes forward.

The lambs are born to butt. One butts a rock. Within seconds,
all five are engaged in a butting orgy. They butt one another, they
butt bushes, and they butt spooks. A sleek youngster with a soft
face races pell-mell toward a slab of sandstone the size of an
upended UPS truck. Without missing a step, he gallops up the
sheer face at full speed, finding footholds invisible to me, defying
gravity as if he were a big gray spider. Another lamb races up and
knocks the first lamb off. Soon more join the game. They sup-
plant one another as if the pinnacle had great significance.

The heat slows them in their play; the entire lamb gang beds
down on the rocky talus, flicking their ears to keep off the flies.
Suddenly, one lamb stands, jumps five feet straight up into the air
from the ground. The other lambs follow suit and the place looks
like popcorn gone berserk.

Mammal young do not play simply because they are cute and

nutty. The exercise strengthens green bones and developing muscles. Each behavior is also an enactment, albeit an immature one, of an adult activity. I especially like to watch the sheep feign surprise at emptiness, or butt the wind, or race madly in circles, or stand up as if a lightbulb had just gone off above their heads. Ethologists refer to these as "vacuum activities"—acting as if doing something toward nothing.

So here I am, broiling my brain amid a bunch of existentialist Caprini.

In camp, day's end pulls the buttery sunlight out of the canyon but does not lessen the furnace effect. High walls of stone hold a radiating heat that will last nearly until morning. I place my sleeping pad close to the river's edge to make use of the swamp cooler effect. It is not unusual to wake up, walk a few yards, and slip into the cool garment of night water.

As the cicadas sing down the day, I think that my work is done. Time to settle down with a chapter on igloo building and polar bears on pack ice. Then one of the older ewes brings the whole lot down to the water for a snack and a drink, and I put my book away.

The lambs act like they have been let out for recess. Nearer to the river, they move with jerky caution, heeling close to a ewe, though the pairing seems random and changes often. A few lambs suckle. Two lambs try to nurse from one ewe. At first, she does not mind. Then she steps over one lamb's neck and moves off.

One of the unmarked ewes is quite elderly: scrawny neck, scruffy fleece, sunken belly below prominent hip and pelvic bones, a bony but sweet face. She moves slowly, a very small lamb at her side. She likely has lambed every year since sexual maturity, having perhaps ten or eleven offspring, her contribution to bringing the band back from near oblivion. This little one may be her last lamb.

The sheep feed in the garden of boulders and willows along the cut bank. From an early age, the lambs nibble at vegetation and increase this activity as they grow. Independence comes early in bighorn sheep life. Already the ewes overtly ignore the nursery, using subtle body language or low *baa-aas* to communicate. The adaptive strategy: Ewes are too small in body size, their horns not lethal, to fend off a large predator. Unless the lamb is but a few weeks old, she generally will not stand in valiant motherly defense. The lamb's best defense is escape. Thus, they are quickly agile after birth.

One would think that the searing heat would paralyze canyon life to a droning hum. Yet the river always moves, a flowing strand of serenity. Two mule deer does feed upstream, their russet bodies set against the smoky green furze of tamarisk. A family of Canada geese floats in, waddles out of the water, and feeds on a gravel bar. The goslings look like middle school–aged kids, gawky and unpredictable, with manic swings between good-natured youth and wretched pricks, their minds somewhere on Jupiter.

Chukars, portly heather brown birds in the same family as quail, zigzag around the legs of a ewe on the riverbank. They have in tow six windup toys—tiny speedy chukar chicks, the avian version of loose electrons.

Chukars, geese, deer, bighorns. An inevitable raven or two if I look over my shoulder to the canyon rim. Cicadas thrumming their thoraxes. The river parting around a rock, a conversation of water and oxygen, stone and eternity. The willows wrap the gray-brown bighorns in emerald greenery dotted with red-orange flower heads of Wyoming paintbrush, the tall, slender-stemmed paintbrush variety that loves to grow near water.

For a moment, the pungent opulence that enfolds us feels like deep jungle. A few yards beyond this margin, into the ricegrass and rabbitbrush, then up-slope into spiked yucca and scattered cactus, all is jagged rock and brutal drought. When they finish eating, that is where the jungle sheep will go for the night—back to the safety of stone.

When they leave, I slip down to my bed near the cool sand, another heat-bitten creature, moving among desert sheep, dreaming of ice.

Mark and I are sleeping with boys.

Earlier the rams wandered along the canyon wall and fed beyond camp. They watched us for a long time, then engaged in a frenzy of body rubbing. They leaned up against slabs of rock and rubbed hard against the surfaces, back and forth. They scratched their ears with a hind leg. After the rubbing, their gray-brown hair stuck out every which way in bovid punk. When they shook, head to tail like dogs, their coats fell into place again.

Rocky Mountain bighorn sheep molt as snow melts and spring warms the high country. Thick clumps of winter fleece break off and dangle in the bushes. Sometimes the hair does not rub off completely, but hangs in matted woolly strips, making the sheep look like cheap mobile rugs. Because desert bighorns live in areas with milder winters and have coats lighter in color and weight, shedding is not as obvious.

Although experts like Dave and Nike can determine the age of a bighorn on sight, gauging from annular rings of horn growth and other physical features, I can only guess. These rams in the canyon tonight may be about four and five years old: long-legged and limber, with elegant strides and flaring helixes around their ears. For some reason, they brought to mind young sheikhs. They were so unbearably handsome after their body buffing, they turned around, all four animals at once, and showed us their south-facing profiles.

Toward dusk, the rams sauntered away from the river and up

the cliff. High on the walls, each pawed a bed, kicking up clouds of dust. They dropped to their knees and lowered their hindquarters, legs tucked beneath them.

Now Mark and I kick and level sand, paw at our tarp, and lie down on our night bed. We are sleeping with the boys. Among the hundreds of nights I have spent on desert rivers over the years, I wonder, how many I have unknowingly spent with wild sheep staring down at the top of my head?

Shortly before the full moon rises above the canyon rim, I push aside the cotton sheet and leave the sleeping pad to sit on a water-smoothed boulder that is half-buried in the sandbar. From here, I think, I will watch rams in moonlight. The lunar orb will flood their beds and brighten their pale haunches in vivid detail.

Are they vigilant at night? Do their heavily horned heads flop over as they sleep? Do they take off their headgear like a helmet when all is dark and no one is looking, then put it back on at first light? Do they have stiff necks in the morning? Do they dream?

The light behind the rimrock grows brighter. Any minute, the pearlescent globe will top it. The boulder feels warm on my legs and bare feet, still holding the day's heat in its mass. The thick darkness hides the river but not its presence. When the moon is up, I think, the water will shatter its light into fragments of liquid silver.

By sky, stone, and creatures, I am thoroughly, irrevocably, and delightfully dwarfed. From the viewpoint of some of my nature-averse fellow human beings, I am in a position of fear, albeit a small, anomalous island of fear. On this relict tract of wild, I am more likely to be killed off by the revelation of my own insignificance than by fanged carnivores.

The fear of being humble has walled all of us into separate geographies. Nature is a place "out there," the not-home place, much as history is "back then," the not-us time. We attend both by random visits. We grab a few souvenirs, then scurry back to our six-inch-thick bulletproof Hummers and race off to the familiar terrain of rampant late-stage capitalism. More often these days, we take both Hummer and paradigm into the "out there" with us. Never has hubris had so much armor.

Under such weight, my bed on the river as I wait for the moon, my immersion in remote refugia, my insistence on an animal life in the everyday world, a crusty resistance to the segregation of human and nonhuman landscapes—all seem but pale and pathetic gestures. Dust bunnies for the nests of tyrant flycatchers. Mercy for a wicked Marxist flicker. Goose rescues. Boojum antidepressants. Calendar markings by a desert tortoise that winters on a plug-in rock. And the long solace of the Blue Door Band, given by a curve of haunch or neck, a flawless climb along the face of my home stone, and the aching hunger to learn a language so unlike my own.

The tamarisk fronds behind me shift in a rogue breeze that suddenly tightens my neck muscles like hackles. The moon rises fat and full, but it is not white. It casts an eerie gray light over the canyon bottom, shadows blurred, rather than sharp, all colors drained. The river flows platinum; the sandstone walls are gilded in gunmetal. Mark is up and we watch the moon's ascent together.

A disk of smoky quartz, the moon is weighed down by the shadow across its face. A dirty moon. I feel a cold, end-of-the-world fear, ice around the heart. As if Earth's lunge through space is not silent but suddenly deafening, as if all life has ceased and, inside this remote chasm, we are the last to know. As if from the avalanche of our own fright, we will slide into the worship of snake gods.

The moment is startling for its sheer lack of intellect, its recognition, by pure sensation, of celestial transit.

Then we know. The moon is in total eclipse.

The people who inhabited the redrock canyons a thousand

years before us were not as ignorant of orbiting spheres. Seldom were they negligent in their tracking. New moon to full moon, the synodic month, and repeated lunar eclipses reassured them of cycles, not apocalypses, and in cycles are solace.

The lunar gray does not illuminate recumbent rams. In the smoky light, I cannot make out any sheep shapes on the rocky ledges above us. Perhaps they have moved to other beds.

Back in our bed on the sand, we watch the darkness slip off the fat orb just a fraction, revealing the slimmest, slightest crescent of light, a rind of luminous white on the charcoal moon.

I dream that the rams line up single file and sneak past us, turning to look. *Are they alive?* one whispers. My dream turns. I am lying amid the legs of bighorn sheep, peering out at sunrise between slender gray columns of hoof, tendon, and muscle. When they drop their muzzles, their exhalations stir the dust.

Members of the tribe Caprini, including true sheep (genus *Ovis*)—the Asiatic urials, for example, the argalis of central Asia, and domestic sheep everywhere—bear twins. Aoudads, not *Ovis*, but a "sheep-goat" of North Africa, are known for multiple births, not just twins but triplets, as well. However, among North American wild sheep, twins are uncommon.

Although desert bighorn sheep have borne twins in captivity, twinning in the wild is infrequent and rarely documented. If twins are born in the wild and one dies shortly thereafter, the seclusion of this event allows no witness. And the ewe mothers have a few tricks of their own.

Downriver from Ram Land, under the blazing morning sun, Mark and I are looking at a big healthy ewe with two robust lambs at heel. We have seen the lambs take turns suckling her. She rejected neither. The ewe lamb is dark, smoky brown. The ram lamb, a little button penis behind his belly, has a gray coat.

According to Nike's records, this ewe and the two lambs have been together since lambing time. Togetherness is not evidence of twinning, however. Maternal bands often have more lambs among them than adult females; when pairs are counted, there are extra lambs. Although it is not the norm, ewes will suckle other ewes' lambs. The reasons for these differences in maternal care are not easily explained.

Upriver, we had seen eight ewes with three lambs. Here, the group has more lambs (six) than ewes (three). Although two miles of river separate the groups, we think they were once together, then jumbled up and separated. The lambs nurse less frequently; they are sturdy and growing up. If the ewes in the two groups have one another's young, nobody appears to be hungry or anxious about separation.

Mark and I are with the lamb-pack group, hoping all will eventually sort itself out. We have tucked ourselves under an overhang, out of the sun's brutal rays and quite a distance from the sheep. With binoculars, we press red rings around our eyes.

The heat chases the group into a shady shelf of stone on their side of the chasm. The lambs butt one another off the top of a rock pile, then off beds as some of them try to settle down. Soon the ledge holds nine resting sheep, a garden of statues with wildly twitching ears.

Parental care of offspring is much like one would expect of wild ungulates. Males have nothing to do with it. The mother forms an immediate bond when she licks and nurses her newborn. Thereafter, both ewe and lamb recognize each other with olfactory, visual, and auditory cues. When a lamb moves in to suckle, the ewe eyes and sniffs it. She will walk away from or butt off a lamb that is not hers. Lambs, too, know their own dam.

The evolutionary value of a single birth and an exclusive lamb-ewe bond, the research suggests, is reproductive success. Ewes cannot afford to invest the extra energy needed to nurse nonkin without risking their own fitness.

Along with these general assumptions, it is worth remembering how socially complex this species can be. A study of transplanted Rocky Mountain bighorns in Montana, for instance, documented patterns of cooperative nursing: ewes that nursed their own as well as a strange lamb, and ewes that lost their own lamb but took on and nursed a foster lamb. The allomothers tended to be older, high-ranking ewes. Somehow they supplied milk to lambs in addition to their own yet maintained their reproductive fitness.

Allomothering among these Rocky Mountain bighorns was believed to be a response to heavy predation by coyotes, an "adjustment" that favored lamb survival under this intense pressure. By letting strange lambs nurse, the ewes kept the nursery group larger and more cohesive and thus less susceptible to predators. Other studies have noted cooperative nursing when lamb mortality was high, and there are suggestions, too, that the allomothers might be investing in kin—that is, selecting lambs that are related to them within the matriarchal band.

For the Blue Door Band, heavy predation is not currently a factor. The nine sheep across from us, as well as their lost contingent upriver, however, typify bighorn organization by matriarchy, a group of closely related individuals, perhaps even less genetically diverse if, since its disappearance, the band grew from a few founders.

Watching this band, we have seen ewes nurse lambs other than their own. And here are these "twins"—a rare double birth, or a ewe with her own lamb and a foster lamb? Has inbreeding in some way affected identifying clues, how lambs smell and how ewes distinguish their odor?

The sheep rise from their beds and pick their way down the cliff. From across the wash comes the upriver group. They merge together, eleven ewes and nine lambs, which find one another in a popcorning bunch that obscures ewe-lamb pairs. With postures

of caution and in a more or less compact group—no stragglers—
the flock heads across an open sand dune toward the river. There
are stops to nibble scattered *Mentzelia,* or blazing star. In the
shimmering heat waves that rise from the pale sand dune, they
look like camels crossing the Sahara.

The nursery seems huge—and somehow reassuring, as if by
entering deep summer alive, the year's lamb crop has crossed a
threshold. The young are out in the world. In their natal bands,
they hang on the canyon walls, learning the rock, growing decid-
uous (milk) teeth, testing the flavor of blazing star, tasting the big
jade river that meanders through their homeland.

Last night's rams fattened up more than fought. The sun turns
the remains of a ram death into leathered flesh, dried femurs, and
bits of fleece among the camelthorn. Still intact, the rib cage arcs
above the sand in delicate curves of white bone, preventing the
wind from leaving the country.

All of this unfolds beyond our understanding. I, for one, am
content with the mysteries. It is as if these highly social creatures
on the river bottom have a dialect all their own, canted in the
tumult of bloodlines, honed by their fidelity to this high, pitched
rock. Time broken by their long years of disappearance somehow
reassembled an ancient desert lineage, making biology more like
story. The profoundest glimpses into their lives come in that instant before logic, like the blind surprise of a lunar eclipse.

As we slip past the ewe on the riverbank, she stands in attention
posture, neck raised and rigid, ears perked forward. Mark ferries
the raft from the river's center to its far shore, giving the animal
as much distance from us as possible. His strokes are deliberately
smooth and quiet. We drift by on a slow current.

The ewe stands on the seam between riparian willows and the
scant cover of the open, beastly hot desert. The sun beats down

from its high-noon zenith, too high to cast shadows. The only shadow is the ewe's own, directly beneath her. In that pool of shade lies a lamb.

The lamb is so big in head, short in nose, and small in body— so newborn in features—at first I wonder if the ewe had given birth nearby, then, pushed by the heat, left seclusion and escape cliffs to drop to the river. She is a two-year-old ewe, alone and far downstream from the large nursery group. Hers is a late-season birth, one of the last of the Blue Door lambs to be born this year.

The lamb stands up. It fits under the ewe's belly with only a slight lowering of its head. The ears swivel. The ewe moves off a few feet to feed, taking her shadow with her, leaving the lamb in the bright sun.

Sweat drips down my temples, forms lakes under my life jacket. The ewe decides we are harmless and floating out of her realm. There is a listlessness to all of us. Summer's cauldron fills the canyon with its magnesium glare. The sky is so open, the pair so far from stone, from the sanctuary of the vertical, I start to look for eagles.

We watch the pair as we drift downriver. Each time the ewe moves to feed, the lamb stands for a moment in the white-hot sun, swivels its ears, then follows the ewe and lies down under her belly, resting in the pool of shade.

JULY

During summer in the desert, smart people mutter excuses, then disappear into darkened dens with frosted cocktail shakers and plasma TVs, and I am sure that I am alone out here with my animal life, treading the thick stillness of heat.

Beneath July's high-pressure system, no one talks of the cloudless clarity of the present, only of the monsoons, still weeks away. Despite this impatience, we know that monsoon rains require architecture: a belly of baked continental air rising, moisture-fat air from Pacific Mexico moving to meet it, and towering thunderheads, violent and local, only when the air masses collide.

Until then, the heat broods. The river shrinks and tamarisks faint into the current, draping feathery green fronds. Melons ripen. Grapes swell and burst. In dirt scraped down to cooler layers, coyotes sprawl, sighing deeply and blowing dust out of their noses. Snow-white datura blossoms fold their deadly beauty away from the daylight. Nights fill with a palpable blackness, languid expectations, and insect sounds I try to separate but can't.

On days that peak in temperatures exceeding one hundred degrees, imminent brain death might be interrupted by random seismic zigzags, a sign that amid the drone some lizard's blink or raven's burp caught but did not hold one's attention. The strongest spikes in the scan happen to align with thoughts of mass murder, which the body, fortuitously plastered to a lawn chair, does not obey.

My notes of "Life with Sheep" follow this metabolic slowdown, periods of breathing and heartbeat punctuated with mirages at the edge of vision. I do not know the sense of things when I see them. This is the pulse of deep summer.

Between the spring rains that never came and the late-summer monsoons of tenuous promise, desert life struggles to stay hydrated. Potholes dry up. Dew never forms. Where sandstone crevices once seeped a slick of moisture down smooth rock faces, only a crust of blackened mineral varnish and desiccated lichens remains.

The Blue Door sheep live by the river. Beyond such a blessing, I wonder if animals are drinking sand. Although wild sheep consume water from freestanding sources, they also meet moisture needs with succulence from their plant foods and a metabolism suited to extreme aridity. Their water must come from somewhere. Camels and oryx they are not.

Nearly a decade of Mars-like drought in this redrock desert has underlined the extraordinary adaptation of this subspecies to its austere geography. Withstanding the heat, the chronic lack of snowpack and rainfall, the drying up of even the most reliable of springs, these sheep are living on the vapors of rain dreams.

Their drought, on the high desert of the Colorado Plateau, is the tropics compared to bighorn habitat in Baja California, Death Valley, the Sonoran Desert, and the southern Mojave and Colorado deserts, where for too many years it can forget to rain at all. Obviously, all four races of desert bighorns have survived cycles of the severest aridity. But no one is sure how.

Wildlife managers have dynamited steep-sided *tinajas* to make them more accessible when water sinks into a low death-trap pit. They have dammed springs, filled aluminum tanks, and built guzzlers—moisture-collection units—to augment natural water sources.

Research shows that guzzlers and other artificial water sources have helped in marginal habitat and where livestock has usurped traditional bighorn water holes. Research also shows that sheep may not use guzzlers even in habitat where water is scarce or unavailable. They simply stick to their own maps.

Years ago, in a *tinaja* in a hotter southwestern desert, water receded to levels so low that the bighorns who came to drink from the tank fell into it and could not climb back up the ten-foot vertical sides and out of the pit. Thirty-four died there and left a boneyard.

A big river flowed only three miles away, but the sheep did not use it. They used the *tinaja* after it filled again. The presence of feral burros and a barrier of tamarisk, where, in the mind of a sheep, a predator might lurk, may have discouraged the animals from going to the river for its unlimited gallons.

During the longest, hottest, driest deep-summer months, most sheep stay within close radius of ancestral water holes. Summer range becomes defined by thirst. For thousands of years, they have lived off their own water secrets, without our intervention.

The windshield frames a brick-colored mesa overlaid with a band of sky so vibrant in its blue, it is neither space nor air, but silence become matter. On the mesa's caprock and upper flanks, pinyon and juniper trees grow close enough to one another to tease the illusion of "forest" from the lips. The conifers—at this density, in a desert more rightly called a woodland—live at altitudes that reach highest toward moisture. The farther down the mesa's flanks, the sparser they become, until the bare rock takes over in a jagged panic of washes and canyons.

The outline of the windshield intensifies this view, as if all would be softer out of the frame and into the rest of the world. I keep my binocular span within the rectangle, pointed toward the mesa, aimed at beige sheep rumps against brick red rock. The windshield has no glass. I can stretch my arm over the dashboard and out to a hood the color of electrocuted parrots, an alarming limes-on-acid green. There is nothing under the hood but air.

I sit on the truck's bucket seat (an overturned bucket) on the driver's side. Little remains of the interior but the hardest of materials—metal and Bakelite. According to a gauge marked with DCH-CHG and faint hatch marks, the battery needs charging. According to the odometer, the truck ended its life at 30,890 miles. Surprisingly, the speedometer needle still moves. The truck has no engine block, tires, or bed, just hood, grille, fenders, and the cab I sit in, perched on a bucket behind a melting steering wheel, watching the mesa.

The windshield frames one scene. No turns to a new angle of view, no lunging through space on a lost American highway. The truck is not moving. It has not moved since about 1965, its work halted, more or less, by a bubble of history.

The electric green Ford truck is one of several vehicle carcasses scattered on the saltbush flats across from the mesa. Most are trucks or the vital organs of trucks, thoroughly cannibalized and stripped, their tires removed or long ago puddled into licorice blobs by the desert sun.

The only sedan is a Buick of an indeterminate color. Its tires and axle have vanished. Its interior is bare to the frame except for a steel column with a chrome handle: the parking brake. The brake is set, as if the car were in danger of rolling downhill on its naked fenders.

Through the frame of the empty windshield, I see a mesa that, below the pinyon-juniper line, is made nearly porous by the gouges, scars, and perforations in its face. Road cuts zigzag to platforms of gravel. The black holes of adits and mine mouths spill aqua cones of uranium tailings over the side of the Chinle Formation, the stratum that yielded the ore.

The mesa is now an in situ dump. Its mined-out innards slide off its face into the red pediment below. By all expectations, the bighorns on this mesa should be easily spotted, especially at night: Day-Glo Caprini.

Given the history of this place, the presence of bighorn sheep is somewhat of a miracle. Like the Blue Door Band, they have inhabited this terrain since deep time. Rock walls and freestanding boulders bear their portraits. They did not escape the wave of pressures that accompanied Euro-American settlement. Against habitat loss, livestock encroachment, disease, and overhunting, bighorn numbers plunged. Then they found themselves living among Cold Warriors.

The broken mesas and buttes accommodate the species with a sense so deeply hereditary, there is hardly a division between land and flesh. Nelson's bighorns are the locals. The human locals had tenets of their own, an ethos that with neither guile nor apology gave such animals no protection.

The abandoned mines and used-up car lot lie in a vast tract of rugged canyon country far to the north of the Blue Door homelands. Since the uranium-mining era ended, the region has become largely empty of all but transient recreationists. The nearest towns lie on fringes too distant to reach before a shower and air conditioning become hallucinatory cravings.

Because of its immensity and isolation, many visitors call this quarter "wilderness." The mines and tailings, the roads, junked vehicles, half-buried cables, and radionuclides in the groundwater are at first invisible. That nearly ten thousand mine workers once swarmed within the broadest boundaries of this region seems improbable unless you are hiking with a Geiger counter. But they were here, roughly from the end of World War II to the mid-1960s, turning the mesas inside out for the core fuel of America's nuclear arsenal.

No bighorn saunters into the framed view of the truck window, only a red-tailed hawk on a listless thermal. The ore truck's cosmotransuranic paint job threatens knicker meltdown, or is the bucket seat on this sizzling July day scalding my butt?

I slip out of the cab and stumble to the shade of a juniper tree. There is no river to cool me. There is no river to drink from. The bighorns in the mesa country survive on delusions: scarce springs, ephemeral potholes, a few guzzlers, dew, cactus juice. If scorn were a sheep emotion, they would look upon the river band as wimps in an easy paradise of flowing water. Up here, water defines where you go and how you die.

I have a water bottle and the patience to wait until the sun drops behind the mesa and leaves the stone cool enough to hike. Note-taking feels as intriguing as recording the hourly gestures of a narcoleptic barnacle. The lead in my sketching pencil softens to a near drip on the drawing pad.

The bighorns live here in half a dozen relict bands scattered north to south along complex mesas and drainages. There are reasons to add them together and call them a metapopulation, the sum of all groups and habitat patches, which are roughly contiguous. Genetic exchange is not entirely hindered by geographical isolation. Where one band might go locally extinct, animals from another could, in theory, recolonize the empty habitat.

Their island is many times larger than the Blue Door Band's canyon fragment, all of it on public lands. Human impact comes by incursion into and out of the area more than from permanent development. Yet despite the country's breadth and its wild character, the sheep bands have stayed small and vulnerable since the mining era.

There are no reliable records of bighorn numbers before the miners arrived in force in the early fifties. But when it happened, the subsequent decline was as unmeasured as it was unchecked. Local anecdote gave the census numbers: The sheep went from "many" to "gone."

Ranchers who used the region for pasture cast the blame

squarely on the local Ute and Navajo. While Indians did hunt bighorns, the same ranchers bragged of their standing order to their hired hands: "Shoot any bighorn sheep you see." The bighorns, the ranchers said, "eat the grass our cattle need." When wildlife biologists first studied the area in the late sixties, they were unequivocal in their conclusion that the number of sheep killed by stockmen and poachers significantly contributed to the decline of the bighorns.

Visitors to the mines at the end of the uranium boom found camps strewn with bighorn sheep bones. We hunted them on our days off, the miners said, "for something to do." They noted that after dynamite blasts in certain areas, the ewes that had once lambed there never came back.

The best ore came from the Shinarump Member of the Chinle Formation, steep faces favored by bighorns for food and escape terrain. A web of roads across talus slopes put more animals in the crosshairs. Feral goats displaced an entire band from its historic range.

Prospectors used camps, but most of the developed mines and mills were manned by workers from towns on the fringes of the mesa country, workers who returned every day to houses, streets, and stores—not exactly the conditions of subsistence hunting.

Yet even the commuting miners claimed to live off the land, since going home to pot roast and Jell-O did not advance an image of rugged independence. In truth, they helped themselves to wildlife within a culture that condoned the custom of doing so. In normal times, such a custom might be sustainable. But there were simply too many hunters and poachers in the area and no curb on their appetite.

By the time a more rigorous science of game management arrived, with censuses, field studies, and a public interest to back them, the mining boom had gone bust. The waning uranium economy, not this armada of "enlightenment," had saved what was left of the sheep bands. The miners found new jobs or other outfits. Shacks, machinery, tailings, and "muck dumps" baked in the desert sun. The usable stuff was hauled away, including the trailer of one uranium miner. Underneath it lay twenty-three bighorn skulls.

While some habitat remained empty, in other places sheep moved into former range. Transplants from Nevada augmented one of the smaller herds. Guzzlers were built in terrain of scant water resources. Officials who called the range "severely over-grazed"—an uncommonly bold honesty for the times—were listened to, sort of, and a few habitat areas were restricted, sort of. (One field researcher noted trespass cattle in a closed area each year of his study.)

In the mid-1980s, animals in the northernmost band in the region began to sicken and die. Within four years, they fell into what was called "a spectacular crash." Sick, coughing, and dying animals were observed in adjacent bands, implying the spread of disease to other reaches of habitat. Although the precise agent was never identified, chronic pneumonia was suspected. Once such an epizootic event has begun, treatment has little effect.

The circumstances of the probable pneumonia die-off added up to the kind of proof that everyone treated like eggshells. What is known is that a rancher, who was also a state legislator, had reactivated his domestic sheep-grazing permit inside known bighorn country after the permit had not been used for a number of years. On two occasions, wild desert bighorn rams were seen among the rancher's flock. Then the first sick bighorns and carcasses were found.

Recovery since the die-off has been slow. The groups hardest hit remain in remnant status. The bands near the uranium mines have stabilized, probably because they were the farthest from the disease epicenter. Although this enormous, largely unbroken expanse of desert appears to be big enough and wild enough, these bands, too, fit the twenty-first-century desert bighorn paradigm: diminished in number, isolated on patches of habitat, counted, collared, managed, moved, more feral than wild. But ever clinging to the stone.

From under the juniper tree, I glass the face of the mesa. Mine tailings cascade off the talus, oxidized and darkened by age, as stolid and enduring as war monuments. I was told that mule deer, bighorns, and other wildlife use water that has surfaced from old mine tunnels, but I am too paralyzed by sanctimoniously obsessive, fluorescent-hair-falling-out terror—too chicken—to look for them there.

To think of the uranium-mining era solely as a kind of hunter's anarchy is to miss the point. The culture that allowed it remains deeply entrenched. Tight-lipped rural communities with defined codes of power. A hardbound work ethic. A self-imposed isolation and insularity that make people fear change. Conformity demanded, imagination undervalued. Distrust of government. Congenital xenophobia. The casting of dissenters as elitists, heretics, even perverts. Belief that public lands and their proteins were created for humans to exploit, that you will somehow fail your God if you do not subdue nature.

There are still trespass cows here, still an overgrazing crisis pushed further into hell by drought, still those who believe that no mining operation need ever be reclaimed, and still people too busy trying to make a living to ever comprehend why you would think of a two-hundred-pound wild herbivore as little other than red meat.

A stratosphere of heat blankets the desert floor, breaking the old truck into shimmering waves of lime green. The mesa's shadow lengthens with a visibly moving edge. It soon engulfs the saltbush flats and the truck, dousing the fluid lines of mirage. When it reaches the juniper and me, the shadow is a mile long. The sun drops behind the mesa. A landscape leached of color by the day's white heat now deepens to bloodred on the flats and molten amber on the highest buttes, which take the last slabs of sunlight.

At day's end, it is not cool, merely less hot. I am not sure if I can move. Actually, I am not exactly *here,* though it may appear so by virtue of the greasy smudge and two forlorn river sandals left under a juniper tree, where androgynous godlike beings from outer space have extruded me through their navels into an Olympus of blue ice, and I am staring at the likeness of the Holy Virgin Mother in a lime popsicle, listening to my hosts—more dryadesque than bug-eyed, antennae-sprouting and gooey, kind of like stoned charioteers in kilts made of gauzy church linens—lean over and whisper, *You are now in Permanent Contact.*

It is bloody hot. I wallow in hallucinations for their promise of ice.

July in the desert without an afternoon monsoon rainstorm to temper the furnace is no time to leave the Blue Door Band and expect to make new sheep friends. Mark and I have camped and hiked in this country, but it hides its animals well. We have seldom seen more than a few animals, some scat, and tracks. They are elusive. Their thirsts are hidden. Their homeland is the size of a small Latin American country.

I wrest myself from the dryads, sling a pack on my back, and hike back to the arroyo where I parked my truck. I drive a back road to a different mesa, park, and pack up again. The coma-inducing heat and perhaps a pinch of atomic pixie dust have deluded me into thinking I am worthy of alien abduction. But tonight, I will be perfectly sensible, rational. I will camp with the Birdheads.

Dig into local oral histories and you may find a story from a range cowboy who works in the desert backcountry. While he was moving stock one day, a bighorn sheep appeared amid the cattle. The cowboy took out his rope and rode toward the ram.

The cattle kind of wadded up and I throwed over the back of the bull at that ram. When I throwed, my horse blowed up and started to buck. I didn't know whether I caught the ram for a ways or not. I didn't care; I was just riding. The rope finally jerked tight and we bucked down there a ways and I got the horse stopped in about a foot of snow. I turned him around and looked down at that rope, and the ram got up out of the snow and shook, and the old horse whirled and started to buck and run again. . . . We took that ram up there and I put him in the pickup because I knew no one would believe that I roped this ram.

I tied him with a little loose rope in there where he could lay down or turn around in the truck. We went ahead and rode all day. My rack from the floor to the top of the rack was six foot, eight inches, and when I rode back up there to that pickup that night, that ram—standing flat-footed in the back of that pickup—jumped six foot, eight inches, and just started over the rack when he hit the end of the rope. Jerked him back in and we pulled him up in the front of the truck, and he got right up against the cab and laid down. . . . I hauled him up to camp and we unloaded him. I tied him down and I took my pocketknife and I cut my brand in his horn. I put +H (Cross H) in his horn and then I told [my partner], "Bring me the bell." He went and got the bell off one of the loose horses, and I put the bell on [the ram] and cut the strap down where it would fit him. Then we turned him loose.

He ran. He ran bad. His hind leg come clear up over his head just kicking at that bell. About six or seven years later . . . he still had the bell on, but the clapper had fell out. He just had a dumb bell on.

When you pay close attention to the small details of your neighborhood, what you thought was particular may in the end give home no immunity from the rest of the world: the cold, lonely estrangement, wild animal and human, the frayed loyalty to the beauty of other life-forms, an entrapment in the cycles of harm.

Deep in canyon country, a work crew built a wildlife guzzler on the side of a high butte. It is a unit of an older style, likely not put together beforehand and delivered by helicopter, but with hand tools and materials hauled in on foot and by pack stock. The collector is a tilted apron of ribbed sheet metal that slides rain and condensation into a gutter. The gutter feeds a buried pipe that runs a considerable distance to a ground-level cement basin on the side of a cliff, out of sight of the sheet-metal collector.

What a breathtaking view from this watering place: a sheep view. Their big eyes can survey at least two Latin American countries. No brush obscures the panorama. The few junipers and pinyons do not make them wary. The promontory is a split-second bolt away from escape terrain. Here they drink quickly and leave.

Wild sheep have come to this guzzler for many years, perhaps because it is safe, perhaps because long ago at least one ewe encoded it on her homeland map and passed the habit down the generations. For reasons that are not clear, they shun other guzzlers and artificial sites. This old guzzler on the butte is bone-dry in this interminable drought. Yet there are fresh tracks and pellets everywhere.

To reach their water, the sheep use trails etched into the cliff-side by the routine of cautious approach. At one point, their trails traverse a petrified forest—logs and stumps strewn everywhere, mineralized and as heavy as marble columns, banded in russet, green, rose, mauve, gold.

Ancient rivers and streams carried the trees here. Where the wood and other organic material formed massive debris piles, uranium minerals, leached by groundwater, clustered. The strata of these old stream channels bear the ore. Mud buried the trees. The trees turned to stone. Erosion exposed them again, and now the sheep move through the ghost forest to their basin of collected rain.

Below the butte is a network of old uranium-mining roads, many of them rutted, eroded, and slumped, but of increasing attraction to a bloating fleet of all-terrain vehicles. Every year, more and more come. Their riders take the machines on and on, moving into the depths of canyon country.

The desert has a pattern: retreating escarpments and labyrinthine canyons. One of the escarpments, a flat-topped mesa, rises sharply, offering no easy purchase but for a broad ledge below the rim. At its foot, the desert unrolls into dawn. The mesa is ten miles long. The desert plain below it is vast enough to bend the Earth.

Except for eroded cuts that have removed great chunks of the ledge, you could walk the entire face of the escarpment on this steplike perch, one side a precipitous slide into talus, the other a blocky wall that forms the rim.

Last evening, I gazed down from the rim to the brassy green crown of a juniper and remembered a story of a ram that, perhaps during the frenzy of the rut, flew off a precipice like this and fell to his death. His skull and bones were found in the top of a juniper tree. Ever since hearing that story, I have looked for bones in junipers.

I scrambled down a rough rockfall from rim to ledge with barely enough light to avoid spiky patches of prickly pear cactus. Surprisingly, some of the cactus was bearing fruit despite the drought. The dark red pear-shaped fruits were lined up in rows along the edges of the waxy green spoon-shaped pads.

I slept at the seam between wall and ledge, tucked well back from the vertigo-inducing drop, but with an unobstructed view.

My bed was a shallow hollow of hard-packed dirt. I did not make it so. A bighorn did, probably decades ago. Perhaps it was not a sheep bed, although it was in the perfect position to be one. Perhaps it was a staging pad for Permanent Contact. I took it because, oddly, it was the only spot with a breeze.

I do not think there are sheep around here any longer. This mesa may be one of the places that lost them during the poaching years or disease epidemics. It is the kind of habitat that makes Nike say, "This place feels so empty."

Now, as morning grows, the day promises to be summer absolute, summer unflawed, sapphire on its ends, blazing white at midday. I can stay here only as long as my water supply lasts, with enough left for the hike out.

The Birdheads line the rock wall behind me. Square-shouldered human figures with birds on top of their heads. Human figures topped with birds instead of heads. Duck-headed anthropomorphs. Duck-headed serpents. Kissing ducks. Kissing geese.

Here the rock artists forgot about the ubiquitous compulsion to etch bighorn sheep. They indulged in birds. I walk the wall for nearly a mile, and the bird petroglyphs never stop in either direction. I find other sheep beds, too, old and abandoned.

The birds on the Birdhead panels look like waterfowl—geese and ducks shown in legless sitting-duck profile, slender birds with long sticklike legs, perhaps ibis, herons, or other wading birds. The nearest body of water is more than thirty miles away, bending inside folds of Triassic rock. The birds of flesh with me today on this high perch are ravens too black to move in the day's waxing heat.

I find potsherds scattered among the boulders below the Bird-head panels, mostly bits of black-on-white pottery. Archaeologists believe that such finely painted ceramics were preserved for ceremonial use—the fancy china, so to speak. The plainer pottery, gray, smooth, and unpainted or with shaped and pressed coils, a style known as corrugated pottery, was everyday kitchenware. When the pots broke, bits of them were saved for ornaments, pendants, game pieces, and other uses.

Among the artifacts left by these cultures is a pair of plain gray potsherds shaped into disks by someone roughly working their edges. The slightly convex sherds were bound together face-to-face with twisted yucca fibers. The string held the sherds flush but for a thin crack. Into the crack you would slip a reed or blade of grass. Head lifted, eyes on a wild sky, you held this clay bird caller to your lips and blew. Your notes would seek a bird's attention.

I sketch some Birdheads and wonder about the time when we were wild, too, when we threw back our heads and with horn or bone used our breath to call to animals. I wonder if the figures with waterbirds on their heads were icons of rain or flight, if they carried hope and prayer to draw the monsoons.

The day is young, but the sun is already fire. It dazzles and scorches. Today, no rain will rescue me from the heat. It is time to rescue myself.

Any water on this mesa is false or hidden. I would die before I found it. Yet a sizable mammal has shaped itself to such places. I lean back on a rock below a Birdhead, close my eyes, and picture a desert sheep.

The water in her rumen is body water. She has sweat glands. For evaporative cooling, she pants. Her woolly coat protects her skin from solar radiation that could elevate her temperature, roast her like walking mutton. She knows how to seek breezes, cooler soil, higher places, an ellipse of shade between wall and ledge, where the old beds lie.

She can trek long distances to find freestanding water. By memory? By hope? She can consume large volumes in one drink, as much as 20 percent of her body weight: one nicely hydrated ewe. She needs more water when she is lactating and thus brings her lamb close to springs and potholes, warier than ever. In deep summer, she can butt a cactus until it cracks open and yields its succulent moisture.

Even with such extraordinary adaptations, what in the world will she do, I wonder, about global warming?

The sledgehammer heat beats down. I feel as if someone is watching me, boring holes into me with his glare. I open my eyes. About seventy feet away, two bighorn ewes stand on a boulder, staring at me. I freeze. They flick their pretty little tails.

Their horns are purple. Their nostrils, muzzles, and lips are stained purplish red. They look like they put on melting lipstick without a mirror.

There are still bighorn sheep on this mesa. They fooled us. They have been up here with the Birdheads, stuffing themselves silly with the purple fruits of prickly pear cactus.

AUGUST

⁓

The range of the California bighorn sheep once extended from the intermountain regions of British Columbia and Washington's Cascade Mountains south to Oregon and the lava beds of north-eastern California and through the Sierra Nevada to the Kern River drainage on the Sierra's southern end—dry, rain-shadow country between coastal ranges and the Great Basin.

Traditionally grouped with the Rocky Mountain bighorn rather than with the desert races, the California bighorn was first described in the nineteenth century and eventually assigned the name *Ovis canadensis californiana* on somewhat shaky taxonomic grounds.

The more sophisticated tools of genetic research have placed the California bighorn under new scrutiny, with suggestions that it is distinct from the Rocky Mountain bighorn by geographic separation rather than by strict taxonomic criteria. Furthermore, the bighorns in the Sierra Nevada show traits that may not fit the conventional *Ovis* classifications. While official revisions of nomenclature are often plodding, this group may ultimately be known as its own subspecies: *Ovis canadensis sierrae*.

Whoever they are, California bighorns usurp my attention, demanding I seek them out. I dump the home band—again. The ewes feed by the river. The lambs grow like weeds. The rams put on fat for the rut. Their hearts will break, missing me.

My new sheep friends, too, reside on islands, remnant habitat that is but a fraction of their former range. The older names for them say where they once lived—rimrock bighorn, lava-beds bighorn—and where we now seek them: Sierra Nevada bighorn. They are, in a way, luring me away from home to go home.

Mark and I load the truck with food, water, camping gear, books. Nelson, the stuffed-toy ram, rides on the headrest, peering over at the devil duckie on the dashboard, a plastic bathtub duck with curving, pointed red horns and scowling, evil eyebrows.

This month, all of America is on vacation. All of America on vacation heads for cool mountains and breezy seashores. We head west for the hottest deserts, the ones that proffer a warning to visitors: "Summer is not recommended."

We cross the Colorado River, then traverse the flaming-red plateaus of the Arizona Strip. Snow-white cauliflower clouds loom over the rimrock, moving toward the polygamist towns on the Utah-Arizona border, announcing the first monsoons. The Colorado Plateau and home may at last see the promise of afternoon thundershowers. Ahead of us, to the west, skies stay clear and superheated.

For a number of miles, the names on the land are biblical—Canaan Mountain, the Tabernacle, Babylon Butte—your last chance before skirting the heathen abodes of Nipple Bench and Satan's Bathtub, then hurling down the interstate across several basins with no choice but to point your doomed virtue into the magnesium glare of Las Vegas. The devil duckie's horns glow crimson.

Somehow we avoid the Las Vegas suction and slip through California's back door of basins and ranges, a plate of rumpled earth astride great quivering faults. We skirt the Cosos, a hazy blue mass crowned with a faultless, clear sky.

On the horizon, the seam between desert and the southern Sierra becomes famously sharp. A sky-scraping spine of granite looms straight up from the Owens Valley, mirrored by an escarpment on the valley's other flank, the Inyo and White mountains.

The Sierra Nevada run nearly four hundred miles north to

south along California's eastern edge. From the crowded Central
Valley on their western flank, they rise in a gradual slope to that
climax of serrated peaks and the abrupt drop into the sparsely
populated Great Basin and Mojave Desert.

The southern end of the Sierra curves westward like the flicked
tail of a northbound rattlesnake—mountains lower in elevation
and less watered than the main rampart of the eastern Sierra, with
forested ridges, broken cliffs of beige granite, and foothills of
grassland and oaks. On an unmarked dirt road, we enter a rough
drainage, mindful of a guidebook that said, "Careful use of a map
is essential to keep yourself located." We do not have a map.

The road dead-ends at a public campground that will be home
for a night. No one else is camped along the rutted loops and
sites overgrown with vegetation, a curious desolation when, by
all expectations, at least half of Los Angeles should be on vacation in the mountains. The bulletin board sags; the wooden out-
houses creak, their many layers of Smokey the Bear reddish brown
paint peeling.

The campground's shabby air has a quiet appeal. We pull into
a site surrounded by live oaks, blue oaks, and digger pines with
silky long needles and shade fragrant with their pitch. A ledge of
granite holds a dozen grinding holes, or fixed mortars, where
early Sierra tribes ground acorns into a fine meal.

The ghostly campground has a host, a bearded, stocky man
who appears to be in his thirties. He is wearing a T-shirt and a
baseball cap. A pistol in a holster is strapped around his ample
girth. He rides up to our site on a motorcycle.

"You can't shoot bears," he announces without introduction.
"It's not bear season."

"Can we camp?" Mark asks.

Somewhat taken aback, he looks around as if he were noticing
his whereabouts for the first time. "Oh. You want to *camp*?"

Always, I am neurotically terrified around guns. Other than in-
stilling a mildly creepy sense that he does not know where he is,

the fellow appears harmless. We, after all, do not know where we are, either. None of us is keeping ourselves located.

"I get trouble from off-season bear hunters," he explains. "All the poachers come from Utah. I saw your truck plates."

Once he is convinced that we are not poachers, he relaxes and gives his name (Arnie), then describes his life as a campground nanny. He has worked at this place for over seven years. He calls the forest rangers—his employers—"ineducated." For the RV crowd, the campground is too primitive. Backpackers forgo these middle elevations for the alpine trails along the Sierra's crest. The campground is seldom used except during hunting season, when hunters harvest some of the area's abundant black bears.

"Utah poachers and Mexicans with too many spray cans, that's what I worry about," Arnie tells us. "When the hunters aren't here, it's usually just me and my dog and my snake."

Arnie keeps a California mountain king snake under his trailer, feeding it the mice he catches in a live trap. Nonpoisonous, handsomely banded in red, black, and cream, a king snake kills prey by constriction. Arnie watches this slow suffocation whenever he feeds his snake. The mouse's eyes bulge, he says.

He knows the drainage well and recommends a hike up a nearby creek. But when I ask about a well-known town ten miles over the ridge, he says he has never heard of it. "Jehovah's Witness protection program," I whisper to Mark after Arnie leaves.

When I lived in these mountains years ago, most of the volunteers, seasonal rangers, and fire lookouts were poets and English literature majors. Visitors irked them. They wanted to be alone with Rilke and Durrell and an unfinished dissertation on prefeminist Edwardian adverbs. They were lanky, nerdy, and armed with notebooks. They lived on pots of brown rice.

Despite having the demeanor of a long-haul trucker on a seven-year coffee break, Arnie fits these wooded foothills with neither affection nor complaint, minding a campground empty of campers in the heart of California's millions. Although their character and motives may have changed, I am pleased to see that the tradition of backcountry loners lives on.

The hunters who use this campground left few signs of their presence. Either Arnie has tidied up after them or their light imprint tells how camping has moved into the habitat of self-contained, enclosed vehicles. The RVs set up a wheeled reproduction of the familiar, the home from which one is allegedly escaping, and a membrane of protection against nature and the messily homicidal "campers" in the sites nearby. The sun-dappled oaks, pines, and creek are but backdrop for a parking space, the picnic table an unused relic, warped and weathered.

During my tenure in these mountains, creeksides like the camp at Arnie's always evoked outdoor spaces of work and nesting, a kind of settling in, for a night or two, in a place with the simple abundance of shade, water, bed, and the exalted peace of exquisite mountain light.

The grinding mortars in the granite outcrops around my home sang with ghosts, ghosts of my mother's family, who knew these stone mortars before me (all of us used them for play), as well as the Indian women who made them. Beside the stones, under the incense cedars, I swore I could hear three hundred years of gossip.

The native people who used the mortars were transient but came back to the same camps year after year. The multiple hand mills in a single slab of rock give us a glimpse of the communal. To sculpt the cuplike depressions, the grinders used handheld fieldstones—pestles unworked except by use or the occasional indentation for finger grips.

At these elevations, the zone of oaks and mixed conifers, creeks glide rather than rush. Minnow noses break the surface of pools under tangled willows, and even the rocks smell green and sweet. Along the water borders, wild ginger and miner's lettuce grow in dense mats.

At camps and cabins, mountain people made small adjustments, rather than bemoaned the lack of amenities. At one of my homes in the farthest reaches of backcountry, my "refrigerator" was a low hand-built stone cave beside a stream. Gravity and a short pipe diverted flow from the stream over the roof of the cave, cooling the fruit, milk, and other food inside. Moss covered the stone with a spongy green cap.

In camp, Mark stashes a bottle of wine in the creek to chill. He rejects my proposal to eat acorn-meal hardtack for dinner. We, too, are slaves to vehicle, cooler, and imported groceries. I brush off a thick layer of pine needles and pollen from the rickety picnic table and set up the two-burner camp stove. Stellar's jays bring splashes of deep blue to the feathery green pine boughs. They are noisy with *glooks* and a cry that sounds like a squeaky wheelbarrow.

Before dinner, we hike up the creek through a quiet ponderosa forest, following fresh bear tracks to a lush meadow ringed by low peaks and an approaching thunderstorm. Cattails surround a small pond, staked out by male redwing blackbirds, their epaulets bright crimson with breeding season plumage.

For a century and a half, these California mountains have been heavily mined for ore, timber, pasture, water, and recreational pleasure. Undoubtedly, livestock grazed in this meadow for many seasons; it is within reach of a rancher's seasonal use. Yet the meadow has all the signs of vegetation recovery: grass up to the waist, diverse wildflowers, no cow tracks, no corrals. To have this meadow entirely to ourselves feels strangely luxurious. Why aren't we whining about crowds and devastation?

The thunderstorm moves in quickly and chases us back to camp. Its first drops send up small clouds of dust as they hit the trail. Bear tracks now overlay the boot tracks we made on our ascent.

For years, too long ago to admit without nostalgic incantations, I lived in the southern Sierra Nevada. I lived there in times of fewer bears and a younger, thoughtless, agile grace. These mountains hold memories of my life held close to the flame. These mountains are family homelands, where homesteading ancestors ranched and ran livestock from the mid-1800s to the mid-1900s.

California sheep men—John Muir called them "muttoneers"— once used the western flank of the Sierra from Yosemite south to the sequoia country for seasonal pasture. In the public domain, this open range was exploited freely and thought to be inexhaustible.

My great-great-great-grandfather summered his flocks in the high country meadows west of Mount Whitney, the highest peak in the Sierra cordillera. His herders were likely Mexican or Paiute, Yokuts, or Tubatulabal, possibly Basque as well. Sierra shepherds formed a distinct rural culture: independent and resourceful, knowledgeable about weather and predators, about mountain passes and plant foods in the next meadow up the slopes, the camps of rest, the creeks that watered the flock after a hard drive. Their job was to make mutton and fleece.

The family muttoneers likely set fires to stimulate forage and clear obstacles for free movement of stock, a common practice at the time. Their sheep grazed five-mile-long meadows and crowded along creeks that were home to golden trout. Their flocks may have been among the earliest wave of domestic sheep to fatally infect native bighorn sheep.

A bighorn sheep band south of the family terrain, unusual for its subalpine habitat and homeland on the far west side of the Sierra's divide, disappeared in the 1870s, victims of a scabies die-off likely related to domestic sheep.

Severe overgrazing exhausted the High Sierra's lush montane meadows. "The sod and verdure are gone—eaten and trodden," noted a visitor as early as 1885, and "gravel is now ascendant." By the early 1900s, in response to widespread range degradation and pressure from cattlemen anxious to use the seasonal pastures for their own herbivores, sheep were excluded from the area. (My family, too, turned from sheep and shepherds to cattle, cow camps, and cowboys.) With the creation of forest reserves and grazing allotments, the federal government took a greater interest in managing the Sierra's public lands.

In my own California days, I frequently hiked that homeland with no awareness whatsoever of its lost native sheep. Their demise and displacement had, after all, been set against the prosperity of miners, loggers, and ranchers like my own family, whose livelihood put food on the table and progress on the agenda.

What kept the idea of wildlife conservation possible during my trekking era was partly attributable to continuing change in the paradigms of land use. A synthetic fleece rather than a wool jacket kept me warm while I read Durrell in camp at night. Brown rice, not lamb chops, simmered in the pot. Muttoneering was out; backpacking was in. So many lovers of the Sierra wanted to bring back the native fauna.

Skulls, historic records, and habitat characteristics give clues to the range once occupied by bighorns in bands along the Sierra's crest and east slope. Of seventeen populations, only nine made it to the twentieth century. By 1948, nine bands dropped to five. By the late 1970s, there were about 250 bighorns in two remote areas on the southern end of the mountain range. A moratorium had prohibited hunting since 1878. Beginning in 1972, the U.S. Forest Service and the National Park Service imposed sanctuary protections to reduce human disturbance.

The extant native sheep lived high on the Sierra's spectacular east scarp. In the early 1980s, their numbers were increasing. Under newly hatched recovery plans, wildlife biologists used stock from these growing populations to restore bighorn sheep to three other historic ranges, bringing today's wild-sheep areas to five. After the reintroductions, Sierra-wide sheep numbers continued to increase.

The animals lived fat and happy on intact, albeit patchy, habitat almost entirely within public lands—rocky, steep, glacier-carved, clear-air country with broad vistas and sheer cliffs of sheep-perfect escape terrain. The hordes of hikers largely respected sanctuary boundaries and regulations. Wildlife agencies worked with stockgrowers to prevent disastrous interactions between domestic and wild sheep. Poaching was practically nonexistent. The 1986 census for bighorn sheep in the Sierra came in at about 310.

In 1995, they numbered only about a hundred—in decline, imperiled, and isolated in bands with, in some cases, an alarming paucity of ewes. The sheep population was collapsing. In early 2000, the federal government officially listed *Ovis canadensis californiana* in the Sierra Nevada as an endangered species.

I have brought the love of my life to a steep slope of granite and foxtail pines. We climbed to these heights along creeks as clear as pain, through patches of pennyroyal that left the scent of mint on our fingertips as we brushed them in passing. The air is thin—we are more than eleven thousand feet above the Pacific—and we have held in our palms glassy chips of jet black obsidian left by Paiute hunters.

The color of the bedrock is engraved in my heart, pale beige in certain light, blue-gray when the light changes. Warm sun on dust and pine needles is the aroma of my bloodlines in these mountains. These slender foxtail pines stand as spare and formal as trees in a Japanese painting, their branches short reaches of green-black needles, their bark a rich cinnamon. The ground beneath our feet is a massive two-mile-high wall of beveled granite, the Sierra's eastern scarp rising above the Great Basin. These mountains are the land's attempt at flight.

Above us, cerulean lakes lie against the rocky headwalls of

alpine cirques—earlier Mark and I hiked up to them and back down to the foxtail trail again—and meadows of emerald sedges, scarlet shooting stars, and gentians with dense blue blossoms. The creeks fall through boulder-strewn gorges so narrow that you could leap over them if they were not so vertical. The cascades have the fresh clarity of glaciers and auras of violet spray.

Somewhere on the cliffs near the timberline are wild sheep on their summer range. We hiked up the mountainside to find them, but I do not care that we didn't. I am here, I think, to speak without words, to tell my Montana-born husband, a man with his own blood mountains, something about the Range of Light. How it strips away the veils of revelation, leaving a purity of image and sensation. How it taught me how to pay attention.

The high passes hold my family ghosts. This is the only land that could make me move away from the redrock desert without fatal heartbreak. These mountains, that desert, coincidentally the homelands of the wild animals that have kept me in thrall all year, are responsible for my nature and its consequences. For few other places is yearning worthy.

The late-afternoon light comes from the bedrock, from within the mountains themselves, pouring amber from granite and dust, wicking up through the trunks and out the branches of the foxtail pines. With apologies to photons and physics, there is no other explanation. Whatever creates this radiance, it is enough simply to breathe it.

We make our way down the steep trail until it switchbacks through the pennyroyal and manzanita and scattered stands of lodgepole pine. Below us, the land becomes drier and drier, with fields of sage and shadscale giving way to the summer brown floor of the desert valley. I remember the story of a pioneer woman from Missouri who hated this rough, arid country so much, each day she walked out of sight of her family and into the rough brush and wept over the lack of green.

As we descend, the shadow of the Sierra traverses the Owens

Valley below us and begins to creep up the stark tawny slopes of the White Mountains on the other side. The shadow is nearly twenty miles across. I once tried to walk on the lip of that shadow as it moved from the abrupt base of the mountains across sagebrush flats, wondering what I would do when I had to slow down for fences, roads, sandy playas, and the Los Angeles Aqueduct, which siphons the eastern Sierra runoff into the city so far south.

The shadow moved more quickly than I could. It sped across the *bajadas* with day's end behind it. Its edge flew over me.

John Muir, conservation godfather, peripatetic mountaineer, rider of storm winds from atop a swaying Douglas fir, devoted an entire chapter of his 1894 book, *The Mountains of California,* to the Sierra Nevada bighorns. He recognized that human activities had usurped wildlife habitat in the valleys and foothills on the Sierra's west slope. But, he wrote, the wild sheep had "little to fear in the remote solitudes of the High Sierras." Their alpine highlands, he assured his readers, their "rocky security," would keep them safe.

In the late 1860s, Muir built a cabin in what is now Yosemite National Park. He made a bed of cedar boughs and let a piece of Yosemite Creek flow along a ditch in the cabin floor. Frogs sang inside and he coaxed ferns through the floor under his window.

Muir had worked in the Sierra as a shepherd, though he would infamously condemn his flocks, all Sierra Nevada flocks, as "hoofed locusts." To a domestic sheep, Muir was not kind. He called it "a dull bundle of something only half alive" and "only a fraction of an animal, a whole flock being required to form an individual."

In contrast to this portrait, Muir gave "Nature's sheep" otherworldly nobility. The bighorns' agility and grace stunned him, purpled his prose, lured him to lofty heights to watch their ascents on craggy walls. To understand the design of such a creature, he wrote, you had to understand the rocks.

Like others, Muir passed on those strange descriptions of bighorns leaping off cliffs headfirst. Although his accounts were secondhand, he relayed the feat of rams diving off precipices and landing on their horns. He clobbered a found skull with his ice ax and declared it nearly impossible to crack. Another witness told Muir about watching a group of sheep jump off the brink of a 150-foot-high cliff. The sheep landed right side up, his informant said. "They just *sailed right off.*"

Like the desert's Blue Door Band, the Sierra Nevada sheep are loyal homebodies. Moreover, within the evolutionary fortress of *home* lies a strong fidelity to seasonal migration. Like good little *Ovis,* they vary their diet and location to take advantage of the most nutritious food available at any particular time.

Vegetation on their ramparts above the desert changes by elevation and season, drawing distinct food lines. Ecologically speaking, munching your way the two miles straight up from foothills to alpine fields would be like munching your way from Dirty Socks Spring, on the Owens Valley flats, thousands of miles north to the Arctic tundra.

During this time of year—late summer—the sheep stay in the rarefied air of the highest rock. They stared down at the tops of our heads as we rested among the foxtail pines near the timberline. They avoid patches of willow and forest and shrub-choked draws, where visibility is poor and predators might succeed. Because the snowfields retreat late in spring and take the first storms of the fall, the plant season at these high altitudes is brief.

In winter, the sheep migrate down the mountainsides to windswept ridges and exposed, often south-facing slopes. Some of the lowest elevations—the Great Basin's grass and scrub zone—offer

the richest diet and broadest vistas. Bitter cold and deep snow are
avoided, although the risk of predation is high. The lower elevations provide good seasonal sheep range. Here the Sierra bands
winter.

Of all the bighorn sheep biologists I have met, the shepherd of
the Sierra flocks is the most migratory. He, too, moves up and
down the mountains with these wild animals and has done so for
nearly thirty years. He believes that animal is *place;* where sheep
are tells a great deal about who they are. Much of what you
would want to know about bighorns in the Range of Light can
be traced to the work of Dr. John Wehausen and his colleagues.

Wehausen, a researcher at the University of California's White
Mountain Research Station in the Owens Valley, is a quintessential field geek. His tall frame is lean from hiking and his mind is
on everything from mitochondrial DNA and plant-digestibility
indexes to the dynamics of rapid extinction and reluctant colo-
nization.

He straps bighorn skulls, bones, and other body parts to his
backpack and carries them out of the backcountry to his work-
room—"the Morgue"—to study them, to find out how an animal
lived and died. He has at times undertaken research without
funding. "How could I stop just because of money?" he asked me.
"I need continuity to understand the biology."

He once drove a battered, duct-taped, runs-on-fumes pickup
to and from trailheads. He trades his uniform of rumpled field
clothes only for the black tuxedo he wears when he plays oboe in
the local chamber orchestra. One of his close friends is a soft-
spoken bronc rider and trapper turned mountain lion tracker. In
the mountains, the tracker finds cat, deer, and sheep signs and,
in the most remote and difficult places, the prints of John's size-
thirteen shoes.

Wehausen grew up in Berkeley and claims he was "bitten by
sheep long ago." The animals "take me to the remotest corners of

North America, and such places are the wellspring of my soul. There is nowhere like the Sierra in this regard."

Although John refers to bighorns, he could easily be speaking of the mountains, too, when he says, "There is something about them that keeps you going back. They are a wonderful reward for hard work."

John watches trends as closely as he watches the bands on their mountain—ewes, subadults, and rams he knows well as groups and individuals. He has found sheep and he has lost sheep.

His science is not as ramcentric as the views of some big-ungulate people, who by a hunting tradition tend to see the animal in the frame of trophy. Yet he marvels at the stunning choreography of the rut, at males presenting their headgear to one another to shake down any ambiguities of dominance. Size is how rams determine hierarchy, John notes. "Rams only know themselves by looking at each other."

When I spoke to him on a random summer day in August, he immediately knew, with psychic telemetry, where to send us to look for animals, to "look for rocks with legs on them." Mark and I climbed to the alpine tarns. The beauty of the place eclipsed the finding, of course, which in the end is the delicious mystery behind the mantra "I walked and walked and I never saw a sheep."

When I first heard John give a talk about his research, he began by saying, "I've spent an extraordinary amount of time collecting sheep shit." Don't let shit fool you. The path from shit to big-picture ecology makes sense.

What the bighorn sheep eat shows up in their scat. Analyses of fecal content reveal much about nutrition. When it comes to nutrition for mountain dwellers like these, elevation matters. They must eat well to fare well. The recent crash of the Sierra Nevada sheep was, John figured, related to food. The sheep made a deliberate choice to eat poorer forage in trade for a gain of some kind.

After predictable seasonal migration patterns repeated over

and over like . . . well, like *sheep,* in the 1980s the Sierra bighorns began to abandon their low-elevation winter range. They stayed higher. In doing so, they did not eat as well. Poor diet influenced vigor, birth rates, and lamb survival. Mortality exceeded recruitment. The Sierra Nevada lost two-thirds of its wild sheep.

John and his colleagues saw certain factors responsible for this shift: drought and hard winters, late storms and quirky soil moisture patterns. They noted another influence strong enough to alter the bighorns' homeland behavior: These sheep had a New Mexico problem—*Puma concolor.*

From the late 1970s to the early 1980s, John's fieldwork had revealed an increase in sheep kills by mountain lions. The preferred cat food was mule deer, but, as efficient opportunists, the lions were taking advantage of other meat by plucking mutton off low-elevation winter range.

Often a small number of mountain lions are responsible for a disproportionate number of kills. Certain mountain lions in the Sierra, John found, had become such "sheep specialists." They worked the winter ranges. Removing the offenders, it was thought, might give the sheep a reprieve and check their crash.

However, *Puma concolor,* too, was a protected animal. By referendum less than a decade earlier, Californians had banned the hunting of mountain lions in the state. The bighorn sheep caretakers in the Sierra had to argue for emergency measures. Eventually, five lions were trapped and removed from sheep range.

John hypothesizes that the Sierra sheep reacted to the escalating lion predation by avoiding their winter habitat. In the mind of a sheep, this range had become too dangerous. Their response to a complex ecosystem shift was to trade food for safety.

The costs of security were high. The sheep gave up better forage, warmer altitudes, and the ease of feeding where there was less snow. Up higher, the cold was more severe. One band lost fifteen animals in an avalanche. A great number of sheep went missing; individuals accounted for in the fall did not return the following summer. Overall, John's field surveys showed high winter losses and, he noted, a mysterious lack of carcasses.

Declining numbers appeared to reduce the comfort of group living, a critical bighorn adaptation strategy. Sheep cannot eat well if they are always worried about being eaten. Instead of snarfing, they are nervously looking about. The smaller bands had fewer eyes and ears for vigilance and perhaps sensed this added vulnerability on their winter range, where predation risk was so high. So they stopped going there.

The emergency lion control, milder winters, the listing of the Sierra sheep as an endangered subspecies, a recovery plan that took into account everything from mountain lion monitoring and winter range security to stricter measures against infection from domestic sheep—all of this, John said, bought animals and biologists some time. "When the Sierra bighorn was listed," he laughed, "I also got a better truck."

From the alarmingly low count of one hundred after the winter of 1995, the bands slowly began to grow again. In 2002, the total number of wild *Ovis* in the Sierra was about three hundred animals. That number had increased slightly by the time Mark and I hiked in the mountains. Their caretakers want to believe that the bighorns have squeezed through their bottleneck.

We pass a water bottle back and forth, gulping but sorely tempted to guzzle. On the broiling *bajada,* there is little shade. Our necks are stiff from looking up to the high peaks above us, to blue-black conifers, glacier-polished rock, patches of snow in the deepest crevices, streams as cool as ice. From one area to the other, there is a difference in temperature of at least twelve degrees, and a difference in altitude of over six thousand feet—straight up.

John recommended another hike to a different pass to look for rocks with legs. Knowing that the sheep hangout cannot be reached until higher elevations does not deter us. Nor does knowing that we will not likely see them even if we climb up there. We are simply running out of energy. The desert entraps us with its heat and our own exertion.

In myth, at least, California evokes an image of love-it-to-death throngs marching up its seductive backcountry trails in long, polite queues. We expected to see at least half the state's population of mobile adults in the High Sierra. No one was at Arnie's campground. They all must be up here, we figured. However, during our foxtail-pine hike and today's death march, we have had the mountains to ourselves.

We were unable to extricate ourselves from town early enough to hike the desert stretch in the cool of morning. Town was busy.

"Why were all those people running around town carrying tickets and little metal tubes?" I ask Mark as he puts away the water bottle.

"Those were backcountry permits and food canisters," he replies. "You put your food in them so bears can't get at it. Permits and canisters are required for overnights."

Oops.

We are freelancing up here. No aluminum tubes. As soon as we reach the first trees, some bear will leap out of a ponderosa and rip my day pack off my shoulders with its claws and teeth, taking out a chunk of my back while taking out our sandwiches and peaches. Who cares? I think as I trudge up the steep incline with lungs screaming like parade bagpipes. I will soon be lying facedown in the dust, making a handy human tabletop for the bear's lunch. I am thankful that I did not bring that plump little muffin, Nelson.

Hikers who camp in the backcountry seal their food inside canisters and follow rigorous protocols for bear deterrence. The local black bears are in a crisis garbage-withdrawal program. They are learning that humans do not mean food. Every granola crumb is under metal. However, we are day users—no plans to camp. We are merely going twelve miles up and down the six-thousand-foot face before dark. Or maybe not.

The chaparral gives way to California black oaks and shade, then a small creek embraced by the slender-leafed arroyo willow. We splash the cool liquid on our hot faces, then sit beside the water and eat our lunch before the bear can. From this spot, we are high enough to see across the valley to the White Mountains. The mountain shadow is hours away.

From crest to crest, the Sierra and the Whites are twenty miles apart. On the Sierra side, *Ovis canadensis californiana* (or *sierrae*). On the White Mountains side, *Ovis canadensis nelsoni,* the desert race of the Mojave, Great Basin, and Colorado Plateau. The races are ecologically distinct. Compared to the desert bighorns, the Sierra sheep have wider skulls and broader horn flares—signs of their isolation, John says.

From their lofty ramparts, the sheep groups peer across the blue air at one another. Maybe they want to just "sail right off." Yet they rarely come in contact with one another. Perhaps one of those "They don't like to get their feet wet" explanations might do. But that discounts the curiosity of John Wehausen.

"The *nelsoni* and *sierrae* races are closer than we think," he once explained to me. "We are finding past evidence of some females crossing both directions between Sierra and Whites and success-fully breeding to leave identifiable genetic lines. They have crossed the Owens Valley, but why they have stayed as distinct as they are is not clear to me.

"One reason I study bighorn sheep is because, for the most part, they can be well defined as populations. Population dynam-ics can be studied more cleanly where immigration and emigra-tion are minimal. However, the closer we look, the less clean it is."

The finest minds have worked with general assumptions about twenty-first-century bighorn sheep: remnant habitat, isolated bands. Hard-hearted homebodies, slow colonizers. Fidelity to

place to the point of doom as well as salvation. But the hoofy little buggers have a few surprises for us.

In the basin and range province of southeastern California, for
instance, sheep considered to be captive on their islands have
moved from one mountain range to adjacent mountains more
readily than anyone thought they would. The animals cross the
desert valleys to reach other patches of suitable mountain habitat.
Their unexpected intermountain travel has prompted biologists
to give philopatry a broader perspective and credence to habitat
conservation on a larger-than-island scale.

Another sheep surprise unfolded on the other side of the
mountains from our resting spot. Sixteen bighorns showed up in
the headwaters of a major Sierra Nevada river. They had eluded
even the most intrepid sheep seeker, John Wehausen. For nearly
thirty years, John has walked the mountains to make ground studies of historic habitat, empty or, if he was lucky, with theretofore-
undocumented bands. And here on a south-facing wall deep in
the Range of Light were sixteen lost sheep.

Were they a Blue Door Band enigma—vanished, thought to
be extirpated, then their numbers increased due to a few survivors, as if sprung from the wilderness itself? Or were they
sheep missing from known bands, sheep that packed up and tiptoed out of known range in order to escape from mountain lions?

During the period of winter range abandonment, one of
John's subgroups disappeared from its expected whereabouts and
did not show up on its summer range. Rams had been sighted on
the "new" area before. Now, ewes, lambs, and yearlings, as well as
rams, were found there.

The movement was remarkable but not unexpected, John
thought. "There is continuity of habitat from their traditional
range to the new area. We just didn't know they would use it.
Too many people treat wild animals as automatons. But these
sheep are making decisions."

Whatever the bighorns did, they did it by themselves. They moved to the deepest rhythms of a world that is so opaque to us, their own complete universe. John Muir believed that we would glimpse this world, begin to understand this animal, "as soon as we make ourselves acquainted with the rocks, and the kind of feet and muscles brought to bear on them."

The creek slides down the ravine. The temperature approaches ninety-five degrees. For now, I do not care about the voracious suck of water by the city of Los Angeles, every last drop once it hits the valley below. Up here, before L.A. can steal it, the water cools our skin and draws ribbons of sun through the willows. A few hummingbirds hurl themselves at our foreheads. Beyond the water borders, the air is lifeless and still. Above the creek, the willow boughs move gently in rills of air created by the flow.

The granite beneath my feet, familiar and lost, the desert spread below us under shimmering thermals, the border of rain-starved mountains beyond: How many lifetimes are needed to earn the landscape merely within this line of vision? Perhaps it is enough to possess the fiercest aspirations. In this country, Mary Austin wrote, "it is possible to live with great zest, to have red blood and delicate joys."

When we are not in the high country, I return again and again to a small museum in a valley town. Under bright ceiling lights and surrounded by a library silence (I am usually the sole visitor), I amble among the fossils, obsidian points, mineral collections, and shelves with cotton-lined boxes of bird eggs, from huge eagle and emu eggs to bushtit eggs the size of jelly beans.

The museum displays maps, guns, saddles, remnants of equipment from now defunct fruit farms, and photographs of mule trains, dusty, treeless main streets, and grumpy-looking men with pale farmer-tan foreheads and woolly-caterpillar mustaches. Newspaper clippings from the early 1900s reveal the tenor of local outrage at the piracy of Owens Valley water by Los Angeles. "Steal my horse, run off with my wife, but damn you, don't touch my water."

I save for next to last a close perusal of the basketry of local natives, an assemblage of winnowing trays, seed beaters, cradles, hats, and wide-rim wheat-colored baskets woven with designs of black lizards, turtles, butterflies, as well as with jagged geometric patterns. Some of the baskets are Paiute. Others were made by the Panamint Shoshone, the people of the Cosos, the people with the world's best rain doctors.

The last stop in the room is what I have come for. I feel like a squirmy kid. When all other treasures have been absorbed, I saunter casually over to a large white wooden box that sits on an old trunk, crowded between display cases. From the top of the box, a stuffed ferruginous hawk casts its raptor gaze at me.

The white box sprouts a fat orange extension cord that slithers cobralike into a hole in the ceiling. Two windows are cut in the face of the box, which is roughly the size of a washing machine. The smaller glass frames a scroll of yellowed canvas. A few lines at a time, the scroll unfurls a hand-lettered narrative. The California Department of Fish and Game, a note informs me, made the exhibit in the 1930s.

The larger second window reveals an intricate color diorama inside the box. A splendid painting of the Sierra crest rising above a deep valley—the landscape just outside the museum's walls—covers the back wall of the diorama. Impressionistic brushstrokes render silver-gray peaks flushed with a puffy delirium of pastels. Pink, rose, lavender, and a horizon the color of jonquils suggest atmosphere and distance. We are way up there on the alpine heights.

The one-dimensional mural flows seamlessly into a three-dimensional landscape, a sculpture of cliffs made from some sort of modeling compound spread over wire mesh. Plant bits and miniature cacti with spines dot the cliffs. Thick blobs of green and pink paint look like lichen on brown rocks.

At the foot of the cliffs are three bighorn sheep. Two of them drink from a pool of water made from a mirror. Partway up the slope, another sheep pokes its head in a shrub. It is hornless and looks tired.

Two more sheep bed down on the steep face of a cliff. A wire protruding from another oval bed indicates a missing sheep, perhaps unglued from its footing, then removed and lost. The sheep figures are about three inches tall, made of plaster or clay, painted yellowish brown. Broken limbs have been carefully repaired. The diorama is, after all, nearly seventy years old.

A flat-topped cliff dominates the center of the diorama. Standing on one side of the cliff, a noble toy ram skylines in an alert position, head raised, stare riveted partly to the viewer and partly to a distant object somewhere outside the frame.

I reach for a chrome toggle-style electric switch on the side of the box. I smile as if I would rather like to bite someone. I flip the switch.

A low-pitched grinding noise fills the room, awakening every last dead person memorialized in this carefully assembled repository of local history. The top window scrolls its story of bighorn sheep in the California mountains: "Even though occupying waste lands, mountain sheep disappeared. No thought was taken for the future of this valuable game animal."

The diorama motor sounds as if it's grinding up fresh loads of zirconium monkeys. The script rolls. "A sufficient breeding stock was not left. Protection came too late. The future of game is in your hands! Are you a conservationist?"

Suddenly, a toy bighorn bursts out from the boulders on one

side of the diorama. Its gender is somewhat indeterminate with a half sweep of horns, but I call it a ram. He moves from right to left along the flat top of the cliff in a jerky mechanical gallop. Inches short of the skylining sheep, he dives headfirst behind the cliff. More monkey pulverizing, and then the ram reappears and leaps along the cliff again. Grind, clunk, leap, gallop, dive, gone. Grind, clunk, leap, gallop, dive, gone.

The toy ram rides his wheel, sprocket, and pulley track again and again until I flip the switch. The sheep-o-matic diorama comes to a rasping halt. Then I leave the museum and walk out into the bright California sun.

SEPTEMBER

Ram 1000 was a mature male, high in withers and muscular in rump, with sturdy legs and few battle scars. He was fond of the cliffs that formed the seam between the curvaceous rust-colored Triassic sandstone along the river and the tilted steel blue limestone of older seabeds, rock with crags and outcrops and a surface so abrasive, it could draw blood.

A life of clash and butt explains much about Ram 1000's skull: two layers of thick bone overlying the brain, forming a double roof of protection against concussion; struts of bone separated by hollow cavities between the bone layers; some of the skull bones spongy, the nasal bones dense and thick—in short, a head with the physics of one big shock absorber. It could take a collision so violent, the ram's entire body would telescope with the force of the blow.

In studied bands, ewes generally outnumber rams as wearers of radio collars and ear tags. Ram 1000 was one of a few Blue Door rams to be marked. His collar was affixed during a capture years earlier, when Dave and Nike began their field research.

Even without a collar, he could easily be recognized. He was not particularly large. (The big ones tend to "burn out and die early," Nike told me.) But he was agile and virile. His curl swooped and flared into tips with a rare lack of brooming. His walk was often a slow-motion prance. Dave and Nike had watched him grow into maturity, fight, and breed.

Dave spoke of this ram with the reverent voices of hunter and biologist. He truly liked this ram. "Number One Thousand was

one of our best rams," he would say. "He had character." Or, "I
think One Thousand was my favorite ram."

A piece of Dave's favorite ram is lying on my dinner plate,
inside a corn tortilla. My fork is poised. I am about to eat him.

It is September now. Summer lingered for a while, still endur-
ingly hot, but with a thin coolness held in the malachite pools of
cottonwood shade. The washes flowed with blow sand and the
peregrine falcons drifted above the river, eyeing morning doves
with the intent to kill.

Hummingbirds whirred against Mark's shirt, trying to sip the
hibiscus on the aloha print. Sluggish and slow, catfish rolled their
pearly bellies in the overwarm shallows of the river, unfazed by
the impishly wild Navajo boys on the cut bank, who quickly
abandoned their fishing lines to swim.

In the garden, I remembered that the Chemehuevi Indians
loved to sing in their melon fields. We harvested cantaloupes so
fat, they were worthy of an opera. The tomatoes rarely made it
from the garden bed to the house. I plucked and ate the plump
red globes in situ with a crushed basil leaf, savoring the sun in
them.

Everyone in town said that a monsoon would break the heat.
In one day, in one rainstorm, we would be an entire season away
from the day before.

And so it came: sky heavier than earth, migraine lightning,
thunder you felt between your shoulder blades. The azure sky
turned the color of granite. A sudden wall of wind preceded not
showers but torrents. Sheets of rain drenched the desert, swelled
the river to an astounding volume, then moved on to New Mexico. Behind the storm, school opened and the kids no longer
went fishing. The pace of life shifted.

Our friend Jackie collected rainwater and began to soak her
desert tortoise, mimicking his natural hydration before hiberna-

tion. She minded what he ate so that he would not enter metabolic limbo with a belly full of undigested plant matter. He could
not go into his burrow dry and stuffed. He had to be a moistur-
ized, empty tortoise.

During the big storm, runoff roared down one of the washes
and fanned into the ranch bottom below our house. The junked
Mercedes in the field stood its ground, doors flung open. The
flash flood entered the north door, then flowed out the south
door, filling the cab with sand clear over the seat bottoms. The
driver's seat now sprouted a wild sunflower, a tall stem of green
behind the ivory steering wheel. The windshield was a spidery
web of aqua and silver cracks. Under the fierce summer sun, the
blue paint turned to the color of tinfoil.

After three months of living on scorched earth, of plots to
escape and inert desperation for relief, the pools of cottonwood
shade finally yielded their balm to the rest of the air. We remembered how hot it was, but not for long. In "Coolness," the Japanese poet Shiki wrote:

> *The plan to steal*
> *melons, that's forgotten too—*
> *how cool I feel!*

After the heat broke, I went to Ram Land for a visit. The bachelor bands, yet to be drawn into ewe range by unabashed lust,
would still display a nonchalant caution, I thought. They would
treat me as if I were just another yucca plant with binoculars. In a
few weeks, the rut would begin and they would become more
aggressive.

I took up a post and with a sorry impatience soon gave up
glassing the cliffs. No sheep. I lounged against a rock, read my
book, yawned. A pesky nip of guilt told me that such laziness
would not likely earn a sighting. *I sat and sat and I never saw a sheep.*
In walked a single ram. He dropped down a steep boulder-

choked draw to drink from the river. He was handsome and sleek and held up the most elegant curl I had ever seen on any Blue Door ram, a flared helix so pure and breathtaking, his head was a work of art.

I saw this attribute as neither trophy nor score sheet in a record book. What I saw was a lightning image of the world without this animal, of the loss not only of flesh and bone but of ritual and mystery imperfectly known to us, a loss of time older than we are and of all of the evolutionary reasons behind head design.

Think of this: no S-necked heron, no crimson throat of a cactus blossom or cinnamon bark on a foxtail pine, no feel of the weight of a falcon's eyes on your skin. Think of the last set of curled keratin atop the head of a rare desert herbivore beside a khaki river. Think of your final glimpse of pale rumps in silent recession toward some distant horizon. Think of losing the exquisite details of a second world. To contemplate this emptiness is the cruelest, loneliest course of the imagination.

The perfect ram saw me across the river's serene flow. He stared at me as if trying to figure me out and report back to his group with his observations. When two more rams joined him, he hardly turned his head.

As John Wehausen had told me in California, rams know themselves by looking at one another. This ram looked and knew who he was: older, beefier, bigger headgear, bigger *cajones*. The enormous testicles on one end and the massive horns on the other were, in fact, a kind of counterweight system. You cannot have uneven rams that tip over and smash their noses. It is far too embarrassing.

All three bighorns pulled leaves from shrubs and chewed. Mr. Perfect leaned against a rough limestone ledge and rubbed against it, moving back and forth like an itchy horse at a scratching post.

Rams were very much on Dave's and Nike's minds as summer

came to a close. Indirectly, the Blue Door rams appeared to be kicking up the winds of change in the band of wild sheep that hung from the stone above the river.

Once the band stepped out from its long years of vanishing, when (if) the last remaining individuals constituted a breeding pair instead of the doom of a single gender, there was the chance of natural recovery. Indeed, the band grew from their fragile remnant. Although accurate counts began long after that turning point, the numbers now told Dave and Nike that, in the past several years at least, the flock had doubled. Individuals were healthy. Recruitment—sheep of reproductive age added each year—remained high.

The ewes stuck to the homeland as if no other sheep paradise existed. The drought sent them to fringes for better food, but few hooves stepped off the map. The rams, however, seemed restless.

Nike had watched a young ram race back and forth along the riverbank, obviously agitated. He jumped into the river, crossed it, and joined a second ram on the opposite bank. So rarely did sheep cross this boundary, we almost never bothered to look for them on that side of the river. Were these two drawn to food unexploited by wild sheep? Had they crossed because other rams had picked on them? Were the reasons important enough to break the bad juju of staying away from that side of the canyon?

Ferdinand the pacifist, the one-horned ram that went across the river and hung out there solo, had not been seen again. (The pair that Nike saw cross the river would return for the rut.) Over the year, on the homeland side, a few rams had roamed perilously close to a flock of domestic sheep. Thus far, they had come back before contact.

Dave and Nike's meticulous observations hinted at a trend. When rams expand beyond their range, they explained, it might be a sign that the herd is reaching carrying capacity. Having rebounded from nearly nothing, the population was leveling off.

The sightings of walkabout rams above the canyon rims, on flatter ground occupied by humans and livestock, disturbed Dave and Nike. Everyone involved with this herd was reminded of the possibility that a single ram could step off the island, nose around a domestic flock, then return, a vector of disease, to infect the band and send it into oblivion. The natives would be gone— again—perhaps, this time, forever.

Dave and Nike talked of putting some bighorns in the bank, so to speak. They immersed themselves in studying the option of splitting the herd, of capturing and moving sheep farther down-river to safer grounds, to remote regions of the greater homeland, historic range of the canyon's bighorns but long empty of sheep.

Factors more complex than God had to be weighed in such a decision, yet the most critical were the most basic. The new habi-tat was superb—food, water, escape terrain. The source herd would not be jeopardized by the loss of selected individuals. The chances of survival were thought to be high. If the transplant were to happen, the work had to be done before the rut.

Across from me, the rams bedded down to rest and ruminate. Each animal's rumen transformed fibrous masses of canyon plants into nutrients, energy, and, out the other end, shiny chocolate pellets with nipples and dents. Mr. Perfect dropped his feathery eyelashes over his liquid amber eyes. How, I wondered, can one sleep with head upright when carrying twenty-five pounds of horns between one's ears?

There were other developments in Ram Land. A year ago, Dave and Nike had determined that their wildlife agency could offer a ram for harvest, the first of the native herd to be hunted (legally) since the band's comeback. The ram-ewe ratio and ram age classes, they thought, could support a single hunt.

Although not all research agrees about the effects of removing older, dominant rams, such selection by hunting is generally accepted as having no long-lasting harm. At eleven years or older,

the rams are thought to be near natural demise and thus expend-
able, not exactly useless, but geezers nonetheless. The hierarchy
of dominance then changes and younger rams become active
breeders.

The wildlife agency auctioned a ram permit for the Blue Door
Band. In a somewhat carpe diem manner, the hunter chose and
shot a ram with a radio collar. Collars are secure but loose and
tend to rub the hair on a sheep's cape. This hunter took home a
trophy with a shaved neck. He gave away the meat. The radio
collar was taken in and retired.

The killed ram was a good ram, not quite a geezer. He left
behind others of sound breeding stock. He was Dave's favorite
ram: Ram 1000. The ram I am about to eat.

Since the hunt, our piece of meat had resided in the freezer, next
to the orange juice. Thawed, it was a deep burgundy red with a
pale white vein of gristle. I stir-fried garlic, poblano chilis, tomatoes, and cilantro from our garden. I sliced the meat, then sizzled
it over the flame. Cooking, it smelled like mutton, tender but neither gamy nor strong.

We had not performed the rituals of a hunter, the wielder of
death and handler of the animal out of whom all life had been
drained. I felt uneasy with this, irresponsible.

Mark lit slim tapers in the silver candleholders that once be-
longed to my grandmother. We rolled up vegetables and meat
into warm corn tortillas and sat down at the table. Desert bighorn
fajitas.

Now, fork hovering over my plate, I think, This is want, not
need. I could have given the meat to our coyotes. I can hunt and
gather in the aisles of grocery stores. I need not kill, eat, and wear
these sheep. I watch, record, and draw them, removed from raw
flesh and blood. I prefer animals that are *animated*—I cannot bear

their stillness. This meal feels like a submerged soul reaching for a deep, deep bond.

The taste of the meat lingers on my tongue. Rain and river. Bedrock to soil to plant to milk to bone, muscle, and sinew. I am eating my canyon. Eating stone.

OCTOBER

Sunrise in the redrock desert has the calm of water. Strange that it be thus in a parched expanse of rock and sand. Yet this is how it comes: a spill of liquid silence, sunlight the color of embers, every surface bathed in it. The heart aches to live to see the start of a day, every day, luminous in the unmoored distance.

How can there be such quiet among a most garrulous species grouped together in space and task—no voices yet? I believe that the quiet prevails because all of us are desert people. We are known gazers into the horizon at early hours. That pause between social discourse and the solitude of the senses feels acute today, a day that will deliver into our hands, briefly, the wildest flesh of the canyon.

Perhaps the quiet is accidental prayer, an attentive stillness that conflates perception with desire. Maybe it is sleepiness at the early hour or the fact that some among our group are quite bashful. The low sun torches the buttes and mesas around us. Each saltbush stands distinctly silver-green on the cayenne red pediment, casting its own violet shadow. The light is what we watch, what steals our voices. When the light changes, when the fire in it passes, we talk.

Dave and Nike brief us on the day's procedure. The helicopter will bring two sheep at a time into the landing area. Two carry teams will move them to the work tent. Three or four people can carry each mesh sling by its handles, maybe more for a big ram. Another person should be on the horns, holding the head upright so the animal doesn't regurgitate its rumen and choke.

Dr. Scott Bender gives instructions, as well. The sleeves of his work shirt are rolled back. An object with tubing sticks out of his back pocket. You could pick him out of a crowd and know that he is a veterinarian. He has assembled an array of medical kits on the tailgate of his pickup. Earlier, he recruited Bill Downey, a friend, and me as his medics. I am to work the blood samples.

Mark works on a carry team. Dave will attach radio collars and punch in ear tags. For two days, Nike will not separate herself from a clipboard with papers that create the first profile of every sheep brought in from the canyon. She has the look on her face this morning of someone holding it all together. At several points, she will ride out with the chopper crew to help locate animals she wants for the translocation, seeking ratios of gender and breeding age for the new band.

Mara Weisenberger is here from the San Andres National Wildlife Refuge in New Mexico. She has brought two colleagues, Guy and Coby, and four aluminum crates that she designed specifically for transporting bighorn sheep. Five others have come from the Navajo Nation Department of Fish and Wildlife.

We will be responsible for the following: blood samples, ear and nasal swabs, mouth drench, inoculations, parasite check, body measurements, body temperature, respiration monitor, physical exam, microchip, radio collar, ear tags.

"Two sheep will come in each load," Scott says. "We'll work them at the same time. I want no more than six minutes per sheep. Our handling should be over and done within six minutes."

We think we have a wait ahead of us: coffee, relaxed postures, quiet talk, the desert silence still an enchantment.

Scott hardly finishes speaking when a pinpoint of sound emerges from the direction of the river. Then it comes quickly, the five-rotor T-tailed yellow bubble and its throaty roar. A cable dangles from the helicopter's belly. At the end of the cable hang double-decker slings, one above the other: upstairs, in silhouette, the curl of a ram's horns; downstairs, two ewes. Three sheep.

After more than a year of preparation, wild sheep are being put into the savings bank. From the band of eighty sheep, twenty-four will be selected, captured, and moved to a release site far downriver. If perils befall the Blue Door Band, bighorns native to this canyon will survive in this second homeland.

The new range is deeper into the backcountry, wilder, and farther from domestic livestock and development. The sheep will have abundant forage. Springs, potholes, and the big river can quench their thirst. The canyon walls provide nearly ideal escape terrain as well as niches and boulder caves for lambing. There are superb views into the Paleozoic chasm. There is room to grow from founder stock and to map a considerable expanse of home range. The new sheep place, in fact, looks like home. It is the habitat of ancestors, a slice of river canyon that has been empty of their kind for thirty or forty years.

You would wish, in a purist's world, that the animals could move to new sheep places by themselves, find their way to wild quarters of their own choosing. Yet their own evolutionary commitment as sedentary specialists—homebodies—makes them reluctant pioneers. And for surrounded, relict bands such as this one, the risk of self-dispersing to the "wrong" place is deemed too great. To colonize safe, unoccupied habitat, twenty-first-century desert sheep need this ark setup and our team of Noahs. They will take a high-tech ride to bighorn paradise.

They will be taken from the canyon of their birth to the nearby work site in mesh slings dangling from the helicopter, undergo less than six minutes of handling, and then be transferred to the San Andres crates. The crates will be trucked overland to a rim high above the canyon bottom, then carried by the chopper to the release site on the riverbank.

Dave and Nike have timed the two-day operation for sheep well-being and transplant success. Lambs are long weaned. The rut has yet to begin; they will not be moving pregnant animals. October bears the gift of clear skies and calm flying weather. Because the day promises to be hot and sunny, we have begun early, reducing the addition of heat stress to the fright of capture. A portable canopy, a sort of minimalist gazebo on tent poles, shades the work tarp, where the medical and tagging work is to be done. Crates sit in the back of pickups, one per truck, ready for sheep storage.

From the work camp, it is impossible to see the chase and capture, the chopper's plucking of an animal from a chasm of vertical stone. About this I am insanely curious yet relieved to miss the split-second crossing from "wild" to "managed" as the net falls over a running animal and it becomes our hostage.

Instead, I imagine fat, temporarily deaf sheep with their noses in bushes, oblivious to a giant metal locust orbiting their heads. They dream a funny dream. They awake in a new place with a *Where the hell am I?* look and start eating again. I envision the old ewe in the San Andres trotting into her wind cave and staying there until every last chopper in the universe goes away.

The helicopter crew works on contract through a private company in Wyoming. Gary, the pilot, is reputed to be the best in the wildlife-capture business. On board with him are a net gunner and two athletic youths known as "muggers." On the ground, a fifth crewman works the cable to its load and drives a fuel tanker.

After Nike briefs them on the lay of the land and desirable captives, Gary and his chase crew fly the canyon's spine until they find sheep—let's say a ewe, since the new band requires more ewes than rams. The ewe bolts and runs with a group that bounds across pinnacles and broken rock. Unlike pronghorn, bighorns are not endurance runners. They are climbers. Their lungs are not built for a long chase. A long chase also risks heat stress and a fatal metabolic disorder known as "capture myopathy."

The ewe may make short dashes, then stop and scramble under an alcove or boulder until the helicopter nudges her out. Gary uses the helicopter as an agile tool, moving up, down, sideways, or at a standstill hover.

Where there should be chopper doors, there is empty space, a wide gap at the craft's sides, where gunner and muggers hang halfway out, held by harnesses and safety straps. When the ewe runs into the open, the gunner fires a cartridge-propelled net over her head. The entanglement holds her. The muggers jump down from the helicopter and approach. They grab the horns, lift the head, and blindfold the ewe. The darkness of the blindfold instantly calms her. The blindfold hides from her the sight of her captors. It spares us from seeing her fear.

The muggers hobble her feet with a webbing strap and secure her into the nylon-mesh sling, her sternum down and her head upright above the sling's top edge: a ewe in a drawstring bag. They attach the cable and reboard the chopper. Gary slowly raises his aircraft and lifts the animal off the ground. Then she is in flight at the end of his pendulum.

The sheep seeking has unfolded quickly. The first round captured two ewes and a ram. Now the helicopter hovers over the landing knoll, spraying us with whirling dust and plant debris. Gary sets his parcels down as if they held the last eggs on Earth; then he lifts off to give safe height to the rotor blades. The carry teams run into the dust cloud and pick up the sheep.

The inexperienced among us glue our antennae to the experienced, learning from them with barely a word passed between us. I see in Mara the grace that keeps her New Mexico flock and hope alive. She is careful, smart, calm. I am amazed by the quiet of this work. No one has told us to whisper and glide our motions, yet we do so as if by instinct.

The hobbled trio lies on the tarp in (one hopes) a comfortable position of sternal recumbence, heads held up, no necks twisted or legs crushed. Scott moves from animal to animal, watching for injury, labored breathing, overheating, drooling, and other signs of stress. Bill administers vaccines. Mara and Coby help Dave affix ear tags and radio collars to the ewes' necks. Nike assigns each collared animal a number and radio frequency.

I hand medical kits to Scott. He passes me a hypodermic needle full of blood. With the needle, I pierce the seal on a glass tube and press blood into it, dividing the rich red fluid among the four vials. Empty, the vial was as cool as an October morning. Blood-filled, it passes the animal's body heat through the glass to my hand.

Mark and Dondi, one of the young Navajo men, are the team's strongest, so they have knelt down on the tarp with the big ram. With a hand on each horn like a calf roper, Mark holds the ram's head. The blindfold hides his eyes. Suddenly, the muscular neck pulses. It could wield a head blow strong enough to break Mark's thigh. With Dondi's help, the ram settles down again.

Epochs pass. We poke and prod them, vampire their veins. My hands are full of glass vials of blood. Bristles of sheep hair cover the front of my shirt. My hands shake. Bill's hands are trembling. We look at each other as if we were the world's most inept and pathetic wildlife handlers. Then we look at Scott's hands. His hands are shaking, too.

The two ewes have been moved into crates. Five people carry the ram to a truck and lift him onto the tailgate, lined up with the crate door. The opening is less than half a sheep high; you do not want the animal to stand and escape as it is moved inside. Once inside, he can stand up. Already there is a ewe in there. Older rams cannot be crated together.

The handlers must remove all restraints as the sheep goes in, a difficult and dangerous maneuver. They compose themselves, look at one another to communicate readiness, then go. Mark detaches the blindfold with one hand as the ram slips through the door. The hobble is off in a blink. Ram in, door shut, no ewe flying out. How they did this all at once—box a few hundred pounds of *Ovis* into a cube of aluminum—no one seems to know.

Along the side of the crates, narrow windows provide ventilation. Jeff covers the windows that face the work site so the sheep cannot see us. They still need that calming. He makes certain they are in the shade.

Scott turns to the crew. We stand before him like limp sock monkey puppets. Silently, Bill mouths to me, *That took an hour.*

"That took five minutes a sheep. Great job," Scott says.

The ram crashes against the crate with one colossal butt. The chopper flies in with four sheep on the end of its tether.

Between sheep deliveries, we move the canopy as the sun's angle changes, keeping the pool of shade as large as possible. October's sun can be fierce at day's peak. Everyone eats dust. Hands no longer shake. Our dance of tagging and treatment becomes nearly flawless, even when Gary brings in four sheep at a time. Mostly, he carries doubles. Scott guides Bill and me with gentle directions. We stay at or under six minutes.

A ram is on watch. One of the muggers told us he fell during the chase and bonked his nose. Scott examines the ram's nose, head, and body twice, then two times more. Once the ram is in a crate, he watches it for a limp, imbalance, or listlessness. Everyone fears injuries during the chase, though the pilot will back off if sheep panic is too frantic. So far, he has brought them in and lowered them to the landing without mishap.

When a ewe struggles on the tarp, Mark talks to her softly. He uses his talking-to-horses voice. I concentrate on refining my hastily acquired art of venipuncture. I hold all four glass tubes between the fingers of my left hand and fill them with the needle in my right hand. The genetic signature in this drawn blood could reveal the lineage of the Blue Door Band, unravel secrets of their bottleneck and missing years.

So far: one bruised ram nose and blood shed only into the vials. When Bill drenches the mouth of a ewe, she spits the water back out. No one blames her. During handling, the rams seem more docile than the ewes. We move some feisty young ewes that try to levitate themselves into freedom during the four seconds between hobble removal and a crate door shut behind them. The haunches that might launch them out of this ordeal are the muscular haunches that propel them up sheer cliffs. I see rumps of steel.

Gary brings in three ewes. I kneel down with one of them as Mark holds her horns. Her pale brown fleece feels coarse and brittle, not curly, a pelage suited to the desert. The undercoat is lighter in color and densely soft. On her face, the hairs are short and glossy. Her black tail is slightly longer than a thumb. She has a scar on her flank, chipped horns, and a torn ear. In my mind I see her eyes beneath the blindfold, for without them she seems incomplete. Her heart beats against my fingertips.

John Muir heaped cottony puffs of praise on the appearance of wild sheep in the Sierra, ever deploring their domestic cousins. "The tame is timid; the wild is bold," he wrote. "The tame is always more or less ruffled and dirty; while the wild is as smooth and clean as the flowers of his mountain pastures."

Less sleek than a deer, this young ewe shows where she lives: in rock and sand and difficult places. She is sturdy, strong, and scruffy. She smells like dust and fear.

These sheep are not flatlanders. Their feet give them away as bovids that no longer roam steppes or grassy plains. This ewe's feet read the stone, find footholds on ledges no wider than an inflated caterpillar. The edges of her pointed black hooves are hard but surprisingly elastic. The divided toes are flexible. One toe can move up, the other down or laterally to meet the irregular contours of rock. The bottoms of the hooves are neither rigid nor flat; they bulge at the posterior in a rounded pad, a cushion of soft tissue for grip and shock absorption.

In their canyon, high on their rock, even under a camera lens, bighorns loom as large as elk, an illusion they seem to have perfected. Up close, they are smaller than you ever expect them to be. To see this optical difference is a shock. This ewe weighs just over a hundred pounds. Running beside a tall person like me, she—her shoulders—would reach my bottom rib.

"Which one is the hot ewe?" Scott asks as he walks over to us from his parked truck. He carries a pack of medical gear.

A ewe on the tarp is overheating. Her sides heave. Mara places an ice pack on her flanks while Coby rubs cool water into her fleece. Scott treats her first, before the other animals, as Bill and I hustle beside him and try to match our work to his skilled speed. Four minutes and we're done.

Nike lifts the radio from her pocket, ready to call pilot and chopper out of the canyon and back to the work site. She asks Scott, "Should we release her? Put her back?"

Scott takes the ewe's temperature and decides that the cooldown has worked. They move her to a shaded crate, where she butts the walls a few times, then settles down. On the radio, Nike and Gary determine that we have enough sheep for the day. It is time to caravan to the canyon rim and release site.

A handsome, slender man in his early twenties, Fernando has the polite reticence of a traditional Navajo. He barely spoke as he worked on his carry team, held heads, loaded animals. When he does speak, his words are soft and brief. One of his jobs is to check on the sheep in the crates. His vigilance seems to me to be quite profound. He moves with the shy, silken grace of a deer. Now, our work finished, he stands near a sheep crate.

The crate window is open because the sheep have settled down and Mara wants them to have ventilation during the truck ride. Most of them are lying down in their crates, choosing a stillness that likely combines self-preservation with the simple reality of confinement.

The largest ram, the one that needed five handlers, stands with his head against the narrow window slot, where he looks out into the arena of his captors. Fernando approaches the crate at an angle, rather than directly across from the crate window. From about six feet away, he watches, arms folded across his chest, body pondstill.

Suppressing the congenital Anglo tendency to babble and fidget, I stand motionless behind Fernando so that I, too, can look at the ram. We do this, I think, because our distance will not spook him. And because the ram has no blindfold and there is in us an uncontainable urge to see his eyes.

The eyes are the color of polished oak. Across them run black irises in that odd horizontal ellipse so distinctive of highly sociable ungulates. Something about that not-round iris implies mischief and teasing. Something about that iris makes goats and sheep look as if they would like to nibble your earlobes with their velvety lips.

The orbs are globe-round, an inch and a half across and slightly protruding. The ram can see behind himself. He can see—instantaneously, up or down a vertical face—where he steps. He moves his head slightly and now he can see us, Fernando and me. Our eyes lock. In my mind I reassure this trapped animal that this silent conversation is not about death.

From the high desert above the river canyon, I can see the entire world: the mesa of the Birdhead petroglyphs to the north, a fifteen-mile-long escarpment the color of blood to the west, buttes and spires of sandstone stranded clear south into Arizona, hazy blue mountain ranges—four islands of them—afloat on the shimmering horizon. Bands of beige and rose slickrock dotted with dark green pinyons and junipers. Creases where the earth gives way to unsteady water and deep, sinuous canyons.

I slowly turn 360 degrees and all around me the views are unbroken, no distance less than sixty miles from me to the seam between land and sky. Distance is a desert rat's addiction.

I choose a direction—that canyon and that blue mountain over there—and take off. Mark grabs the back of my collar. "Stay here. We have work to do."

One of the creases in the distance is the rim of the river canyon. Below it, on a debris fan, lies the release site. For the helicopter work, we must stay up on top, on the flats, wrapped in this dizzy, dreamy view.

Our caravan made its way down the highway, passing travelers who did not know that they were driving by twelve rare desert bighorns with needle marks in their butts. From the highway we took a dirt road. Scattered houses and corrals gave way to uninhabited desert.

Mark maneuvered the truck carefully over ruts and bumps, trying not to shake up the ewes and ram in the crate on the pickup bed. I looked back at the load often and gave myself a stiff neck. I remembered the last time I had hauled sheep, years ago: domestic Rambouillet wethers hog-tied in the back of an open pickup, bouncing over the rugged Montana prairie on a friend's ranch, Mozart playing as I drove them to a stock truck and their doom. It was but a blip in the ancient bargain of domestication, of animals husbanded and eaten.

These wild sheep are in our hands only briefly, once in their lifetime, and as far as I know, there are no plans to eat them. The protection of rare animals marks a new kind of bargain, one that runs contrary to the historical imperative to press everything alive, dead, inert, or otherwise into human service.

This ark business is still a rough jewel in the modern psyche. It signifies an act of conscience, a fragile ascendance toward the notion of intrinsic worth, that wild creatures have value independent of human measure. Some of the people we passed on the highway would hardly know the difference between a gazelle and a leggy duck, yet this translocation, these desert creatures, would excite and move them beyond words.

Leaving the dirt road, we followed a barely discernible two-track path until it came to a dead end on the top of the mesa. Gary will now lift the crates off the parked trucks and fly them down to the river one at a time on the cable. Scott has checked each animal. They remain unharmed, but he feels their captivity—by now about five hours long—must come to an end. He wants them out on the rocks with food, water, space, and one another. When our backs are turned, the sheep stare out the window slots at us.

Nike ties hot-pink streamers to a truck's antenna so that Gary can see the wind direction on the ground. The midday thermals and a slight breeze have picked up, but he flies in smoothly, lands, and lets out the muggers.

The muggers escort Dave, Nike, Dondi, and Pam, a Navajo wildlife biologist, to the aircraft, guiding them safely beneath the whirling blades. Gary flies the foursome down to the river site, where they will receive the crates and release the sheep.

As we wait, Coby and Mara hand out a snack. From New Mexico they brought the meat of one of the animals hunted on the White Sands Missile Range: oryx jerky. We stand on the Colorado Plateau eating an African antelope.

The muggers join us, removing their bulbous white helmets and emptying sand from their boots. I ask the younger mugger, a lean, wiry nineteen-year-old, what he does in Wyoming when he isn't working wildlife contracts.

"Rodeo bull riding," he replies.

As jobs go, mugging and bull riding make sense. Ride an acrobatic, highly inflammable helicopter, grapple frightened horned, hooved animals on craggy walls and narrow ledges above rocky chasms. Shake your spine like a Slinky on the back of angry male beef.

In the hustle of work, I refrained from asking Mara about the old ewe in the San Andres Mountains. Months have passed since I visited the New Mexico refuge and, with Kevin Cobble, the refuge manager, listened to the ewe's radio-collar blip as she stood on her mountain. I fear that Mara will tell me that the ewe lost the odds against her—the predators, her advanced age, the generals deciding that she threatened national security.

Mara knows her sheep and her mountains. She knows about SAE 067. But I do not want her to tell me that the last native bighorn sheep in the Chihuahuan Desert has died. That passage would press on us a great weight.

I gnaw oryx. Then I ask, "Mara, how is the old ewe?"

A breeze flutters the pink streamers on the truck antenna. The far-flung mountains shiver atop heat waves.

"She is still alive," Mara replies. "She had her lamb this year, a ewe lamb."

"The transplants? The Kofa sheep and the others?"

"We lost a few to mountain lions, but not as many as we expected during the first few months. There's a new crop of lambs. We think the transplant will take."

The crates await Gary's pickup. On their silver walls, petroglyph-style bighorns in black paint leap around the U.S. Fish and Wildlife Service stickers. Inside, the real sheep lie quietly with their legs tucked under them. Air moves through the open vents. Without a sound, Fernando slips over and checks them.

Mara describes the crate design. "We tried to cover everything to the last bolt, all from a sheep's point of view."

She and Kevin even sat inside the crates as truck and trailer hauled them down the highway on test runs. "We wanted to see how they rode, where the noise came from. We wrapped cables and chains in tape so they wouldn't rattle and cause more stimulation than the sheep already experience."

Several wildlife managers in Nevada copied her crate design, she says. "They told me, 'You've got these figured out down to a gnat's ass.'"

The half door gets sheep inside without breakouts. For the release, the door opens at full height to an inviting panorama of freedom. Handlers wait behind the back wall, not wanting to startle or prod the animal, but allow it to bolt out on its own and find its way to safe terrain.

Mara recalls the "sensitive release" of a large ram. She unlatched the door and hid so she would not disturb his exit. The ram sat in the box for an hour. He would not move. She wiggled the crate. She rocked and tipped the crate. The ram sat, door wide open. Finally, he stood up, whirled around, and butted the back wall, where she was crouching.

Gary buzzes in and hovers over a crate. The muggers attach the cable and the chopper lifts the crate off the back of the truck and flies off. We watch the crate spin a few times. The weight of the sheep inside appears to cause a twirl. Gary tries to correct it by varying his speed; then aircraft and load disappear over the lip of the canyon. Too much spin, Mara worries. Already, in her head, she is designing foils or some way to stabilize the crates for the next time.

One by one, Gary flies the crates to the release site. He lines them up in a neat row on a sandy patch of open ground on the debris fan. The crate doors face up-canyon toward secure terrain.

A hundred yards away from the crates, the river flows over its ancient bed, a sunlit ribbon of jade water unbroken but for lacy ripples over submerged rocks. I see the place in my mind because I have passed it many times in a boat. I have explored its face of cliffs, where hanging springs drape emerald foliage over terracotta rock and brass-colored frogs hide behind maidenhair ferns, their bodies moist and cool. The steep, broken country is sheep heaven. It is but a remnant wild; rugged, out of reach, a taste of all of the wild that we have lost to our own hubris.

Nike and her crew stand behind the crates and open the doors. Twelve desert bighorns leap into the warm October air and race upriver, the first natives to return to a place that suddenly does not feel so empty.

Paul Shepard writes,

Wild animals are not our friends. They are uncompromisingly not us nor mindful of us, just as they differ among themselves. They are the last undevoured riches of the planet, what novelist Romain Gary called "the roots of heaven." . . . As a fauna only the wild are a mirror of the multifold strangeness of the human self. We know this. It is why we scrutinize and inspect and remark on them, make them the subject of our art and thought, and sometimes kill and eat them with mindful formality, being in place with our own otherness.

How can this young bighorn ram, whose blood has spilled on my hands, not be "mindful" of us? We rob him of his mobility, his best weapon against predation. We incite terror. There is no way to explain that this capture is temporary and that sheep paradise— succulent plants, exquisitely edible stone, estrous ewes, the river— will soon surround him.

At the end of this second day of the translocation, the chase will be over.

The needle's draw has leaked sticky red blood all over my fingers. In spite of the leak, I still have enough blood to fill the four vials that Scott needs for his lab work. I try to cant the needle inside the glass tube so that I do not press the plunger too firmly and "blast" the cells, ruining them for the tests.

Today we have relaxed teams and feistier sheep. A young ewe

with a pelage the color of ash spooks in her crate and tries to bash it to bits, despite blocked-out windows that are meant to diminish her fright. When I lean against the truck, I feel the vibration of her hooves through the metal.

Dondi is full of teasing Navajo humor. He tries to convince Dave that yesterday's released sheep hiked upriver all night long, many, many miles, to return to their homeland. Using Pam's binoculars, he glasses the cliffs near the work site. "Dave! They're back."

Out in the air above the canyon, the pilot spots fewer animals to match Nike's selection. The sheep have become more wary. Some hide behind rocks when they hear the chopper, for which you can hardly blame them. If I were a bighorn, I'd dress up like an antelope and hitchhike to the Mexican border. Nike does not want animals that already have collars. Many are older females. Two are barren. On the radio, she tells Gary that we have enough rams and asks him to find young females.

The chopper crew chases a band of ewes and a ram. When two ewes are netted and airlifted away, the ram tries to follow, as if his entire sex life were fluttering heavenward.

On a ledge above the river, the gunner nets a lamb. The muggers hobble her small feet and wrap her head in a blindfold the size of a handkerchief. Instead of dangling her sling from the cable, they put her inside the chopper. The lamb limo flies a few minutes longer, nets a ewe, then brings them both in. The lamb is so small, Dondi carries her to the work tarp by himself.

She is about six months old, progeny of a fall rut I watched and a springtime birth during the weeks of my quixotic attention. She was one among the year's crop of popcorning fluff beside the river, now weaned, lankier, and destined to run with the ewe band in their new terrain. She still has oversize ears and short devilish horns. Her black Y-shaped nostrils are so delicate, they hardly seem possible. Her docility and petite size incite an epidemic of tenderness among the men.

Gary brings in a single ewe, the twenty-fourth capture and the last of the Blue Door Band to be transplanted. For this singleton, too, there is the leisure of awe but not of time. Although she is the last and there are many hands to work her, we stay under the six-minute rule.

She is a beautiful ewe, robust and unscarred. She has the slender-bodied musculature of the Blue Door Band phenotype. She shakes uncontrollably from head to tail, the first and only animal to do so. Her mute trembling bears a message of fear so profound, it borders on grief, and I am not certain that I can move beyond it. Pam holds the ewe's head up by the horns while her nose rests in the palm of my hand.

Out on the mesa with the view of the entire world, we tie streamers to the antenna to give the pilot a read on the wind. We snack on smoked oryx meat. For the New Mexico crew, I name the landmarks around us. They live on the Rio Grande, in the harsher Chihuahuan Desert, so, like all dwellers in extreme landscapes, this is the first thing they want to know: Where is the water? I describe a confluence of rivers hidden in folds of stone, a spring on the side of the mountain in land so holy, you must sing every footstep you place on it.

Relieved that the operation is nearly over and no animals were harmed, Dave and Nike shift to postcapture fretting. The clinical signs of capture myopathy—renal failure, shock, ruptured muscle tissue, ataxia, death—can show up within hours (none had) or a week or two after the transplant. Hidden on the canyon's stairstep terraces, animals with capture myopathy or fatal injuries would be invisible; their mortality signal would come through, but not all of the animals have the new radio collars.

What if the bighorns break their legs? Climb the rims, race very far overland to domestic sheep, poachers, highways, Wal-Marts? Will they take to habitat that is much like their old ground, with water, galleta grass, singleleaf ash, blackbrush, the tasty petals of Indian paintbrush, the lush fruits of prickly pear cactus? Will the rams wander afar or, because they are on the eve of the rut, forget everything but crazed copulation?

Will the sheep be blessed with winter rains, clumsy mountain lions that eat only deer, healthy vegetation, lambs next spring, growing numbers? How will the source herd, the fifty-six sheep that remain upriver, respond? Dave and Nike will not be able to track the new band thoroughly for several weeks, and this worries them. I feel optimistic. But what do I know?

When we finish today, sixteen ewes and eight rams will be safely deposited in the bank, in habitat that greatly favors their survival. If the Blue Door Band far upriver succumbs to scabies, pneumonia, or some other catastrophe, these transplants will keep the native line unbroken.

Their lineage is ice-age deep. Their ancestral fiber interweaves with millennia of human witness. If you compared the DNA from the bone of a bighorn sheep made into a hide-scraper tool by an aboriginal hunter in this desert a thousand years ago with that of one of the animals we touched today, you would find a genetic link.

The new band reoccupies land emptied of their kind. No one knows how or when the old population disappeared, but with them they took their maps of the canyon—the lambing grounds, the dangerous places, the paths of descent and ascent on walls so precipitous, they seem to have no paths. The extirpation interrupted the intricate social mechanisms that pass information on home ranges from generation to generation.

A ewe or a few of the translocated ewes will reestablish such threads, describe the homeland with hooves and instinct, keen eyesight and memory. Others will follow. They are, after all, a follower species. The rams will define bachelor range, where they can strut about and bash heads and look at one another to know who they are.

To watch these twenty-four sheep stake out their place, establishing their fidelity to it, for the first time would be to witness everything that makes this animal what it is, its evolution and its hunger, its seamless, nearly molecular bond to landscape. To see how they map the stone would be to know this canyon with extraordinary intimacy. To see how they do it would be truly to learn something.

The muggers escort four of our crew to the helicopter, which will fly them to the canyon bottom to open the doors and free the sheep. With a flash of panic, I watch my husband inside the bubble cockpit of a mad-locust Hughes 500D, harnessed next to the pilot and, with Mara, Jeff, and Scott, whisked off into the general direction of Canada. I wonder if Mark will hang out the open door like Mara does.

At the canyon's rim, the ground fell out from beneath him, Mark will tell me later: the classic stomach-between-the-ears, plunging-elevator sensation. Next thing he knew, he was beside the river, in a familiar place, the high red cliffs and emerald springs, the sandy spill of rabbitbrush and sand fanning out from the side canyon into stream-bank willows and gravel bars.

Gary shuttled the crates down to them, setting each one on the ground like Irish crystal inside a box made of butterfly wings. The sheep, Mark reported, looked a bit airsick. They all had hiccups. None leaped out when the doors opened. They just sat there until little sheep lightbulbs went off in their heads. Then they bounded out and ran upriver, swiftly and together, climbing talus and crossing boulder fields, laying their tracks over the tracks of the bighorns released the day before.

Her nose lay in my palm. The warmth of her breath spread to every nerve in my hand. The short gray-brown hairs were silky along the muzzle, velvet and white near the apertures and cleft of her black nostrils. Her nose ran a clear mucus, and sand clung to the moisture. Her nostrils were ringed with a rime of red sand from the canyon.

Finally, her trembling ceased. Despite her fear, her exhalations grew steady and unlabored. The fright lay in her eyes, the great golden orbs hidden behind a cloth blindfold. Darkness stilled her limbs. Strangely, it curbed all instinct to kick or twist herself upright. Stillness was not as much surrender as it was an instinct of passivity, as if eye contact with her captors would kill her.

How has this come about? I wondered. How have I come to a piece of October desert with the nose of a rare bighorn resting in my hand?

All year long, I had never crossed the agreed boundary between the Blue Door Band and me. I sat on a rock, my mind on Hopi Heheyas, while a ram studied the top of my head. I deserted the herd for phantom *borregos* in Mexico and rain doctors in California. Sometimes the ewe bands appeared on the talus and came close for inspection. They milled about and cocked their heads, as if I looked much better to them sideways. When the lambs grew to the strength of a nursery pack, the ewes brought them to my sandy alluvial fan by the river.

Now I feel as if I have crossed a threshold. The privilege humbles me. This would be the intimacy of the hunter, although against the hunter's hand there would be no heartbeat, no breath. I have touched her, this impossible survivor of a near extinction. I have placed my fingers on her flesh in a sacrament of trespass.

The blindfold stays her terror, stills her limbs. If I could see those eyes, I would see the wild, the second world. Her fear would cripple me. The palm of the hand is a most sensitive human organ. On it, the warmth of a breathing animal is pure solace.

THE LAST UNDEVOURED RICHES

Practitioners of phrenology, a "science" that was popular in the mid-nineteenth century, claimed that the brain was a mosaic of "little organs" that governed everything from vision and language to shyness and wonder. They believed that these phrenological faculties could be read and analyzed by studying the head's shape and protuberances.

Medical diagrams made at the time illustrate the brain's interior functions. An engraving from England, for instance, dated 1840, shows a human head in profile and cross-sectioned into thirty stamp-size compartments, each with a miniature scene rendered in colorful detail.

For some of the brain sectors, the artist could find no pictorial equivalent, so words mark them: *Form, Comparison, History.* Some are blank—air space or lurking unmentionables? Most of the scenes hint at allegory or symbolism. A man stands at an easel, painting a landscape (*Imitation*). A naked boy holds a monkey's head (*Mirthfulness*). Toward the back of the skull is *Self-Esteem:* A plump man in a top hat puffs up his chest and casts a haughty gaze over the tops of everyone's heads. The diagram depicts brain sectors for *Sublimity* (birds, water, trees), *Amativeness* (a cupid), and, above the left ear, the largest sector of all: *Alimentiveness* (two men at a table, one drinking, the other carving a roast).

When I envision the contents of my own not very bumpy head, I see compartments that are simpler and fewer than those in the phrenologist's diagram. There is the implication of a laboratory of some kind, or the nether quarters of a natural history

museum with stuffed otters and finches—a sheep-o-matic diorama sort of interior, curated by a pack of unruly imps.

The brain imps walk sideways like Egyptians, although their
kilts are the plaids of my Scots ancestors. On their feet, inexplica-
bly, they wear Mexican huaraches. The imps are running quite a
spectacle: yearning, restlessness, wonder, trouble, terror of bore-
dom, sniveling, curiosity.

The smug little neuron-munchers think they know the biological functions of art and music: the senses giving the brain small
bursts of pleasure. A mob of imps, tongue in cheek, teams up
with the mustachioed imps of sarcasm and caricature, making my
tales a playful hell for the literal-minded. But the imps in the language and memory sectors are gray-haired and decrepit, shuf-
fling along in orthopedic huaraches, wreaking havoc, turning the
contents of my cranium into moon cheese.

What I fear is acute perception and sensory passion gone
bland, like a flatlined heartbeat: a cerebral attic chamber, a cube
of a room, painted government green, with a dimming bulb and
dust motes. As long as the void does not come too swiftly, I shall
surrender gracefully to the moon cheese, to the inevitability of
my own biodegradability.

The rescue line comes from intimate witness to nature's genius,
to the pure facts of the nonhuman lives that are still possible in
this far-off desert. To learn something, to jolt the imps and get
along in a world whose wild grows increasingly thin with each
passing year, I must, metaphorically speaking, listen to bats.

One summer night on a sandy riverbank at dusk, as bats
swooped and fed in the air above camp, a zoologist friend handed
me a battery-operated device that picked up the bats' ultrasonic
echo-locating calls. Because of its high frequency, the naked
human ear cannot detect this chatter. But the bat detector opened
to us the sound track heard by the creatures themselves.

While I watched what had been, without the detector, a silent
aerial display, the bats showered my ears with faint clicks. I heard

warbles and whistles, random clicks and fluid clicks that ran together in strings, followed by a burst of sound as a bat found food. If an insect shifted from a leaf, if a moth flexed its wings, the bat that heard it sent out a sonic stream.

What could be seen only faintly with our eyes—the careening flight of winged mammals as night absorbed all light—came as sounds of extraordinary complexity. Above my head, small brown mammals were yelling. Above my head lay an entire world of which I was not aware.

The human spirit, it is said, yearns for glimpses into the "interiority" of a being that is different, not us, something not quite comprehensible, something that moves in its own complete universe. To bat-listen, to touch an otherworld with more than one sense, to reclaim daily the notion of layered miracles, I followed the seasons of the locals. I fed the imps the glories of the stone-eaters, who, inside their big river canyon, unfolded another year.

By the time Dave and Nike took their first look at the transplanted sheep—I named them the Downcanyon Band—it was nearly December and the Colorado Plateau had settled into winter. We entered the sheep range by the river.

Ice stiffened the bowlines and the wind carried a knife's edge of polar air. At its low angle, the sun reached the canyon bottom for only a few hours during the day. Most of the time, we floated and camped in the refrigerated shadow between the massive walls of rock.

Deep in the canyon, Dave and Nike pulled out their telemetry equipment and began to listen for radio-collared sheep. We did not know where the animals had gone after being released. Some might be lost or beyond range. We dreaded a mortality signal from a sheep that had perished. Had any animals died of capture myopathy? Fallen off unfamiliar precipices?

Compared to the old homeland, the rock in this terrain was

redder, blockier, and more consolidated, the walls steeper and with fewer rockfall chutes and draws for ascent and descent. The sheep could be invisible, midway between river and rim on a wedding-cake tier, moving horizontally along the canyon wall, with plenty of food and water from springs and potholes. To travel vertically, to come down to the river from this middle world, few passages could be found on cliff faces so smooth and sheer that they seemed sliced.

Dave and Nike preferred to back up each radio signal with a confirmed sighting. In this way, they could also track and count the unmarked animals in the groups. However, this rugged landscape offered formidable challenges—an easy wildness for sheep, but difficult for biologists. "We will pick up radio signals," Dave said, "but we may not see the sheep."

Several miles upriver from the release site, the first signals came in. Nike matched their frequencies with her notes: two ewes and a ram. We floated farther downstream and received clear bleeps from the rest of the collars. A rush of excitement rode a wave of relief. All marked animals in the Downcanyon Band were present and accounted for. The helicopter rides and handling had not harmed them. They had survived us.

At one camp, we hiked to a perch on the canyon wall opposite the sheep range, high above a river fringed with ice and coral-colored sand. With her headset and twirling antenna, Nike appeared to be listening to another planet. But she drew in signals on two collars, and we all grabbed our binoculars. For the first time since their bolt from the transport crates, live sheep came into view.

A ram, one of the largest we had moved, fed on a talus with five ewes. All six animals were fat, sleek, and a bit glassy-eyed with the rut. Although breeding season held them to this piece of canyon, they were likely still wandering; where we found them would not necessarily be where they would stay. Eventually, the males would figure out their Ram Land. The ewes would map lambing grounds and places of safe descent to the river when summer's heat came and they took their young to the water.

For now, they fed quietly in sheep heaven under the cold, dry clarity of a heliotrope sky. We watched them for a long time. The ram had no male company at the moment, so we hoped he and his plump love bunnies were making new little sheep like crazy, bringing the wild back to the high red stone that had been empty of their kind for so long.

In our last camp on the winter river, Mark dreamed that we were transplanting canyon wrens, gray-feathered denizens of the redrock country. We gave them tiny radio collars, rolled them up in miniature mattresses, and carried them to crevices near springs. Upon release, they fluffed up and sang their lucid melody of descending notes.

I dreamed of a sheep band on the run, alarmed by a predator or an unseen spook but clearly racing in a panic for safe ground. They rushed up a high slope. From their side of the rise, they were blind to a sheer drop-off on the other side. But I could see it; I could see that they were heading toward a cliff that could not be descended, not even by agile bighorn sheep. I feared they would rush to the edge and pour over it in a waterfall of broken bodies.

They ran up the rise, oblivious to the looming precipice, ewes and lambs crowded together in a side-heaving run. I tried to warn them, but I wore the cement shoes of a dream.

Less than ten feet from the abyss, at the last possible second, the lead ewe turned in a dead run. The turn was neither panicked nor abrupt, merely taken as if she were rounding a bend in a well-marked trail. She did not break her pace, and the others followed in a smooth stream that dismissed the chasm of space beyond their withers as mere scenery.

When I awoke from my dream, I wondered, Are the new sheep on ground so strange, unmapped, and unmemorized, they will not anticipate its perils? Will they know when to turn?

For bighorns, topography is memory, enhanced by acute vision. They can anticipate the land's every contour—when to leap, where to climb, when to turn, which footholds will support their muscular bodies. To survive, this is what the band would have to do: make this perfect match of flesh to earth.

Scott, the veterinarian, reported back to Dave and Nike on the tests that he had performed during the capture. The results showed the herd to be in good condition. He said he had never seen such "clean" sheep. Mites, parasites, pathogens, sinusitis— none of these presented serious problems. The native stock was healthy stock.

Soon after the winter trip, when the rut had ended, one of the older rams crossed the river, climbed out of the other side of the canyon, and wandered far to the north. He took another ram with him and left younger rams behind with the ewes. He sent no postcards. Although he frequented an escarpment well away from domestic sheep, Dave and Nike kept an eye on him. The fall rut— his blood instinct for access to mates through the ritual of head bashing—might bring him back to the canyon again.

In the spring, the radio on one of the ewes sent a mortality signal. Her carcass lay on an impossible (for human hikers) precipice and could not be reached for a necropsy. Nike speculated that she had fallen, a victim, perhaps, of still-unknown terrain, a turn not taken in time, a misstep or miscalculated leap. Now she was raven food.

The ewe's death and the walkabout rams left twenty-one of the twenty-four transplants coming out of winter in their new habitat. By late spring, the ewes brought seven more to the water, seven healthy lambs.

On a midsummer trip, Mark and I floated past a group on the banks: two lambless ewes, two ewes with their young of the year, and a long-legged young ram so handsome and virile, he seemed destined to become the Downcanyon Band's Mr. Perfect. As we floated, they walked along the river in the same direction, stopping occasionally to feed on hackberry leaves. Eventually, we lost sight of them and camped eight miles downstream.

In the morning, we awoke to find all seven sheep directly across from us, a hundred feet up on a narrow ledge, dozing in their beds. Somewhere along the way, they had picked up an extra lamb. This young female seemed unattached to any adults. (When we told Nike about the extra lamb, she wondered if it might be the orphan of the dead ewe, old enough to feed and climb and rejoin her matrilineal band.)

From their perch, the sheep watched us as we sipped coffee on the beach and did our camp chores. I set Nelson, the toy ram, out on a boulder to stare back at them. I could see the horizontal black irises in their amber eyes; they were that close, a choice of resting place that seemed almost deliberate. "They followed us," I told Mark; "they wanted to be with us." *That chopper crap,* they said, *all is forgiven!*

A band of lemon yellow sun illuminated the sheep on their morning ledge. Ears twitched. Necks were scratched. The sheep acted as if they had lived on these walls forever, with no memory of the Blue Door range. One of the recumbent lambs rested his head on his mother's rear flank. She was approaching her prime, a well-conformed four-year-old with a pale, smooth nose that had rested in the palm of my hand. For this gift, for the wildness that she surrendered to my intrusion, I had still found no reciprocation.

A stubborn survivor of mountain lions, drought, captures, a broken leg, and an epidemic of disease, San Andres Ewe 067 had lived on her New Mexico mountaintop alone after the catastrophic die-off of desert bighorns on the San Andres Wildlife Refuge. Later, she was joined by sentinel rams, her own offspring, and the transplanted stock, which brought with them the promise of wild sheep back in the mountain range again.

In her fourteenth year, the last indigenous bighorn sheep in southern New Mexico died one winter day on a steep slope above the shimmering white playas of the Tularosa Basin.

Mara Weisenberger, the refuge biologist, tried to piece together the circumstances of the old ewe's death. I found myself reading her note with a wildly beating heart.

"We knew she had been on borrowed time for the past few years and were expecting her life to end at any time," Mara wrote. "But it didn't come any easier when it actually happened."

When she and Kevin Cobble examined the death site, a nearby leg snare held a sixty-pound female mountain lion. "Kevin gently pulled [the ewe's] carcass just away enough from the lion so that we could perform a necropsy. It was surreal as we worked, with the lion a few feet distant, hissing at us, and only wanting to get away."

The site showed no blood in the area, no sign of a struggle or the hemorrhaging of a neck wound, things that typify predation. Her radio collar bore no scratches or scrapes. The carcass had been dragged a short distance. Only her heart and lungs had been eaten.

They found a compound fracture in the ewe's front leg, the same leg that had been broken in a capture ten years earlier. Mara didn't think the second fracture was a fresh or debilitating break. "The ewe had fat on her internal organs and her bone marrow looked good, indicating she was in good condition. She was pregnant with a ram lamb."

Mara and her colleagues could not determine with certainty how the old ewe had died. Had a mountain lion attacked and killed her, or had she died in some other way—in her sleep, her eyes closed and heart stopped—and then a lion scavenged her carcass?

"We're not sure how she died," Mara said. "What we do know is that the loss of this ewe marked the end of the original San Andres Mountains desert bighorn sheep herd."

Inseminated by one of the sentinel rams put on the refuge after her years of solitude, SAE 067 had given birth to a ram lamb, the leaping half a lamb in the photograph that Mara had given me. The following year, she bore a ewe lamb. These two sheep still climbed the cloud-raking rock of the San Andres Mountains. Fortunately, Mara said, they would pass on some of the old ewe's wisdom and genes. Perhaps they, too, knew the native routes and ledges, the rocks and the escape moves that would allow them to survive for a long time.

Because Kevin and Mara could make no clear assumptions about the ewe's death, they had to take the ewe off the mountain for further evaluation.

Kevin carried the ewe's carcass down the steep terrain, then headed to the truck. I carried her across the *bajada* to meet Kevin. In a way that I don't fully understand, it was a cathartic experience. I carried her down the mountain on my back, with her front legs wrapped around my neck, like giving someone a piggyback ride. For a fleeting moment it was just the ewe, the mountain, and me.

I hope someday to comprehend that mixture of respect, relief, loss of an old friend, loss of a part of the system, forever, in this passing of the last of the indigenous herd. The death was not only the ewe's, but also of something more.

And what can be reported of the sheep I'd named the Blue Door Band, the source herd for the translocation project and my companions over the year?

They were sheep who bred like rabbits.

By late spring, twenty lambs were added to the population, leaving little question—this year at least—that the band had replenished itself after a couple dozen herd mates disappeared on the end of a rope attached to a helicopter.

Although it is not common to breed so young, a number of the band's yearling ewes bore lambs. Also in the lamb crop were two sets of twins, although only one set survived. Dave and Nike marveled at how their bovid wards contradicted the statistical rarity of twinning by desert bighorns.

The mystery of the Blue Door Band's disappearance and return, its genetic profile, inbreeding, and hard-bound fidelity to the river canyon—to this was added still another seasonal cycle and, for Dave and Nike, a rich thicket of study material.

Nike sorted through diet, weather, herd density, age of females, and other factors that might have influenced the robust size of the lamb crop. She continued to study the band's somewhat unusual maternal behavior, the signs of allomothering, of females who nursed lambs other than their own. Each seemingly minute response to environment, each extraordinary efficiency of instinct, added up to a prodigious ice-age will.

Sometimes the sheep in this band acted like the textbook mountain sheep in the mounds of scientific literature about their species. Sometimes they surprised us. Always they instilled a tense hope, a hope that there never would be a return to the years of near extinction, a desire to be assured that when we went down the river or to a remote watching post on the rim, the wild sheep would always be there, living inside their redrock gorge.

On a summer morning of bright, piercing sun, I threw together gear for a day with the Blue Door Band. I packed spotting scope and binoculars, water and a book, Nelson and lunch.

I tucked two sketches into the pages of my book. One was a

drawing of an Anasazi petroglyph on a red sandstone wall, an image of a bighorn sheep with a wavy line emerging from its mouth—its conversation with the universe, its trail of breath. For her survival and tenacity, for her wild, complete world, I had made this image, in my mind, the San Andres ewe.

The other sketch, a bighorn with backward horns, came from the Cosos, from a brown-black basalt ravine amid the blue layers of basin and range, drawing rain from the Sierra Nevada with the power of dreams.

Within that basalt canyon lay confirmation of our species's instinctive love of metaphor, one that, ironically, seemed prereligious, an innate human need to express the inexpressible, the something more. This, I thought, was not unlike the *more* that Mara felt as she carried on her back, across the *bajada,* the animal that had been the last, yet which had kept the mountains from being so empty.

As I loaded my daypack, it struck me that these forays into sheep country were futile and delusional. The end of the wild world, the emptiness, will come—indeed, has arrived. The absence may not be one of actual bodies, a physical loss of this bird or that mammal, a river of native fish or a band of homeland ungulates. Rather, it is a reduction of diverse nature into a simplified biota that is entirely managed and dependent. It is a loss of autonomous beings, the self-willed fauna that gave us metaphor, that shaped human minds capable of identity with all existence.

Sometimes I picture this moment in history, a moment with which my own lifetime chances to coincide, as a gate that we have been closing for some time. On the other side of the gate, deep landscape falls farther and farther away, always at the point of loss. The spellbound threshold between humanity and the rest of nature is very nearly pulled shut to the latching point. Soon we shall turn our backs and walk away entirely, place-blind and terribly lonely.

I remember going to Mexico to not find and not see any desert bighorns but to be in the place where they live and to try to learn something. And so now there was no better journey than to the outward, to the edge of things.

This is a good day, I thought, to take Nelson to lunch.

The animal-longing sector of my brain remains indefatigable. I set the shreds of my imagination to go the distance with all of nature's creation. I hunger for the quiet rapture of observation, the measure of time by the clock of blood, the exaltation that comes with the intimacy of beings so unlike ourselves in home-lands so unlike our own.

Humans are creatures in search of exaltation. We crave, some-one once said, the occasions when jolts from the universe fly open. This jolt, in this desert with these animals, is a belonging so overwhelming, it can put deep cracks in your heart.

The sun climbed. I was losing the cool of the morning. It will be hot out there, I thought. The heat will rise from the canyon and break the air into shimmering liquid waves. Across the stone, in gaits and patterns older than time, the fine-limbed, amber-eyed animals will move.

SELECTED REFERENCES

Bleich, V. C., J. D. Wehausen, and S. A. Holl. "Desert-Dwelling Mountain Sheep: Conservation Implications of a Naturally Fragmented Distribution." *Conservation Biology* 4 (1990): 383–94.

Burrus, Ernest J. *Jesuit Relations, Baja California, 1716–1762.* Los Angeles: Dawson's Book Shop, 1984.

DeForge, James. "A Four-Year Study of Cause-Specific Mortality of Desert Bighorn Lambs Near an Urban Interface and a Community Response." Abstract. Desert Bighorn Society. *Transactions* 46 (2002): 3–4.

Desert Bighorn Society. *Transactions.* Vols. 1–46. 1962–2002.

Geist, Valerius. *Mountain Sheep: A Study in Behavior and Evolution.* Chicago: University of Chicago Press, 1971.

Goodson, N. J., D. R. Stevens, J. Cole, P. Kyselka, and K. McCoy. "Survival Rates and Causes of Mortality in a Desert Bighorn Sheep Population on the Navajo Nation." Desert Bighorn Society. *Transactions* 46 (2002): 18–24.

Grant, Campbell, James W. Baird, and J. Kenneth Pringle. *Rock Drawings of the Coso Range.* Ridgecrest, Calif.: Maturango Press, 1987.

Hass, C. C. "Alternative Maternal-Care Patterns in Two Herds of Bighorn Sheep." *Journal of Mammology* 71, no. 1 (1990): 24–35.

Krausman, Paul R. "Exit of the Last Wild Mountain Sheep." In *Counting Sheep,* edited by Gary Paul Nabhan. Tucson: University of Arizona Press, 1993.

———, ed. "Special Issue: Bighorn Sheep Restoration," *Restoration Ecology* 8, no. 48 (2000).

Logan, Kenneth, and Linda Sweanor. *Desert Puma.* Washington, D.C.: Island Press, 2001.

McCarty, Craig W., and James A. Bailey. *Habitat Requirements of Desert Bighorn Sheep.* Colorado Division of Wildlife Report no. 69. 1994.

Monson, Gale, and Lowell Sumner, eds. *The Desert Bighorn.* 4th edition. Tucson: University of Arizona Press, 1990.

Palmer, Mikki. "High Desert Cowboy." *Blue Mountain Shadows* 10 (1992): 18–36.

Ramey, R. R. "Mitochondrial DNA Variation, Population Structure, and the Evaluation of Mountain Sheep in the Southwestern U.S. and Mexico." *Molecular Ecology* 4 (1995): 429–39.

Schaller, George B. *Mountain Monarchs.* Chicago: University of Chicago Press, 1977.

Singer, Francis J., and M. A. Gudorf. *Restoration of Bighorn Sheep Metapopulations in and Near 15 National Parks.* U.S. Geological Survey Open File Report 99-102. 1999.

U.S. Fish and Wildlife Service. *Mountain Lion Management to Protect the State Endangered Desert Bighorn Sheep, New Mexico.* Final Environmental Assessment, September 2002.

———. *Recovery Plan for the Sierra Nevada Bighorn Sheep (Ovis canadensis californiana).* Draft Environmental Assessment, May 2003.

Valdez, R., and P. R. Krausman, eds. *Mountain Sheep of North America.* Tucson: University of Arizona Press, 1999. (Additional references were found in this volume's comprehensive bibliography.)

Wehausen, John D. "Comment on Desert Bighorn as Relicts: Further Considerations." *Wildlife Society Bulletin* 12 (1984): 82–85.

———. "Effects of Mountain Lion Predation on Bighorn Sheep in the Sierra Nevada and Granite Mountains of California." *Wildlife Society Bulletin* 24 (1996): pp. 471–79.

Welles, Ralph E., and Florence B. Welles. *The Bighorn of Death Valley.* U.S. National Park Service Fauna Series, no. 6. 1961.

Whitley, David S., ed. *Reader in Archaeological Theory.* London and New York: Routledge, 1998.

Wilson, Lanny O. *Distribution and Ecology of Desert Bighorn Sheep in Southeastern Utah.* Utah Department of Natural Resources Publication, no. 68-5. 1968.

Younkin, Elva, ed. *Coso Rock Art.* Ridgecrest, Calif.: Maturango Press, 1998.

ACKNOWLEDGMENTS

I am grateful to Kevin Cobble, Kenneth Pringle, Peggy Schoaf, Jackie Warren, and Joe Pachak for their time and generosity, and to Joan Benner for refuge at Benner Base Camp in the Owens Valley. Katie Lee, thank you for the songline map of Baja.

I am also indebted to Jeff Cole, Pam Kyselka, Gloria Tom, and the Navajo Nation Department of Fish and Wildlife. Helpful to my research were conversations with Guy Wallace and Charlie DeLorme.

For fieldwork and dedication to wildlife, there are few better than John Wehausen and Mara Weisenberger.

Dave Stevens and Nike Goodson Stevens let me shadow them in the canyons and explore their thoughts and work. For their trust, I am profoundly grateful.

My touchstones in the book world are Nora Gallagher; my incomparable agent, Flip Brophy; and Jane Garrett, the editor every writer dreams of.

For Mark my love is deeper than the days of white sand, turquoise water, and *cardón bajadas* on the far beaches of El Rosario and Mexia.

About the Author

Ellen Meloy, a recipient of a Whiting Foundation Award in 1997, was a native of the West and has lived in California, Montana, and Utah. Her *Anthropology of Turquoise: Meditations on Landscape, Art, and Spirit* was a finalist for the Pulitzer Prize and the winner of the Utah Book Award and the Banff Mountain Book Festival Award for the best book in the adventure and travel category. She was also the author of *Raven's Exile: A Season on the Green River* and *The Last Cheater's Waltz: Beauty and Violence in the Desert Southwest*. Meloy spent most of her life in wild, remote places; at the time of her sudden death in November 2004 (three months after completing *Eating Stone*), she and her husband lived in southern Utah.

A Note on the Type

The text of this book was set in Monotype Columbus, a contemporary face designed specifically for digital typesetting by Patricia Saunders. Named for Christopher Columbus, and released on the quincentenary of his 1492 voyage from Spain to the Americas, Monotype Columbus has a distinctly Spanish flavor to its letter forms. Saunders did, in fact, draw inspiration from fonts created by Jorge Coci in sixteenth-century Spain, as well as from italic fonts by the brilliant typographer Robert Granjon, to create this lively and highly readable new face.

Composed by North Market Street Graphics, Lancaster, Pennsylvania
Printed and bound by R. R. Donnelley & Sons, Harrisonburg, Virginia
Designed by M. Kristen Bearse